The H ia _ _oo'box

The Historian's Toolbox introduces students to the theory, craft, and methods of history and equips them with a series of tools to research and understand the past. Written in an engaging and entertaining style, and filled with fascinating examples, this best-selling "how to" book opens up the exciting world behind historical research and writing.

This fourth edition expands the repertory of tools and techniques available to students entering the workshop of history. These include materials on the Kennedy assassination, the litigation of Van Gogh's *Night Café*, local town histories, contemporary history, Twitter, and the contemplation of the end of history as well as the Sixth Extinction in a new epilogue. The book demonstrates the relevance and expanding possibilities of the study of history in our cacophonous information age of tweetstorms and fake news; it emphasises the increasing value of critical thinking, facts and evidence in the face of political lies and conspiracy theories. Material added to the fourth edition will resonate with a new generation of computer-literate readers in the face of climate change.

The Historian's Toolbox continues to be a seminal text for supporting students throughout their study of history and an accessible teaching tool for instructors.

Robert C. Williams is Vail Professor of History Emeritus at Davidson College. He has taught Russian, European, and American history at Williams and Bates Colleges and at Washington University in St. Louis. He is the author of numerous books and articles, ' ' *American Money* (1980), nominated by Harvard Pulitzer Prize.

The Historian's Toolbox
A Student's Guide to the Theory and Craft of History

Fourth Edition

Robert C. Williams

Routledge
Taylor & Francis Group

NEW YORK AND LONDON

Fourth edition published 2020
by Routledge
52 Vanderbilt Avenue, New York, NY 10017

and by Routledge
2 Park Square, Milton Park, Abingdon, Oxon, OX14 4RN

Routledge is an imprint of the Taylor & Francis Group, an informa business

First edition published by M.E. Sharpe 2006
Fourth edition published by Routledge 2020

Library of Congress Cataloging-in-Publication Data
Names: Williams, Robert C, author.
Title: The historian's toolbox : a student's guide to the theory and
craft of history / Robert C Williams.
Other titles: Student's guide to the theory and craft of history
Description: Fourth Edition. | New York, NY : Routledge, 2020. |
Includes bibliographical references and index.
Identifiers: LCCN 2019039095 (print) | LCCN 2019039096 (ebook) |
ISBN 9781138632165 (hardback) | ISBN 9781138632172 (paperback) |
ISBN 9780429345302 (ebook)
Subjects: LCSH: History–Methodology. | History–Research.
Classification: LCC D16 .W62 2020 (print) | LCC D16 (ebook) | DDC
907.2–dc23
LC record available at https://lccn.loc.gov/2019039095
LC ebook record available at https://lccn.loc.gov/2019039096

ISBN: 978-1-138-63216-5 (hbk)
ISBN: 978-1-138-63217-2 (pbk)
ISBN: 978-0-429-34530-2 (ebk)

Typeset in Bembo
by Swales & Willis, Exeter, Devon, UK

Printed and bound by CPI Group (UK) Ltd, Croydon, CR0 4YY

History as a Discussion without End

You come late. When you arrive, others have long preceded you, and they are engaged in a heated discussion, a discussion too heated for them to pause and tell you exactly what it is about. In fact, the discussion had already begun long before any of them got there, so that no one present is qualified to retrace for you all the steps that had gone before. You listen for a while, until you decide that you have caught the tenor of the argument; then you put in your oar. Someone answers you; you answer her; another comes to your defence; another aligns herself against you, to either the embarrassment or gratification of your opponent, depending upon the quality of your ally's assistance. However, the discussion is interminable. The hour grows late, you must depart. And you do depart, with the discussion still vigorously in progress.

—Kenneth Burke, *The Philosophy of Literary Form*

Contents

PART III
The Relevance of History   **127**

Illustrations and Tables

Illustrations

Tables

History as Fun

Doing history is fun, even though the past offers us much tragedy, as well as comedy and farce. History involves the study of the past. History is not really an art, nor a science, but a craft. The craft of doing history—as opposed to reading history—involves a further intellectual process of research, writing, and revision. Doing history is hard work and requires tools of the trade: some internal to the discipline, others borrowed from related disciplines.

The purpose of issuing a fourth edition of the *Historian's Toolbox* is to help history students, and even other historians, understand the tools of the intellectual process and craft of history. The tools in the toolbox (Part II) provide a number of techniques common to reading, research, and writing, as well as some current controversies in the historical profession. These are simply my personal reflections and selections, with the usual limits of race, class, and gender; but they at least reflect the hindsight of a practitioner of the craft.

A fourth edition reminds us that doing history involves not simply a search for evidence about the past, but ongoing research, a second (or third, or fourth) look at the evidence. When we approach a text again, we often see a new landscape of meaning, based on our new experiences, new evidence, and continuing thinking. History is the study of change over time in the past. The past may be over, but its history itself changes over time. Memories change. So do interpretations of past events, and the selection of the significant from the apparently insignificant.

60 years ago, I turned away from studying science to doing history with the view that history was a subtle, complex, and endlessly fascinating way of understanding the human condition over time. Today I still believe that. What I have learned about history has come from reading, rereading, writing, and doing my own research. There is no better way to understand a craft than to pursue it yourself. Most people, of course, are not professional historians; but they may be quite fascinated with reading history, seeing historical films, and visiting historical sites. History is all

around us and speaks to us all. We all do some history every day without realizing it, but doing history professionally is another matter.

Looking at the evolution of history as a craft, I believe that history is here to stay. History will survive even the assaults of antihistory and postmodernism, of fictional history and "what if?" speculation. Telling true stories about the human past is an inherent part of human culture. So is simple curiosity about what actually happened in the past, and why. One ignores history at one's peril. For history can help us understand not just the past, but the present and the future as well. As long as *Homo sapiens* survives, there will be historians to chronicle its survival.

History is an argument without end, as Dutch historian Peter Geyl put it. The controversies are never really over. (A former colleague of mine once said that history is what any six dead people agree on.) Thus, historical revision—the modification of conventional wisdom based on new interpretations or new evidence—is a permanent characteristic of doing history. Historians often disagree about their interpretation of the past, even when looking at the same body of evidence.

As I have revised my own views of history over the years, I owe a great deal to my colleagues and students at Harvard University, Williams College, Washington University in St. Louis, Bates College, and Davidson College. They all have taught me as much as I have taught them, and they challenged me to rethink history every semester. I am also grateful to Phil Cantelon and my colleagues at History Associates Incorporated, who have proven that history can be both professional and useful in the marketplace. My debt to Ann Williams is immeasurable; and my editors, first, Andrew Gyory, and then Steve Drummond, have made this book better than it might have been. Kevin Murphy of Columbia University helped add stimulating sections on the Internet, event analysis, public analysis, public history, oral history, and material culture. I am likewise indebted to Routledge for encouraging me to produce a fourth edition of this book, and to its skilled editors, Kim Smith and Zoe Forbes, for helping me improve and enlarge the manuscript.

The year 2001 was once the subject of a popular film by director Stanley Kubrick about future space travel. Now 2001 is history. The events of September 11—suicidal Saudi jihadists crashing into New York buildings using civilian aircraft—certainly have changed our world. But how? Shockingly new and unexpected at the time, "9/11" is now the historical subject of endless reports, memoirs, and histories. So the killing of Osama bin Laden by U.S. Special Forces in Pakistan ten years later, on May 1, 2011, will soon be considered past history. And thus the election of Donald J. Trump as U.S. President (POTUS 45) in 2016 will soon be history.

It is a sign of the times that the research for this fourth edition has been performed almost entirely at my desk using a computer and accessing the Internet. Okay, so I did read a few more books (though not on a Kindle) to enlarge my horizon in time and space. This time I have used the virtually unlimited evidence available online (see Chapter 21, "TMI: Too Much Information") and the selective power of search engines to educate myself about the new tools of history, notably geographic information systems (GIS) and crime scene investigation (CSI) forensics, and to explore the private lives of U.S. presidents and the history of WikiLeaks. I have added material on world history, local history, the Kennedy assassination, the fossil record, and mass extinctions.

Books themselves are often available online, and a search will now take us to a particular page and highlight the name or topic of interest. Information, data, and evidence are ever increasing, but our historical research becomes ever more powerful. We access our unregulated Internet database of documents, obscenities, and fake news with a growing number of apps and search engines. We try to select new nuggets of information and scholarship from the garbage heap of social media rantings. Tweets are new historical documents, acceptable as evidence in court. What used to take up historians' time, energy, and money for travel to libraries and collections can now often be accomplished at the desktop in seconds. The tools of history may change and improve our efficiency, but the fundamental principles remain the same. I hope you find this new edition of the *Historian's Toolbox* useful.

In 2020, historians still inhabit a world of global climate change, wars, revolutions, fire, flood, diseases, and other disasters of Biblical proportions. Some historians say we live in the midst of the Sixth Extinction of species on earth, including perhaps our own. We also enjoy greater longevity, improvements in medicine and science, and efforts by individuals world-wide to assist others in surviving these disasters. Equally alarming is a worldwide rise of authoritarian nationalist strongmen who seek to dismantle democracy, build walls to halt immigration, and manipulate history for their own purposes. The long argument without end over an accurate account of the past, based on evidence and facts, faces a growing challenge from sceptics, true believers, ideologues, and outright liars. The result is a world of fake news, alternate facts, and postmodern relativism that turns history into a wilderness of falsehood and entertainment. What is true and what is false about the past? History and truth are under attack. But we have never seen such a proliferation of excellent history, biography, genealogy, and film as well.

History began as a discipline grounded in the biographies of "great men" and the nation-state. Nations and their achievements were the foundation of history after the French Revolution. Currently history is increasingly global, not national. Diseases, cyberspace, space exploration, the law of the sea, radioactive and toxic waste, and refugee movements to escape war and famine are just a few of the current historical topics that cut across national boundaries. The Ebola virus, the Chernobyl nuclear plant accident, glacial melting, hurricanes and monsoons, terror, and air pollution may begin in one part of the globe but soon have worldwide effects. After 350,000 years, the existence of *Homo sapiens* can no longer be taken for granted on the planet it seeks to exploit, dominate, and develop. With a bang or a whimper, human history will vanish when there is no human left to tell its story.

Today's history was yesterday's future. So what is the craft of history? And what are its tools? What does it mean to try to narrate and explain what happened in the past? By confronting those questions, this book serves as a guide to understanding the purpose of history, the evolution of historical thought, and how the tools of history can be identified and used.

For Further Reading

Good recent general introductions to the study of history include Mark T. Gilderhus, *History and Historians: A Historiographical Introduction*, 7th ed. (Upper Saddle River, NJ: Prentice Hall, 2010); Jules R. Benjamin, *A Student's Guide to History*, 11th ed. (Boston: Bedford Books, 2009); and Norman J. Wilson, *History in Crisis? Recent Directions in Historiography* (Upper Saddle River, NJ: Prentice Hall, 1999).

Another good introduction is John Tosh, *The Pursuit of History: Aims, Methods, and New Directions in the Study of Modern History*, 5th ed. (London: Longman, 2010). Then there is the dated, but still useful, E.H. Carr, *What Is History?* (New York: Alfred A. Knopf, 1961).

James Gleick has set modern information theory in a historical context with his *The Information: A History, a Theory, a Flood* (New York: Pantheon Books, 2011). For the long view of human history, see Yuval Noah Harari, *Sapiens: A Brief History of Humankind* (New York: Random House, 2014).

Part I
The Craft of History

1 The Past

In the beginning was the past. There really was a "then." The past consisted of events, people, natural surroundings, and the landscape. The past of planet earth goes back 14 billion years. *Homo sapiens* (*Wise Men*) appeared a few million years ago. In the distant past, time was measured in seasons and by the cyclic alteration of day and night, light and darkness. In most cultures, time was cyclic and repetitive, rather than linear. There was cosmos but no history, clocks, or calendars. Most humans in the past lived lives of "ceaseless repetition of gestures initiated by others."[1] Replication, not invention, was the norm. They imitated celestial archetypes in rituals of eternal recurrence, repeating acts of gods or heroes, abolishing history and time. Events were meaningless except as periodic ceremonies of regeneration or repetition of primal events of creation, such as the great battle between the Babylonian god Marduk and the sea monster Tiamat. There was no real sense of history. The *past* is not *history*. The past may be lost without a trace. Or it may be remembered or continually reinvented or imagined as story. The *past* may be absent or present only through *history* as a reasonably true account or as useful fiction.

In the case of the Trobriand Islands people of the Pacific, their language had no verb tenses. They simply did not understand the meaning of past, present, and future. While they certainly *had* a history, their understanding of history differed from that of other cultures.

Our senses—smell, taste, hearing, and sight—and our memories remind us of the past. We remember, and sometimes reinvent, the past that we think we do not forget. We remember things that happened in sequence, before or after, but rarely at any particular time. Material objects in the present remind us of the past: leaking poison gas canisters from the two world wars in France and Germany; the DNA of disinterred bodies; fossils; ancient pollen; old photographs; battlefields; bones. I once encountered dried bloodstains of the Russian revolutionary leader Leon Trotsky (1879–1940) on top of some of his papers in a Harvard University archive, vivid evidence of the past, if not exactly history. (History reminded me that he was killed in 1940 by an ice axe blow to the head while hunched over his desk editing his papers in Mexico City.) We remember now, but it happened then. The past existed once and is not invalidated by our approximate, incorrect, or disappearing memories of that past now, in the present. Perhaps this is what President Abraham Lincoln (1809–1865) meant by our "mystic chords of memory." There really was a past. We even may remember some of it. We may suppress or forget other parts of it. Or we may simply not know part of the past.

Historians and other people often use the past to sanction present structures of authority, religious, or secular. But alternative histories may also justify overthrowing that same authority. Power and rebellion both exploit history. Genealogy legitimates monarchy and nobility or provides a guarantee of future salvation (for the Mormons, or Church of Jesus Christ of Latter-day Saints). Marxist history legitimates class struggle and revolution, not capitalist authority, as the final and inevitable product of history. The past may be used to explain the present and predict the future. No matter how the past is used and altered in the present, it was once there and then.[2] We seek traces of the past in the evidence we find in the present.

The past is intimately connected with *time*, a mysterious entity that we measure metaphorically in terms of space (a long or a short time). Early on, people developed calendars to help them keep track of past, present, and future time. Calendars are based on the motions of the natural world (sun, moon, stars, earth) and on a beginning of time (birth of a hero, founding of a religion or a nation, creation of the world, etc.). They contain both cyclic (hours, days, weeks, months, years) and linear (sequential years) elements. Cultures keep track of calendar time in many different systems. But calendars are a culturally defined measure of past time. The Mayans measured time in terms of days, years, and *katuns* (7,200 days, or about 20 years). Mayan time was both linear and cyclic, so that knowledge of recurrent patterns of events gave power and authority to the priests and wise men and women who understood the past. One historian of calendar time defines time as "interconnected hoops rolling up a great hill of progress."[3] Western time (like Chinese time) is linear. But for many different cultures, time was cyclic, a wheel and not an arrow, eternal recurrence and not linear progress.

We all have remembered pasts. I ask my students to give an accurate account of what they ate for breakfast. I then ask them to suggest various ways in which they might obtain *evidence* about that breakfast (eyewitness testimony, receipts, fragments found, etc.) that would prove that their account was true. The results can be messy but so is history. For human history involves historians and their human subjects in our common fate, that is, in what the German philosopher Immanuel Kant (1724–1804) called the "crooked timber of humanity." Unlike scientists, historians resemble the objects of their all too human study of the past. We do not need to get bent out of shape by the fact that we are all crooked timber. We understand others in the past precisely because they too, like us, were human beings. We can empathize with their triumphs and tragedies. We can imagine what we might have done in their situation.

The past, then, is not history. The past and its traces provide the raw material of history. History gives an account of the past in the present. We might well have begun with the evidence, those traces of the past that are accessible to us now, in the present. Evidence is the raw material of history, the texts, fossils, images, manuscripts, and artifacts that help us tell a story or make an argument. But without the raw material evidence from the past, there would be no surviving evidence in the present to be examined and questioned, no story to tell, and no history to discover and construct. Thus, we begin with the past and with the root word of history, *story*.

Notes

1 Mircea Eliade, *Cosmos and History: The Myth of the Eternal Return* (New York: Harper and Row, 1959), 5.
2 J.H. Plumb, *The Death of the Past* (Boston: Houghton Mifflin, 1970).
3 Anthony Aveni, *Empires of Time: Calendars, Clocks, and Cultures* (New York: Basic Books, 1989), 332.

For Further Reading

On the idea of the past, see especially Mircea Eliade, *Cosmos and History: The Myth of the Eternal Return* (New York: Harper and Row, 1959). The historian J.H. Plumb explores the difference between past and history in *The Death of the Past* (Boston: Houghton Mifflin, 1970). On time, see Anthony Aveni, *Empires of Time: Calendars, Clocks and Cultures* (New York: Basic Books, 1989). See also, from an art history perspective, George Kubler, *The Shape of Time* (New Haven: Yale University Press, 1962), as well as G.J. Whitrow, *Time in History* (Oxford: Oxford University Press, 1988).

An interesting recent study of memory in relating past and history is Patrick H. Hutton, *History and the Art of Memory* (Hanover, NH: University Press of New England, 1993). For contemporary history, try Ian Kershaw, *The Global Age. Europe 1950–2017* (London: Penguin Books, 2019).

2   Story

Once upon a time, as we say, human beings maintained their family and community, in part, by telling stories about the past. They still do. Stories were generally oral, not written. Stories often contained as much fiction as fact. The storyteller might also be a healer or a magician. Today, literary critics talk of narratives more than stories. But *story* and *narrative* form the same linked chains of tales about the past. Stories tell of the past in ways that give meaning and coherence to the present.

Story in any culture forms the basis of *myth*, where gods and humans interact in a way that explains the natural world. The Greek poet Homer (c. eighth century B.C.E) in the *Iliad* and *Odyssey*, and the Roman poet Virgil (70–19 B.C.E) in his *Aeneid*, provide memorable examples of the impulse to write down stories from a world of oral folk tales as epic poems. (We are not even certain that Homer was a real person, rather than a compilation of oral accounts.) There are many stories and gods in the polytheist universe of ancient Greece and Rome. Myths keep the collective unconscious alive by telling stories of gods and humans interacting in love and war. Native American Wabenaki stories abound of their legendary creator, Gluskap. Many Chinese myths and stories claim to predict the future. We often live by such stories, which are told and retold with variations over and over. Stories give meaning to our lives.

One particular Greek story links history with women. Clio was one of nine daughters of Zeus, god of the heavens, and Mnemosyne, goddess of memory. In time, Clio took on the role of the "proclaimer" of the past, or the muse of history. She ultimately became the patron of all historians. In the West, the story of history as a discipline begins with the Greek goddess Clio.

A story generally exhibits a plot that develops from a beginning through a middle section to an end. Think of this triad as past, present, and future. Good stories may or may not end happily ever after, but they surely do end. The Hebrew Scriptures and the New Testament are examples of oral traditions that have become written stories in which God is the main stage director and narrator of human events, keeping the Hebrews to their covenant and promising salvation to Christians at the end of time, and in eternity beyond death. God speaks and makes promises. God hears and accepts sacrifices. God reveals the truth at the end of time.

Stories exist to entertain, to moralize, and to teach us about life. The *Iliad* glorifies war and exemplifies the Hellenic code of the hero. The *Aeneid* tells of the genealogy of empire and the transfer of empire from Troy to Rome. The Florentine poet Dante and his Renaissance townsman, Boccaccio, were great storytellers who drew on the rich traditions of both pagans and Christians to portray the divine and human comedies. The Arthurian legends of late-medieval France and England told stories of knights and ladies, magic, and the quest for the Holy Grail. The Renaissance writer Christine de Pizan told stories about her imagined and liberated City of Ladies, unhindered by patriarchs. The Grimm brothers collected and reinvented German fairy tales. The British writer Katherine Mansfield (1888–1923) and the Russian Anton Chekhov (1860–1914) helped make the short story a modern art form. So did Stephen King and Toni Morrison. Stories persist as part of our culture. They articulate cultural norms of right and wrong, good and evil. Stories reflect our morality—and immorality.

> "I am always at a loss to know how much to believe of my own stories," said American writer Washington Irving (1783–1859) in his *Tales of a Traveler* (1824).

Stories normally contain more elements of fiction than are allowed historians.

History was originally an attempt to tell a true story, then to get the facts straight, in order to explain and give meaning to the past. But in recent years the line between story and explanation, literature and history, has blurred. Some postmodern literary critics consider all the past a text and historians merely tellers of a relatively meaningful (or meaningless) story that they construct from textual fragments found. Texts are not necessarily fictions, of course. But our most important stories, especially stories about ourselves, may also be true or at least grounded in truth. Historians remain doggedly concerned with approximating the truth about the past on the basis of available evidence. Yet historians recognize, as they always have, their own present situation and inclinations. Recognizing their limitations, historians still want to tell true stories, not make up a fictional past. They want to figure out what probably happened, not what we might imagine happened. They abhor fake history.

Stories are like instructions or blueprints or manuals for the craft of history. They narrate the step-by-step process of construction in sequence. But stories do not give us the raw materials unless they are true, nor do they provide the tools for construction. They are a useful beginning, and we should know them before we settle down to work. Fake news and conspiracy theories are the enemies of history as a reasonably true story of the past.

We are, to paraphrase Aristotle, storytelling animals. But, as the contemporary writer of Vietnam War stories, Tim O'Brien, reminds us, stories blur the line between truth and fiction. Stories are normally fictional. They do not necessarily intend to tell the truth about the past. Truth and fiction may at times seem indistinguishable. *Story* is the root word for *history*. But stories about the past are not yet history, because they are not necessarily true. Stories imagine what might have been. History seeks to explain and understand a past that actually was. What, then, do we really mean by the word *history*?

For Further Reading

Story and history are closely related. My favorite analysis of the relationship is Norman Maclean, *Young Men and Fire* (Chicago: University of Chicago Press, 1992). Maclean tells his story of trying to discover and reconstruct the history of smoke jumpers killed in a fire that blew up in Montana in August 1949. The writer Tim O'Brien explores the similarities and differences between story and history regarding the Vietnam War in *The Things They Carried: A Work of Fiction* (New York: Penguin, 1990). John H. Arnold, in his book *History: A Very Short Introduction* (Oxford: Oxford University Press, 2000), provides some enthusiastic examples of history as "true stories" about the past. See also John Lewis Gaddis, *The Landscape of History: How Historians Map the Past* (Oxford: Oxford University Press, 2002).

3 History

The Register of Knowledge of Fact is called History

—Thomas Hobbes, 1651

History is philosophy teaching by example

—Bolingbroke, 1735

Historical research is a process of discovery and construction. The historian investigates what happened in the past by *researching the available evidence* in order to establish the facts and the chronology of events. This evidence may include written records, archives, manuscripts, maps, and documents, but also unwritten evidence—photographs, paintings, coins, records, tapes, videos, computer hard drives, fossils, and so on. The garbage of the past is everywhere. But from the very beginning, the historian must select and distinguish what is important and significant from what is unimportant and ephemeral. We *discover* evidence, but we *construct* a history.

History aspires to construct and tell true stories about the discovered evidence of the past. Of course, truth about the past remains elusive and approximate. We can never be certain that we have understood the past correctly. But historians always *seek the truth* about the past insofar as that is possible. Truth is that not quite attainable straight line that is never precisely straight. As craftsmen, historians construct their story on the basis of evidence by selecting and arranging the facts (or ideas, values, images, or artifacts) in a chronological sequence that has a beginning, middle, and end. Where the story begins and ends is a matter of interpretation, as well as discovery. In this process, past facts become present statements of fact, narrated after the fact by the historian.

In addition, history seeks to understand and explain past events by interpreting their meaning. The historian seeks to *discover* order and structure in the chaos and messiness of the past. The historian also *constructs* order and structure by creating a narrative or an argument, based on verifiable evidence. Historians know they live in a present where bias and interpretation of the past abound. They understand their own bias. Yet they try to be objective.

In addition to telling a story, *they develop a persuasive argument* on the basis of the evidence, an argument that they believe is reasonable and accurate. They write about context, as well as text. They identify causes that will help *explain* how or why events happened the way they did. They seek *understanding* and *empathy* with individuals in another time and place. They persist in asking questions about the past: Why and how did events happen? What caused an event? Which individuals play important roles? And *what is the meaning* of the events studied, in terms of both past and present?

Why have I italicized some selected words and passages above? Because I think they are very important in understanding history.

Most histories began as *chronicles* or narratives of wars by men who had fought in those wars—the two Greek generals Herodotus (485–425 B.C.E.) on the Persian Wars and Thucydides (460–400 B.C.E.) on the Peloponnesian Wars, for example. These early historians tried to narrate the story of events that actually happened. They were participants. They tried to get the *facts* straight. They made explicit the evidence and sources for their statements of fact. They tried to be objective, even when they invented or imagined some of the evidence according to what others told them. They accepted some wild stories on faith and made up speeches they never heard in person. In Thucydides's account of public speeches in ancient Greece, for example, he made up what he "thought the situation demanded."

> History is the witness that testifies to the passing of times; it illuminates reality, vitalizes memory, provides guidance in daily life, and brings us tidings of antiquity. The first law for the historian is that he shall never dare utter an untruth. The second is that he shall suppress nothing that is true. Moreover, there shall be no suspicion of partiality in his writings, or of malice.
>
> —Cicero (106–43 B.C.E.)

The Greeks invented history by trying to tell true stories about the past. They realized that truth was grounded in evidence. But history was often more *cyclic* than *linear*, going nowhere. In contrast to the Greeks, the Hebrews made history meaningful and linear by making it *monotheistic*. The Hebrew Scriptures comprised a series of stories that told of God's covenant with the people of Abraham and Israel, his chosen people who promised to obey God's commandments and laws. God spoke to his people through burning bushes or at sacrifices. Historical time was linear, not cyclical, beginning with the creation of the world (Genesis) and ending with the coming of the Messiah (Revelations). In between lay nomadic wandering and endless suffering for the Israelites. Prophets predicted the coming Messiah and a river crossing to the land of milk and honey. One God gave *meaning* to the terror, the wandering, and the suffering of history.

Christian history was also monotheistic and linear but added a *central sacred event* between the beginning and end of history, namely, the appearance of Jesus Christ as the Son of God. Christians replaced Jews as the chosen people in the New Testament, fulfilling the promise of a coming Messiah. History began with the Garden of Eden and the creation of the world and with Adam and Eve's big mistake, original sin. Free will could be dangerous. At the end of history, Christ would come again to judge the quick and the dead after a final battle between the forces of Christ and Antichrist, God, and Satan. History would have a meaningful end in which Christians would find eternal life and salvation from sin in Heaven, or else eternal death in Hell. Likewise, Islam offers the sacred event through the life of the Prophet, Muhammad.

Christian history in the Middle Ages was often a *chronicle*, a listing of wars, kings, queens, baptisms, plagues, and marriages. *Chronicle* meant *chronology*, a listing in order over time of important events. But monks also wrote and copied down Christian accounts of historical events. Behind events stood only one cause—the will of an omniscient and omnipresent God. History was moral drama, a story of God's judgment and a battle between God and Satan for the control of human souls, a battle between good and evil. Events conveyed moral meaning and value. Medieval histories are full of the stories of good men and bad, saintly women and wicked hags, chivalry and perfidy. "History records good things of good men," wrote the Venerable Bede (673–735) in the eighth century, and "evil of wicked men." Bede used multiple sources and cross-checked them; he also believed that what a bishop said about saintly bodies that allegedly did not decay simply had to be true because of divine authority.[1] The bishop on God's authority knew right from wrong, and truth from heresy. *Moral judgment* was a crucial element in medieval history, in which God was omniscient, omnipotent, and omnipresent.

Medieval Christian history was above all *dualist*. History was a battle between two forces—God and Satan, light and darkness, body and soul, Heaven and Hell. St. Augustine (354–430) portrayed history as a story of the City of God and the City of Man. But some medieval history after around 1100 A.D. was also *triadic*. Purgatory became a third place between Heaven and Hell. The twelfth-century monk Joachim of Fiore developed a scheme of history that divided all time into three ages that reflected the Father, the Son, and the Holy Spirit. The scheme sounded a lot like past, present, and future. And Joachite thinking became the archetype for later tripartite schemes of the nineteenth century, including the thesis-antithesis-synthesis logic of the Prussian philosopher Georg Wilhelm Friedrich Hegel (1770–1831) and the feudalism-capitalism-socialism stages of history described by the radical social thinker Karl Marx (1818–1883). The line between medieval and modern history was more continuous, and less sharp, than the moderns initially pretended.

Medieval history also meant *genealogy*, a family history that justified ruling authority through a line of royalty, or nobility through marriage and descent. Virgil's great account of the genealogy of Rome, how Aeneas fled burning Troy to found Rome (despite an affair with Dido, shipwrecks, and a descent to the underworld), provided a model of a genealogical epic of a founding father. Virgil also hoped to please his contemporary patron, Emperor Caesar Augustus. In the late Middle Ages, an entire profession of genealogists emerged to chart, and sometimes to forge or fake, lines of noble descent. Genealogy was not simply a form of history, but a claim or road to power.

The words *history* and *historian* only appeared in English around 1500. A *historian*, as distinct from a chronicler or annalist, tried to provide a true, written narrative of past events, not simply a year-by-year listing. Historians began to distinguish between primary (direct) and secondary (second-hand, or indirect) sources. But most historians were simply people who wrote history as a hobby. Griots, shamans, and storytellers were the first professional historians. But historians did not organize themselves professionally as a group until the end of the nineteenth century. Until then, history was the pastime of gentlemen, not the occupation of professionals.

> A *primary source* is a document, image, or artifact that provides us with evidence about the past. A *secondary source* is a book, film, article, or museum that displays primary sources selectively in order to interpret the past.

The Renaissance and the Enlightenment gradually made human beings and human actions more central to human history. History was not revelation, but reason. History became in part the study of change over time, more accurate, more systematic, more focused on human, rather than divine, activities. In time, the practice of history divided into two varieties—call them *positivist* and *idealist*—which viewed history as science or as art.

Science by the eighteenth century gave history two quite different sets of metaphors to employ in the language of narrative and explanation, *mechanical* and *organic*. Mechanical metaphors involved words like *force, mass, energy, inertia, revolution, rise,* and *fall*. These words came largely from physics and Newtonian mechanics. (Russian revolutionary Leon Trotsky used to talk about the locomotive of history racing down the tracks of time.) Organic metaphors involved words like *birth, life, death, growth, culture, evolution,* and *decay*. (The German philosopher Johann Gottfried Herder (1744–1803), whose ideas on culture and peoples influenced later romantic and nationalist historians, distinguished between mechanical *civilization* and organic *culture*, a distinction of enormous importance to later German and Russian thought.) Historians today employ both mechanical and organic metaphors, often quite unconsciously. Watch out for them in your reading!

After the Enlightenment, some historians claimed to be practicing a kind of science, seeking to sift and weigh evidence critically, to test the validity of sources by cross-examination, and to classify and organize evidence in the manner of a geologist or palaeontologist. Some critics called them *positivists*. They were positive about what they could and could not know, using the tools of reason and science. The German historian Leopold von Ranke (1795–1886) epitomized this impulse when he offered seminars on historical method to university students in Germany. Ranke claimed that history sought to explain, to understand, as well as narrate, the past "as it really was." To do this, historians needed to empathize with people of another time and place, to put themselves in their place, and to get the facts straight. In Native American terms, historians needed to walk in the shoes of their subjects of study. Some claimed that history would "speak for itself." Others claimed that history, like science, could establish laws of human behavior over time. History, proclaimed the British historian J.B. Bury around 1900, was "herself simply a science, no less and no more."[2]

Other historians and philosophers of history—notably Wilhelm Dilthey (1833–1911), Benedetto Croce (1866–1952), and Robin G. Collingwood (1889–1943)—became *idealists*. That is, they emphasized that history was really contemporary, here in the present, and autobiographical, about the historian's mind and ideas in the present as much as about the historian's topic in the past. They focused on what people thought, felt, and imagined as much as on what they did. They showed that ideas and ideologies were causes of actions in the past. Some became intellectual historians, historians of ideas. Many believed that ideas shaped events—and the interpretation of events.

The idealist historian sought to understand the past by getting imaginatively inside the minds of individuals in the past. Collingwood in his book *The Idea of History* (1943) distinguished between the inside and outside of events. The outside of events meant simply actions, bodies in motions, what people actually did. The inside of events meant the thoughts, values, and ideas of the human actors who made history. The purpose of history was empathy and understanding of others. By studying the mental world of the past, historians sought to inhabit the minds of their subjects, knowing that to empathize requires imagination inspired by evidence. The historian could then re-enact past actions the way those who performed them were thought to act. Historians needed empathy as a tool in their toolbox.

Positivist ("scientific") historians claim that history provides a scientific explanation of past actions and events. Some philosophers argue that such explanations presume a "covering law." For example, to explain the 1917 Russian Revolution in terms of two main causes—the disastrous effects of World War I and the presence of an organized conspiratorial political party, the Bolsheviks, ready to seize power—is to presume a law something like this: "Whenever a society experiences defeat and destruction in war and contains a political party organized to overthrow the government, a revolution will result." Thus, positivists believe that explanation is equivalent to prediction. The statement "x and y caused z" is equivalent to the statement "If x and y, then z." Explanation implies a power of prediction that most historians would deny, but may themselves imply. Historians generalize, but rarely claim to be discovering a law.

Most historians simply accept that history is part science and part art. They can only try to explain the causes of past events. They work to understand the intentions and motives of historical personages. But they can be certain about neither. Both scientific explanation and imaginative reconstruction remain elusive goals. Objectivity in writing history remains a "noble dream," as one historian put it. The point is simply to try to explain and understand past events by testing a general hypothesis against particular and specific evidence, to try to be as objective and accurate as possible. The result must always be contingent and subject to revision.

> *Historiography* involves the study of the writing of history. It describes historical arguments, theories, and interpretations over time, how schools of thought on particular events change over time—like history.

For example, historians continually argue about, debate, and revise our understanding of the causes of the American Civil War. They usually distinguish between causes that were necessary and those that were sufficient to cause a civil war. Necessary causes include sectional differences between North and South, the existence of slavery as an institution, the moral and political critique of slavery, and the dispute over the tariff. Given the existence of these necessary causes, then other causes were in the end sufficient to lead to a civil war—the Kansas-Nebraska Act of 1854, the election of Abraham Lincoln as president in 1860, or the federal decision to resupply Fort Sumter in Charleston Harbor in 1861, followed by the southern firing on the fort. Without the necessary causes, the sufficient causes would probably not have been sufficient. With them, they produced war and endless suffering—and monumental changes—in both North and South. (See the longer example of causation and the Civil War in Chapter 11 of the toolbox section of this book.) Historians rarely make their causal models explicit. But they often assume and employ them.

Causation is like an explosion. Necessary causes are like dynamite, plutonium, or hydrogen—that is, the fuel. Sufficient causes are like the fuse, match, implosion lenses, or atomic trigger—that is, the ignition device. Ignition causes explosion—but only because the fuel is present.

After the middle of the nineteenth century, the idealistic impulse of some historians shifted to a form of history that sought to find the ultimate meaning of historical events within, rather than outside, history; in human action rather than divine intervention, in large patterns and forces operating over time. Recent critics have dubbed this trend *metahistory*. If historians are generally trying to understand the subtleties and complexities of many things, metahistorians are trying to understand THE ONE BIG THING that gives meaning to history.

Notes

1 Venerable Bede, *Ecclesiastical History of the English People* (London: Penguin Books, 1990), 41–43.
2 Quoted in Fritz J. Stern, *The Varieties of History: From Voltaire to the Present* (New York: William Collins, 1956), 223.

For Further Reading

A good selection of philosophical writings on history is Fritz J. Stern, *The Varieties of History: From Voltaire to the Present* (New York: William Collins, 1956). See also Patrick Gardiner, *Theories of History* (New York: Free Press, 1959).

A classic positivist view by a leader of the *Annales* school is Marc Bloch, *The Historian's Craft* (New York: Alfred A. Knopf, 1953). A more recent exposition is Fernand Braudel, *On History* (Chicago: University of Chicago Press, 1980). On the history of the positivist dream about scientific history, see Peter Novick, *That Noble Dream: The "Objectivity Question" and the American Historical Profession* (New York: Cambridge University Press, 1988).

For the idealist counterpoint, see Robin G. Collingwood, *The Idea of History* (New York: Oxford University Press, 1943). A more specialized, but brilliant, essay on history, free will, and determinism is Isaiah Berlin, *The Hedgehog and the Fox: An Essay on Tolstoy's View of History* (New York: Mentor, 1957).

On historians as a breed, see J. H. Hexter, *On Historians* (Cambridge, MA: Harvard University Press, 1979), and *The History Primer* (New York: Basic Books, 1971).

A fascinating collection of essays on history as mystery is Robin W. Winks, ed., *The Historian as Detective* (New York: Harper and Row, 1968). In the same vein of historical fun, see David Hackett Fischer, *Historians' Fallacies: Toward a Logic of Historical Thought* (New York: Harper and Row, 1970).

4   Metahistory

The history of the world is none other than the progress of the consciousness of freedom.
—G.W.F. Hegel

The history of all hitherto existing societies is the history of class struggle.
—Karl Marx

Metahistory seeks to find one all-encompassing meaning in history.[1]
Metahistorians and system builders believe that history has its own meaning internally. Historians can thus discover meaningful laws and patterns in
history over time. The intellectual revolutions initiated by the British
naturalist Charles Darwin (1809–1882) and the German philosopher
Friedrich Nietzsche (1844–1900) made God extraneous to history, if not
entirely dead. Judaism, Islam, and Christianity provide powerful divine
metahistories. But after 1850, the idea of God's will and design acting in
history gave way to ideas of the survival of the fittest species by natural
selection, to class struggle, and to the will to power of the Overman. But
Darwinian natural selection and Nietzschean escape from the prison of
history were only two varieties of *historicism*, the view that history has its
own meaning and pattern and laws. Historians merely had to discover
those meanings, patterns, and laws. Metahistorians wanted to discover (or
construct) the Big Idea behind history.

Metahistory emphasizes ideal patterns and regularities. Some metahistorians leaned toward science and system. The so-called positivists, especially the French philosopher Auguste Comte (1798–1857), believed that
the study of history was, or could become, a science. Comte too believed
in historical stages. The past was not only meaningful but also law-like
(the iron law of wages, the law of business cycles, laws of the rise and fall
of civilizations, and so on). In part, metahistory derived from medieval and
early modern natural law theory, divine in origin but knowable through
human reason. History was often repetitive (e.g., as tragedy and farce) and
therefore knowable and discoverable. In this sense, metahistory extended

and transformed the Christian view of history as meaningful and linear. But history was secular, not sacred. History, not God, contained the great design of the universe, the Big Idea.

The German philosopher Hegel was a metahistorian. He replaced God with the Absolute and saw history as an evolving process of progress toward freedom. All quests for truth were dialectical in that they began by stating a thesis, then developed its antithesis, or opposite, and finally resolved them in a synthesis. The dialectic was Hegel's Big Idea. Karl Marx studied Hegel's method and became a materialist, seeing material possessions as the basis of culture and society. Marx considered all history the history of class struggle and oppression—the thesis— leading to revolution—the antithesis—and the seizure of political and economic power by the working class (proletariat) from the capitalist class that owned the means of production (bourgeoisie)—the synthesis. Class struggle was Marx's Big Idea. (Ironically, the term *revolution*, borrowed from physics, initially implied not linear development, but cyclic return, the recovery of rights lost.) In England, the so-called Whig view of history extended the Enlightenment project to see all history as continuing rational progress toward a happier future of the greatest good for the greatest number based on complete knowledge of the world. History meant progress, for individuals and for societies. Life was simply getting better and better. Progress was the Whig Big Idea.

Other thinkers claimed that all history was biography. They emphasized the individual lives of great men and women who "made history" in the past—Henry VIII, Frederick the Great, Elizabeth I, Catherine the Great, Napoleon, and Winston Churchill. Still other historians traced the rise of peoples and nations—Treitschke and Droysen in Prussia, Macaulay and Trevelyan in England, Soloviev and Kliuchevsky in Russia, Guizot and Michelet in France, Parkman and Bancroft in the United States—and gave nationalist meaning to history. Nations were like individuals. They were born, they developed, and they perished, like other living organisms. The nation-state was the primary object of historical study. History also became a means of defining and asserting national identity through a real or imagined national past. Politically, nationalism, liberalism, and socialism informed nineteenth-century metahistory after the revolutions of 1848. So, historians naturally turned to studies of nations, individuals, and social classes. Liberalism and socialism also created master narratives of progress and revolutionary emancipation.

> History and memory are closely connected. We cannot afford amnesia if we are to function in the present. The memory hole (a term coined by British writer George Orwell [1903–1950] for eliminating inconvenient history) can destroy both truth and identity, as well as function.

By 1900, metahistory turned to the ideological and irrational in history. Sigmund Freud (1856–1939) and Carl Jung (1875–1961) opened up the subterranean world of the irrational and the unconscious to psychoanalysis and psychohistory. All history was the history of neurosis resulting from mankind's perpetual struggle to repress unconscious urges, longings, and desires, notably those of sex. Jung interpreted history in terms of persistent archetypes in the collective unconscious. Dreams became evidence for analysis of the psyche. "The riddle of history," the Freudian philosopher Norman O. Brown wrote later, "is not in Reason but in Desire; not in labor but in love."[2] Psychoanalysis offered a way out of history, freedom from the burdens of a repressed past, the sublimated instincts of Eros and Thanatos, love and death, liberation from repression.

Metahistory also turned more speculative. In the wake of World War I, Oswald Spengler (1880–1936) wrote his massive *Decline of the West* (which he dictated on a machine), describing the organic laws of the rise and fall of civilizations and of what he called Apollonian, Magian, and Faustian cultures within Western civilization. He produced two almost unreadable volumes. Arnold Toynbee followed with his massive study of the rise and fall of civilizations according to rules of challenge and response to crises. Both looked for law-like explanations for the collapse of the West after a terrible war. Likewise, after World War II, theologian Reinhold Niebuhr (1892–1971) articulated a modern Protestant vision of history by reinstating God as sovereign maker of history and its "one story," full of irony and paradox. Niebuhr again placed meaning outside of history and in religion.

Unfortunately, some metahistory also nurtured totalitarianism. Metahistory provided the underpinnings of two monstrous dictatorships of the twentieth century in Europe: Nazi Germany and Soviet Russia. German leader Adolf Hitler and Soviet leader Joseph Stalin based their two police states on race and class, anti-Semitism and Marxism, respectively. Racist thinkers in Germany explored the history of the so-called Aryan race and predicted future Aryan domination over non-Aryan races. Marxist thinkers in Soviet Russia reduced all history to formulas of class struggle. The ideologies of anti-Semitism and class struggle dominated all thought and reduced individuals to pawns in an evil chess game. Individuals went to the gas chamber or the gulag labor camps simply because they stood in the way of history. Aryanism and anti-Semitism were the Big Ideas behind National Socialism. Communism was the Big Idea behind the Soviet Union (1917–1991). White Supremacy was the Big Idea motivating U.S. President Donald J. Trump.

Nazis and Marxists also rewrote, or altered, history to suit the party line, not the truth. The Aryan race and the working class became the collective heroes of a deadly new kind of official history. Historians criticized the official approach at their peril. (Subscribers to the *Great Soviet Encyclopedia* were once surprised to receive in the mail a razor blade and an article on "berylium" to replace the inconvenient entry on "Beria" after police chief Lavrenty Beria was shot and killed following Stalin's death in 1953. Beria became an unperson—literally written out of history.) Historians had to make their work conform to the established orthodoxies of the party line, Nazi or Communist. If they did not, they became—as Soviet leader Nikita Khrushchev once put it—"dangerous people." The party line, not factual evidence, defined truth.

In the case of the great French medievalist and historian Marc Bloch (1886–1944), who helped found the journal *Annales* and reinvent history as a social science, metahistory literally killed history. The Gestapo tortured and murdered Bloch for his work with the French Resistance during World War II. Millions of others lost their lives because they failed to conform to the standards of metahistory or dared to criticize that metahistory as defined by Nazi or Soviet leaders. Critical thinking and individualism threatened metahistory and could not be tolerated.

But metahistory not only created ideologies. It subverted them as well. Marx, Darwin, and Freud were great demystifiers of history. They concluded that history was not what it appeared to be, not simply the story of individual agents making choices over time. History was a mystery to be revealed. They had revealed that mystery. They were realists, not romantics. History was really a struggle determined by a single force—a struggle to eliminate class inequities and injustices, a struggle to enable the fittest species to survive, or a struggle to repress or sublimate sexual desires by creating civilization. Individuals were not independent agents, but members of groups. Groups made history. Winners in power wrote history. To explain history as it really was meant to strip away the repressive language of ruling elites and other groups in power and to discover and reveal the real and true meaning, the metahistory, underneath that deceptive discourse.

Twentieth-century metahistorians took a "linguistic turn" (following the philosophers), reducing history to a kind of language game. Postmodernism, in addition to deconstructing the language of power, created its own language to replace the organic and mechanical metaphors of the past—*body, other, colonial, imperial, space, border, discourse, narrative, empowerment*, and *text*, to name a few choice words. By claiming that history was merely a form of text, the postmodernists annoyed most historians with their relativism, scepticism, and language games. They also contributed valuable insights into the importance of language in historical studies and into the craft of history itself.

A recent, and more benign, example of metahistory involves evolutionary biology and genetics. Some call it *memetics*. By this theory, cultures evolve in a process of natural selection that favors the most durable *memes* (cultural genes, or viruses). A *meme* is a cultural unit such as an idea, a value, or a fashion fad. Some memes catch on immediately and "go viral" on the Internet. Some become quickly extinct. History develops organically and has a pattern. DNA determines the outcome of history as cultural evolution. Cultural evolution follows Darwinian logic. History exhibits symptoms that can be studied scientifically—the epidemiology of core ideas and values. One speculative thinker thus concludes that "both organic and human history involve the playing of ever-more-numerous, ever-larger, and ever-more-elaborate nonzero-sum [winning does not necessarily mean losing, and vice versa] games."[3]

Another example of metahistory is the current concept of "Jihad versus McWorld," which interprets contemporary history as a struggle between the forces of tribal nationalism and holy war, Islamic Jihad, on one side, and the forces of global integration and international corporations on the other. The deadly attack on New York's World Trade Center and on the Pentagon on September 11, 2001, epitomized that struggle. So too did the terror and violence in the Middle East, from Afghanistan and Iraq to the Gaza Strip and Lebanon. The ideas of freedom and democracy growing out of the Enlightenment encountered the martyrdom of suicide bombers and the terrorist death cult of Al-Qaeda. The "war on terror" confronted "death to America." The wars in Afghanistan, Syria, and Yemen still go on. A war between the U.S. and Iran threatens.

In any event, metahistory, which began as a philosophical effort to fill the metaphysical void left by the death of God in the nineteenth century, became speculative. At its best, metahistory helped historians and readers see the larger meaning of history. At its worst, metahistory provided the ideological justification for totalitarianism and terror. Politicians distorted history to justify nationalism, genocide, fake news, and ethnic cleansing. We are not yet done with the great simplifiers who have used history to serve their own ideological ends. Metahistory breeds martyrdom and self-sacrifice in the name of a Big Idea.

In the meantime, historians sought to analyze, rather than simply narrate, the story of the past without making any grand assumptions about meaning. History became less positivist, more empirical, and more probabilistic, more pragmatic in its approach. Historians and metahistorians went their separate ways. "To analyze a complex phenomenon," as one contemporary historian observes, "a single theory, however rich and multivariate, will seldom suffice. Complex events usually have multiple causes."[4] The age of metahistory and great speculative theories about the past seems to be waning. But there will always be those who claim to understand the one big thing that gives meaning to history. Terrorism, "Too Much Information," and the "war on terror" are simply the latest version of the Big Idea that underlies metahistory.

Notes

1 Hayden White used the term *metahistory* in his book *Metahistory: The Historical Imagination in Nineteenth-Century Europe* (Baltimore: Johns Hopkins University Press, 1973). White defines history as "a verbal structure in the form of a narrative prose discourse" and "a specifically Western prejudice by which

the presumed superiority of modern, industrial society can be retroactively substantiated" (ix, 2). Few historians accept White's view.

2 Norman O. Brown, *Life against Death* (Middletown, CT: Wesleyan University Press, 1957), 16.

3 Robert Wright, *Nonzero: The Logic of Human Destiny* (New York: Vintage, 2000), 6.

4 Victoria E. Bonnell, *Roots of Rebellion: Workers' Politics and Organizations in St. Petersburg and Moscow, 1900–1914* (Berkeley: University of California Press, 1983), 17.

For Further Reading

The place to start is with a massive study rejected by most historians, Hayden White's *Metahistory: The Historical Imagination in Nineteenth-Century Europe* (Baltimore: Johns Hopkins University Press, 1973). The classic liberal Whig interpretation is the subject of Herbert Butterfield, *The Whig Interpretation of History* (London: Penguin Books, 1931). A modern Christian metahistory essay is Nikolai Berdyaev, *The Meaning of History* (Cleveland: Meridian, 1962 [1936]). Arnold Toynbee portrays history as the challenge and response of great civilizations in *A Study of History* (New York: Oxford University Press, 1957).

On history as narrative, text, and virtual reality, see Hayden White, *The Content of the Form: Narrative Discourse and Historical Representation* (Baltimore: Johns Hopkins University Press, 1987).

Paul Costello summarizes the work of twentieth-century metahistorians (H.G. Wells, Spengler, Toynbee, Pitrim Sorokin, Lewis Mumford, and William McNeill) in his *World Historians and Their Goals: Twentieth-Century Answers to Modernism* (DeKalb: Northern Illinois University Press, 1993).

On the new cultural evolution approach to history, see Susan Blackmore, *The Meme Machine* (New York: Oxford University Press, 1999). On history as information, see the book by James Gleick on information cited in the introduction.

5   Antihistory

The unhistorical and the superhistorical are the natural antidotes against the over-powering of life by history; they are the cures of the historical disease.
—Friedrich Nietzsche, *The Use and Abuse of History*, 1874

The only grounds for preferring one [historical interpretation] over another are moral or aesthetic ones.
—Hayden White, *The Content of the Form*, 1987

As long as there has been history, there have been those who opposed or denied history. The English poet Matthew Arnold (1822–1888) wrote of "that huge Mississippi of falsehood called history." Stephen Daedelus in Irish novelist James Joyce's *Portrait of the Artist as a Young Man* called history "a nightmare from which I am trying to awake." History is a basically rational enterprise. Thus, the currents of irrationality that flooded Europe in the twentieth century also inundated the historical profession. The central threats to those who sought to tell the truth about history were excessive idealism and relativism.

Historians are notorious for asking questions: Who? What? When? Where? How? Why? Question-framing is crucial to the historian's craft. Without a significant question, one is unlikely to get a significant answer. Idealism had its roots in the philosophy of Bishop George Berkeley (1685–1753) and Immanuel Kant, the notion that ideas (like Platonic forms) had reality and that history was essentially the history of ideas. All history was intellectual history, the history of thought. History was not science, but art. Artists would paint whatever picture they chose. Nietzsche argued that future "supermen" would substitute their own ideas for religion to manipulate the herd of humanity, narcissist Trump's suckers. The point was not to remember the past, but to forget it, and liberate our true selves. History was simply an idea, not a reality. And ideas were only true relative to the person who thought those ideas.

There is certainly nothing wrong with emphasizing ideas, understanding, and empathy in doing history. But to emphasize the idea at the expense of the evidence is inappropriate. So, if there were many historians, then there would be many ideas of history. Historical truth was no longer absolute, but relative to the historian. Every man was his own historian, as American historian Carl Becker (1873–1945) put it around 1930. Relativism meant that there was simply no way to choose which of two or more competing histories of the same events was preferable. There was no absolute truth, simply relative truths that pragmatically worked for different historians. The facts and the meaning were impossible to agree upon. Interpretation was all.

In some cases, historicism gave way to skepticism and postmodernism. History, in the opinion of the anti-Semitic automobile manufacturer Henry Ford, was bunk—except his own malicious version. If all interpretations of history were equally valid, or meaningless, why not choose the one that worked? Ford believed in the spurious anti-Semitic forgery known as the *Protocols of the Elders of Zion*, which explained the history of the modern world in terms of a Jewish conspiracy, and he disseminated these views widely in the 1920s. (See Section 13.4, "Forgeries and Facsimiles," in the toolbox.)

Some idealists and relativists turned to fascism. Benedetto Croce admired Italian fascist dictator Benito Mussolini (1883–1945). The German philosopher Martin Heidegger (1889–1976) became a member of the Nazi party. The Belgian literary "deconstructionist" Paul de Man (1919–1983) wrote for Nazi journals during World War II. The French philosopher Jean-Paul Sartre (1905–1980) went along with Stalinism in the Soviet Union. And after the war, existentialism produced a literature of despair in which history was a meaningless struggle for existence, Sisyphus endlessly rolling his rock up the hill, the stranger wandering in the void. Despair bred nihilism and relativism. History seemed a tale of sound and fury, signifying nothing, as Shakespeare and William Faulkner put it.

> In writing history, you should be true to the facts, report your sources accurately, write in the past tense, avoid "I," be as objective as possible, make passive sentences active, and choose your words carefully. Do not be vague, wordy, pretentious, or gender specific. Organize well. Be brief.

Fortunately, historians generally tended to resist totalitarianism, not to collaborate with it. If they could not resist, they sometimes refused to go along with the party line and "wrote for the drawer," waiting until a freer time to publish their findings.

During the Cold War, censorship and secrecy became the enemies of history. Classification of secret documents in closed archives made crucial evidence off limits to historians not cleared to see such information. Government control of information proliferated. Under the Official Secrets Act, "weeders" routinely eliminated inconvenient documents and files in British archives. (Not everything in the Public Record Office, as one bureaucrat put it, was open to the public.) Whole archives were closed or disappeared into shredders. History fell down the "memory hole," as British writer George Orwell described it. In the Soviet Union, not only people, but also history in general, was purged, cleansed, revised to suit the party line. Historians were afraid to publish their findings for fear of arrest or worse. Only in the United States did the Freedom of Information Act (1966) finally come to the aid of historians and reopen secret archives to public scrutiny. Even then—and even today—bureaucrats have found ways to subvert or delay the release of previously classified information.

I once discovered the secret 1950 "confession" of British atomic spy Klaus Fuchs in the Truman Presidential Library. The German-born Fuchs worked at Los Alamos, New Mexico, the super-secret center of the Manhattan Project to build the atomic bomb during World War II. Fuchs passed information on nuclear weapons to the Soviet Union via contacts in Santa Fe, Boston, and New York. The document recording his confession to British intelligence interrogators was classified "top secret" in Britain. But Fuchs's confession was internal to an unclassified memorandum to President Truman in the United States from Sidney Souers, Truman's national security adviser. I published the confession in my biography of Fuchs in the early 1980s. Shortly afterward the American document was reclassified. Such is the wilderness of mirrors of classification and secrecy.

The most recent example of antihistory is the idea that fiction and nonfiction are identical. Some postmodern thinkers and ill-informed politicians consider all history a form of text or narrative to be manipulated for their own purposes. The past does not exist. Reality does not exist. Truth does not exist. Time does not exist. The facts do not exist. History is a story constructed (not discovered) by the historian. One story is as good as another. No story is falsifiable. Take your pick:

- The Holocaust never happened.
- A massive conspiracy killed President John F. Kennedy in 1963.
- Alger Hiss was completely innocent of all charges.
- Ancient Greek civilization came from black Africa because Aristotle stole his ideas from Africans in the library at Alexandria, Egypt.
- A Blair Witch Project existed in Burkettsville, Maryland.
- Japanese soldiers did not torture, rape, and kill hundreds of thousands of people in Nanking, China, in 1937–1938.
- The biographer Edmund Morris grew up with Ronald Reagan in the 1920s.
- President Barack Obama was not born in the United States.

These are all erroneous statements of fact. There is no evidence to support any of them. There is much evidence to contradict them. But many people believe them. Who wants to choose between competing lies?

So, the difference between fact and fiction is central to doing history. Yet some literary critics proclaim all history a text or a useful fiction.

History is all about interpretation. Historians make up details that suit their narrative. Biographers (such as Edmund Morris) insert themselves into the biography of another person as if they had known him or her. Films perpetuate completely discredited historical theories about events (director Oliver Stone based his film *JFK* on a discredited report on the Kennedy assassination; see Section 13.6). Historians even write books on what might have happened, rather than what did happen, confusing prophecy and vivid imagination with history.[1]

The most notorious example of antihistory is historical denial. Historical denial asserts that a well-known event never really happened or that a well-known person never existed. In accordance with relativism, those who deny history assert that all views of history are equally valid, just a bit different. They claim that their denial is just as valid as any other historical account. Thus, the Holocaust, a series of events and actions that killed six million Jews and other "subhumans" during World War II, either happened or did not happen. Take your pick. The "revisionists" deny that it happened at all. People usually deny that past events happened for present political reasons. They ignore the normal rules of science, reason, and logic. They distort, or take out of context, selected facts that suit their opinion or argument. They ignore all evidence that contradicts their claim. They exaggerate claims based on one piece of evidence, not many. They substitute bias for open-mindedness toward the past. They cite discredited sources that agree with their point of view. Historical denial is *not* historical revision, a perfectly acceptable way of rethinking the past. Denial is pseudohistory and antihistory.

> A single fact neither proves nor disproves a historical argument. History is grounded in multiple facts and sources, streams of evidence pointing to a single conclusion. Denying one fact proves nothing.

Historians themselves are not immune to the virus of extreme relativism and useful fiction. Historian Simon Schama joins the language game of antihistory by introducing into his histories "purely imagined fiction" and "purely fictitious dialogues" along with a true account of events. Thus, Schama transforms history into a partly fictional work of the imagination "worked up from my own understanding of the sources as to how such a scene might have taken place."[2] (See the example of Schama's fictitious British soldier's account of scaling the cliffs of Quebec in Section 13.2.)

Of course, once we begin mixing history and fiction, we may well invalidate history as a whole. If one fact is made up, why not the next? And the next? And the next? U.S. President Donald J. Trump creates antihistory daily from his own world of lies, half-truths, and fake news that ignores history for his own malignant narcissism. (Trump produced over ten thousand lies since he became president in 2017, according to the latest count.) Trump claimed President Barak Obama was politically illegitimate because he was not born in the United States, which Obama was. Politicians lie about the past. However brilliant and well written, antihistory is speculation, conspiracy theory, or fiction, not history.

Notes

1 For example, Robert Cowley, ed., *What If? The World's Foremost Military Historians Imagine What Might Have Been* (New York: Putnam, 1999). These essays imagine "likely outcomes had history gone differently"—Hitler deciding not to attack the Soviet Union in 1941, Atlantic storms hitting the Normandy beachheads for one additional day in June 1944, the Confederacy winning the Civil War, Nazi Germany occupying Great Britain, and so forth.
2 Simon Schama, *Dead Certainties* (New York: Vintage, 1991), 327. Schama admits that the observations of one of General Wolfe's soldiers prior to the Battle of Quebec are "pure inventions based, however, on what the documents suggest," but denies that he would ever "scorn the boundary between fact and fiction," that is, history (322).

For Further Reading

On the denial of history, see especially Deborah Lipstadt, *Denying the Holocaust: The Growing Assault on Truth and Memory* (New York: Free Press, 1993), and more recently Michael Shermer and Alex Grobman, *Denying History: Who Says the Holocaust Never Happened and Why Do They Say It?* (Berkeley: University of California Press, 2000).

Postmodernism has had a greater impact on literary criticism than on philosophy or history. For a favourably inclined collection of essays, see Keith Jenkins, *The Postmodern History Reader* (London: Routledge, 1997), and his more recent *Refiguring History: New Thoughts on an Old Discipline* (London: Routledge, 2003). A more hostile response to postmodernism is Keith Windschuttle, *The Killing of History: How a Discipline Is Being Murdered by Literary Critics and Social Criticism* (Paddington, Australia: Macleay, 1996). The title says it all. A more balanced account is in Mark Poster, *Cultural History and Postmodernity: Disciplinary Readings and Challenges* (New York: Columbia University Press, 1997).

For more recent accounts of postmodernism and its impact on the writing of history, see Elizabeth Clark, *History, Theory, Text: Historians and the Linguistic Turn* (Cambridge, MA: Harvard University Press, 2004), and Jonathan Clark, *Our Shadowed Present: Modernism, Postmodernism, and History* (Stanford, CA: Stanford University Press, 2003).

6   The Present

All history is contemporary history.

—Benedetto Croce

What I offer you here is in part my invention, but held tightly in check by the voices of the past.

—Natalie Zemon Davis, *The Return of Martin Guerre*, 1983

Present and past interact in the mind of the historian. But when does the past end and the present begin? Perhaps the past ends with one's own birth year or, perhaps, yesterday. Agreement is impossible. There is no clear way to distinguish contemporary history from past history. Besides, history has always involved the historian in the present describing a past that once existed but now needs to be discovered and reconstructed. History has even been defined as the "simultaneous perception of difference and similarity between past and present."[1] What can the past teach us about the present? How does our present inform our view of the past?

Some idealist historians claim that all history is present, or contemporary. History is a product of the life and mind of the historian here and now. Some positivists claim that history is a weak science of description, if not prediction, that can approximate the truth about a past that really existed. But history is a large tent under which sit many historians of different interests, from intellectual history to material culture, from cultural history to economic history. There is room for all, except perhaps for those who wish to tear down the tent. Or for hungry camels.

> Legitimate *revision* of history involves filling a gap in the literature, changing an accepted interpretation by presenting new facts, or rearranging old facts to provide new interpretation of the past.

Professional historians, of course, are a community of practitioners. They are craftsmen and craftswomen. They continue to research and write history essentially the way they always have. Many remain blissfully ignorant of, and uninterested in, the theoretical dogfights that rage around them. They simply go on doing history.

Historical interpretations meanwhile undergo periodic revision. New schools of history (sometimes fads, or fashions) develop to fill gaps in the literature or to open up new fields—economic history, quantitative history, psychohistory, postcolonial studies, cultural studies, and so on. Historians continue to employ useful methods from other disciplines, notably sociology, economics, linguistics, and anthropology. Historical journals and online historical websites proliferate. Teams of historians revise the conventional wisdom of old topics. Biography and film bring history alive in new and exciting ways, conveying history to a broad audience untouched by the average scholarly monograph.

In recent years, historians have also become less elitist and more inclusive. The men's club that was history now is an equal opportunity, even affirmative action, employer. Historians now include more women, minorities, and LGBTQ people than ever before. Many have their own organizations and special interest groups. History has expanded its topics to include women's history, African American history, labor history, queer history, the history of the body, the insane, and the differently abled. Virtually everyone is now the subject of historical study. Anyone can become a historian. The workshop and craft of history are open to all.

> Historians study continuity and change over time. They look for long-term trends, as well as short-term turning points. They study what did not change, as well as what did change, social structures as well as events.

In the twentieth century, the school of French historians grouped around the journal *Annales* had an enormous impact on researching and writing history. These historians sought to achieve more scientific history by examining very long periods of time *(longue durée)*, a worldwide geographic perspective in space (*l'histoire totale*), the mental world (*mentalités*) of people in the past, and any and all evidence that might bear on the structure of society—weather reports, linguistic terms and phrases, aerial photographs, crop production, prices, and geography, for example. (In one case, a historian used archival statistics on the number of candles burned in particular French churches in the Middle Ages to look at regional variations in religious enthusiasms!)

> The past cannot speak except through the sources after interrogation. But historians of recent events can interview subjects who are still alive and willing to speak. Oral interviews are a significant historical source, because the historian can cross-examine a witness to events who is living, not dead.

The *Annales* historians and their successors have tried to return history to its scientific origins and to shift historical study away from politics and foreign policy to society and culture, including material culture. While they do not ignore political events, they focus on social history. They are partly responsible for the general shift in historical studies toward social and global history, and away from narrative to analysis. What matters to them is not the history of events, but the structure of society that changes very slowly over time.

Present-day historians develop a number of useful skills that will help them in virtually any future career or activity:

- Research—finding, selecting, and weighing evidence.
- Judgment—distinguishing good evidence and arguments from bad.
- Persuasive argument.
- Good, close reading of written texts.
- Good, concise writing of logical narratives and analysis.
- Question-framing that is significant.
- Simple and direct presentation of a case study.

One historian, David Potter, characterized all historians as either *lumpers* or *splitters*, people who put things together or take them apart. More likely, historians begin with some simple assumptions that tend to lump things together, then encounter the incredible complexity and diversity of the past, then try to find their way through to a new way to lump things together that provides a better explanation than has been provided to date. Put in another way, historians encounter data, frame a hypothesis, and modify that hypothesis if they encounter new data that require such modification. In any case, historians develop useful skills of investigation and expression.

Living in the present, rather than the past, also raises the question of *bias*. How can the historian overcome present opinions and personal predilections to write a reasonably objective account of the past? Contrary to the notion that all history is autobiography, historians need to understand and empathize with people and cultures of other times and places. They are less likely to study themselves than the other, the stranger, the kind of person they never will be because they lived in another time and place. Current identity politics tends to steer historians toward topics of race, class, and gender and to characterize individuals in terms of a group or social class. Historians can never overcome present politics entirely. But they should make the attempt. And they should make their own bias explicit for the reader as part of their approach to doing history.

Today, historians continue to break new ground in our knowledge of the past. They may fill a gap by studying an unknown topic or individual. They may synthesize existing sources that concern a sprawling, interdisciplinary topic like the history of New York City. They may rearrange knowledge by studying what happened in a particular year, say, 1831. They may study new and "forbidden" topics such as the history of contraception. They may reinterpret a familiar subject such as Abraham Lincoln in a new way, perhaps emphasizing his religious views or gender. They may re-examine a famous primary source, such as the Declaration of Independence. They may look at the lives of ordinary people "from below" in extraordinary times, such as Stalin's purges of the 1930s. They may launch a team effort to have many historians re-examine a well-known event, such as the American Civil War or the Boxer Rebellion in China or the Iraq War. Or they may turn to a study of the language or discourse of the past to understand political culture and folkways.[2]

In 2016, I became interested in the Russian connections of Donald J. Trump whose links with Russian and Eurasian organized crime went back to his first marriage to a Czech émigré and his Trump Tower hotel complex in Manhattan. Trump was a well-known playboy and realtor in New York who enjoyed manipulating the media. As a Russian historian, I found that my background provided tools for investigating such a contemporary topic. Using open and online sources, I was able to write an account of Trump's links with Vladimir Putin's kleptocracy that helped explain Trump's presidential run in the present with inconvenient evidence from the past. My account preceded the official (and heavily redacted) report to the Justice Department by Robert S. Muller. Moreover, I was not obliged to limit my investigation to Trump's 2016 political campaign (Trump thought he would lose). I could explore Trump's real estate operations that enabled Eurasian oligarchs to move their money abroad after the collapse of the Soviet Union in 1991. History helped explain the present. As a Russian historian, I could shed light on Trump's links to Russian oligarchs and Eurasian criminals.

But Trump is not easy to fathom. As a "gaslighter," he produces a tweetstorm of lies, misdirections, misstatements and denials whose fog leaves his target audience full of self-doubt and confusion, waiting for the next topic shift. Nothing he says can be fathomed or even denied by the historian. Facts and evidence to refute his lies simply do not exist, because there is nothing to refute. Trumpland is outside history.

History has always been partly a product of the present historian, as well as the past. Historians living in the present choose what to research and write about, when and where to begin and end their story, and how to construct a true narrative. They do not, or should not, invent useful and dramatic fictions or leave out and suppress inconvenient evidence in the archives. They should use their tools wisely and maintain them in good condition, like any other craftsmen. Historians cannot escape the fact that they live in the present, but they should always seek to understand and empathize with those who once lived in the past. The present should give us perspective on history, but not intrude upon historical analysis, argument, and narrative grounded in evidence from the past. And history helps us understand the present, even when it is full of lies, deceptions, and denials.

Notes

1 Jacques Barzun, *From Dawn to Decadence: Five Hundred Years of Western Cultural Life* (New York: HarperCollins, 2000), 47.
2 See Maria Diedrich, *Love Across the Color Lines: Ottilie Assing and Frederick Douglass* (New York: Hill and Wang, 1999); Edwin G. Burrows and Mike Wallace, *Gotham: A History of New York City to 1898* (New York: Oxford University Press, 1999); Louis P. Masur, *1831: Year of Eclipse* (New York: Hill and Wang, 2001); Andrea Tone, *Devices and Desires: A History of Contraceptives in America* (New York: Hill and Wang, 2001); Allen C. Guelzo, *Abraham Lincoln: Redeemer President* (Grand Rapids: Eerdmans, 1999); Pauline Maier, *American Scripture: Making the Declaration of Independence* (New York: Alfred A. Knopf, 1997); Sheila Fitzpatrick, *Everyday Stalinism: Ordinary Life in Extraordinary Times: Soviet Russia in the 1930s* (New York: Oxford University Press, 1999); Gabor S. Borritt, ed., *Why the Civil War Came* (New York: Oxford University Press, 1996); Kenneth Cmiel, *Democratic Eloquence: The Fight over Popular Speech in Nineteenth-Century America* (Berkeley: University of California Press, 1990).

For Further Reading

The journal *History and Theory: Studies in the Philosophy of History* is an excellent place to start discovering how philosophers, critics, and historians think about history today. A good overview of historical thinking by a practicing historian is Richard Evans, *In Defence of History* (New York: W.W. Norton, 1999). See also Joyce Appleby, Lynn Hunt, and Margaret Jacob, *Telling the Truth about History* (New York: W.W. Norton, 1994). Philosophically inclined students will appreciate William H. Dray, *Philosophy of History*, 2nd ed. (Englewood Cliffs, NJ: Prentice Hall, 1993). A good history of twentieth-century trends in historiography is George Iggers, *Historiography in the Twentieth Century: From Scientific Objectivity to the Postmodern Challenge* (Middletown, CT: Wesleyan University Press, 1997).

For a good case study on how history can be entangled in present politics and painful memories of the living, see Edward T. Linenthal and Tom Engelhardt, eds., *History Wars: The Enola Gay and Other Battles for the American Past* (New York: Henry Holt, 1996).

On history as a male enterprise, see the history of women in the profession by Bonnie G. Smith, *The Gender of History: Men, Women, and the Practice of History* (Cambridge, MA: Harvard University Press, 1998). Also, see Joan Scott, *Gender and the Politics of History* (New York: Columbia University Press, 1989).

On contemporary history and present politics, see my book *Useful Assets. The Trump Family, the Russians and Eurasian Organized Crime* (Pittsburgh: Dorrance Publishers, 2019).

7 The Future

Historians do not make very good futurists. The so-called futurists of the European avant-garde before World War I imagined a coming world of racing cars more beautiful than ancient Greek sculpture. (Maybe they were right, given the popularity of NASCAR.) They disdained everyone over the age of 30. Many of them died violently in the mud and trenches of the Great War. Historians failed to predict the rise of Nazi Germany in the 1930s or the fall of the Soviet Union in 1991. But history is not a craft of prediction, like meteorology. We cannot predict for certain that the future of history itself holds promise. Historians disagree in that regard.

Although history is not predictive, it can offer some useful perspectives and counsel prudence for decision makers in the present. History provides marvelous critical tools for puncturing inflated analogies—for example, between two different centuries, Donald Trump's presidency and the rise of Hitler, the origins of very different wars. (Bismarck's comment that the Balkans were not worth the bones of a Prussian soldier was once popular. So is the analogy between the Maginot Line and the Star Wars antimissile system, or between the medieval assassins of Central Asia and present-day terrorists.) Decision makers who have read history widely and deeply may well have better virtual historical experience for making decisions than someone quite ignorant of the past. But they may also be tempted to use the expression "history shows" to precede an inaccurate, uninformed, or misleading statement.

> History cannot predict the future. Unlike science, history does not study laws of nature but specific events in the past. History cannot run controlled experiments. Fortunately, we are not condemned to repeat history, but free to make the best of it.

History will continue to survive in the natural selection process that creates and destroys modes of knowing. History as a species of knowledge is deeply rooted in the human condition, our need for true stories about the past. Particular forms of history, however, have become, and will continue to become, extinct. Hagiography (laudatory lives of saints) has pretty much disappeared, except in the biographies of dictators like Saddam Hussein and Muammar Gadhafi, or the campaign biographies of American presidential candidates, or the pop memoirs of sports heroes and rock stars. (Come to think of it, maybe hagiography is still alive and well …). We do have our modern heroes—Michael Jackson, Elvis Presley, Lady Gaga, Harriet Tubman, Martin Luther King, Ruth Bader Ginsburg. But historians no longer assume the primacy of individuals or even of politics, policy, and diplomacy. Intellectual history has given way, at least temporarily, to social history and cultural studies. Even postmodernism has probably had its day, relatively speaking, except in the lies and useful fictions of politicians.

The field of evolutionary biology has provided historians with a new word, the *meme*. Memes are like genomes or perhaps computer viruses. They are replicators. They convey information and send messages that determine which memes will survive in the meme pool and which will not. Memes may be ideas, slogans, tunes, poems, or clothing fashions. Imitation means survival. Otherwise they will become extinct, like the concept of the ether, or the Absolute, or Great Men, or the Edsel. Genomes survive, but computer viruses can be eliminated. In this model, history is a meme that will survive the struggle for existence. History has enormous powers of both replication and adaptation. Despite the assault of postmodernism, history as a discipline is here to stay.[1]

History will probably remain partly art and partly science, construction and discovery. Historians cannot simply paint whatever picture they imagine. Nor can they run controlled experiments in the present to verify hypotheses about the past. Rather, they continue to construct products for the marketplace of historically curious readers, using the materials of the past, the blueprint of story and narrative, supplies of evidence, and the rules of the trade. Readers (and reviewers) of history in the end will determine which history survives, becomes popular, is relegated to the scholarly journals, or disappears.

> A source may be both primary and secondary, depending on its use. For example, Joyce Appleby's *Liberalism and Republicanism in the Historical Imagination* (1992) is a secondary source about liberal and republican thought. But it is also a primary source about Joyce Appleby, women historians, and American historians in the late twentieth century. Our purpose partly determines whether a source is primary, secondary, or both.

Thus, the historical profession will continue to adapt and change. Historians will work within existing paradigms or establish new ones. Students of history will not be clones of their mentors, but voyagers on a new and exciting journey of their own. We know only that they will go to times and spaces that we have not yet seen. They will employ new methods, study new topics, and revise our view of what we thought we knew.

The Internet offers exciting new opportunities for historians. It provides a global data base, powerful search engines, access to the card catalogues of distant libraries (I often pay a virtual visit to Harvard, Dartmouth, or the Library of Congress via the Internet before heading there to do research on-site), chat rooms, e-mail, blogs, and the opportunity to submit and edit a journal article entirely online. Yet there is also a downside to the Internet. There is often no peer review. Garbage, conspiracy, ideology, alternative facts, and erroneous information abound. There is no editing or cross-checking, no guarantee of accuracy. The Internet is a powerful tool for research.[2] But it is also misleading and incomplete. Historians tend to use it only as an ancillary tool or a starting point for research.

The Internet puts a vast amount of information and evidence on the historian's desktop. Primary sources in distant archives and secondary sources from the distant past may all be online. The Internet is always worth checking, especially because one website often links to others in an endless network of historical texts and images. And blogs make the views of many historians—good or bad—instantly accessible online. If you do not like what you read, you can often put in your own two cents worth of opinion. As usual, you should approach the Internet with the same caution and critical viewpoint that you bring to any source. The traditional tools—selection, verification, significance, cross-checking, judgment, comparison, and consistency—are still effective in cyberspace.

There is ample evidence that history is alive and well. Television has a channel devoted to nothing but history. The television series *The History Detectives* brings the methods of the historian to an audience of millions. The documentary films of Ken Burns testify to a deep American need to rediscover the past through visual and musical historical materials. The History Book Club has wide readership. Millions read history for fun and pleasure. Companies research and write history for interested clients; for example, History Associates Incorporated (with which I have had the good fortune to be affiliated) provides litigation support, archival services, and historical research and writing for corporate and government clients.[3]

Historical controversies over issues such as the arsenic-laden hair of Napoleon, the bones and DNA of dead tsars and presidents, and the Holocaust become front-page news. Daniel Goldhagen's book *Hitler's Willing Executioners: Ordinary Germans and the Holocaust* (New York: Knopf, 1996) created a furor in Germany and the United States by arguing that ordinary Germans, not just Hitler and the Nazis, participated actively in killing Jews.[4] Historical preservation groups in virtually every community fight to save and restore old buildings or monuments, to collect historical artifacts from families, to publish anniversary accounts of towns and regions.

We also have people apologizing for past historical injustices. Everywhere political and religious leaders apologize (and sometimes pay reparations) for past crimes against humanity—the Crusades, Galileo's imprisonment, slavery, Confederate rebellion, the American internment of Japanese-Americans during World War II, Stalin's purges, and Hitler's Holocaust. In this way, history becomes public mythology. That mythology too is subject to revision. Apologizing for history has become a postmodern growth industry of late capitalism. If history offends, apologize. Or pay reparations. Or tear down monuments. And bring on the lawyers!

History exists both in the knowable past and in the present mind of the historian. History is neither scientific fact nor relativist fiction. Historians both discover and describe the past through narrative and persuasive argument, or interpretation. They are detectives and writers, craftsmen, not scientists or artists. In explaining the course of a past event—how and why it happened—historians provide an interpretation that is provisional and temporary. History is continually tested and revised by other historians. History involves revision, not denial, of statements of fact about the past, based on new facts or new interpretations of old facts, not on present politics. The community of historians produces converging lines of evidence that create a testable hypothesis about the past. Historians then test, examine, and rethink that hypothesis in the complex craft that is history. On occasion, they may even rethink the paradigm of history itself.

Like a lawyer, the historian builds a case upon the historical evidence, although seeking a true account of the past, not a courtroom victory for the client. Like a detective, the historian seeks clues to solve a mystery, if not to convict a criminal. Like an artist, the historian paints a picture that expresses a personal vision while portraying a real world. Like a scientist, the historian frames and tests falsifiable hypotheses against the data. But in the end, the workshop of the historian perhaps most resembles the workshop of the craftsman. The historian aims to make history a true and readable account of the past limited only by the materials, the plans, and the design. That account must ultimately be grounded in fact, not fiction.

As long as human beings survive to tell stories and ask questions about the past, history will survive. History is not just narrative and text. Nor is it likely to become, well, just history. History is a durable and venerable branch of knowledge in a liberal arts curriculum. But it is also a craft whose knowledge and tools will serve students well in any occupation or career over the changing course of their lifetime. Most students will not become professional historians. But they will use the historian's tools, consciously or unconsciously, every day of their lives. And they will read history for enjoyment and understanding. Remember that. And write it down.

Notes

1 On memes (a word coined by geneticist Richard Dawkins in 1976), see especially Richard Brodie, *The Virus of the Mind: The New Science of the Meme* (Seattle: Integral Press, 2001).
2 A good history website is www.ukans.edu/history/VL/, which has numerous links to other historical and archival sites.
3 See, for example, Philip L. Cantelon, *The History of MCI: The Early Years, 1968–1988* (Dallas: Heritage Press, 1993); Richard Hewlett, *Jesse Ball du Pont* (Gainesville: University of Florida Press, 1992); Joan Zenzen, *Battling for Manassas: The Fifty-Year Preservation Struggle at Manassas Battlefield Park* (State College: Pennsylvania State University Press, 1998).
4 For a historical study of a historical controversy. see Geoff Eley, *The "Goldhagen Effect": History, Memory, Nazism—Facing the German Past* (Ann Arbor: University of Michigan Press, 2001).

For Further Reading

On the limited uses of history for decision makers, see Richard E. Neustadt and Ernest R. May, *Thinking in Time: The Uses of History for Decision-Makers* (New York: Free Press, 1985). On history as analogous to film and photography, see Siegfried Kracauer, *History: The Last Things Before the Last* (New York: Oxford University Press, 1969).

For an excellent guide to the Internet for historians, see Dennis A. Trinkle and Scott A. Merriman, eds., *The History Highway*, 4th ed. (Armonk, NY: M.E. Sharpe, 2006).

Part II

The Tools of History

8 Doing History

An Overview

The best way to understand history is to try to do some history yourself. The following examples should help you to choose a good research topic, begin your reading, take good notes, and write a good final paper. In time, you will discover other tools and hone them for yourself.

8.1 Choosing a Good Paper Topic

Choosing a good paper topic is a challenge and an important first tool in researching and writing history. How big should the topic be? How small? Can you do the topic justice in the short period you have to research and write it? Here are some friendly questions to ask yourself when choosing a paper topic:

1 Will this topic maintain my interest and curiosity over a long period of time?
2 Do I have the necessary background in reading and course work to undertake research about this topic?
3 Is this a topic about which other historians have written (historiography) rather than simply a topic of personal interest to me?
4 Is this topic feasible in the sense that there are primary sources (documents, correspondence, autobiographies, records, etc.) available to me for research purposes?
5 Is the topic really historical (say, before I was born), or is it so contemporary that historians have not yet explored it?
6 Is the scope of the topic too big and broad (modern Russia), too small and narrow (Lenin's speech at the Finland Station, April 1917), or just about right (the response of the Bolsheviks to the Provisional Government in 1917)?
7 Does the topic present a significant question that can be reasonably answered in this case?
8 Will this paper contribute anything original to the historical discussion? Fill a gap in the literature? Or at least take sides in an ongoing historical debate?

9   Will I have fun researching and writing about this topic? Will it make a good story, as well as a convincing argument?

10   Can I explain to my niece, nephew, parent, elevator companion, or friend what the topic is and why it should be of any interest to that person?

Task: Write a brief account of how and why you actually chose your topic for a recent history paper. Which of these criteria did you satisfy? Which did you not satisfy?

8.2 Reading History

Reading is another critical tool in doing history. You should read as much history as you can. Try to distinguish good history from bad. Reading history is different from reading novels, or poetry, or essays, or scientific articles in a technical journal. The volume of work on any historical topic is normally so large that it could take the better part of a lifetime to read through it with any care. What should you read? How should you read works of history? What techniques can help you know when and how to skim, or read carefully, or selectively?

Historians rarely start at the beginning of a book and read through to the end. This kind of reading is pleasurable. But the sheer volume of sources makes it impossible for historians to read everything completely. Rather, they approach each source with specific questions or interests in mind that automatically limit the amount of material that will be relevant to them.

Historians will often start with the index of a book to see what entries might be of interest to them and related to their topic or question. They may then move on to the bibliography, which tells them how thorough and relevant the book's "database" is to their own research. They may look up and read only selected passages. Is the book up to date on historiography? Has the author consulted all the relevant sources? A glance at the introduction and acknowledgements can also be useful. Who has assisted in the research and writing of the book? Who has read the manuscript prior to publication? A book's bibliography then becomes part of the historians' virtual bibliography they are constructing as they read more and more about a topic.

Historians also learn to skim a book briefly to see what its scope and quality offer to them. The table of contents and a look at relevant sections as indicated in the bibliography should suffice. They may find a brief section or two of some value and decide to copy it for later use. But you should avoid copying in the early stages of your reading until you have a clear question and focus in mind.

As you read history, you should simultaneously be thinking about your topic and how the reading relates to it. This will help you read selectively and quickly. You should also get in the habit of rereading. Historians often consult a work more than once. Each time they reread that work they may see a new dimension helpful to them. Rereading primary sources from the archives can be especially important.

This morning I began to think about this selection. What might appeal to students? What would be a good example of historical reading? With that purpose in mind, I chose a book to reread, Franklin Ford's *Political Murder: From Tyrannicide to Terrorism* (Cambridge, MA: Harvard University Press, 1985). I thought the example of President Lincoln's assassination by the actor John Wilkes Booth on April 14, 1865, in Ford's Theater in Washington, DC, might be interesting to students. I used the index to find an entry on Lincoln on pages 350–353. I decided to copy a brief paragraph (350) after I skimmed those pages. The example follows:

> Booth's devotion to the Confederacy appears to have been sincere enough, albeit grounded in emotion and melodramatically expressed. In the months following Gettysburg, and still more after the President's reelection in 1864, as Grant's and Sherman's armies applied ever more relentless pressure upon an exhausted South, Booth's anti-Union sentiments became correspondingly stronger. His hatred of Lincoln in particular drew added virulence from much that a biased observer could pick up even in the North from an environment poisoned by the seemingly endless war, with its casualties, draft riots, shortages, and disappointments. In October 1864, just a month before Booth appeared for the last time on stage with his brothers, Edwin and Junius, Jr., playing the part of Mark Antony in *Julius Caesar* before an audience of two thousand at New York's Winter Garden Theatre, he began a series of trips to Montreal for clandestine meetings with Confederate representatives in Canada. There, in collaboration with desperate Southern agents, he conceived in its original form his plan to help reverse the tide of Union victories.

This selection intrigued me partly because of the passage about Booth's trip to Montreal to meet Confederate agents. There are several recent books on the topic of the Confederate secret service and the Lincoln assassination. I wanted to recall more about Booth's trip to Montreal and his meetings there. The whole question of Confederate complicity in Booth's plan to kill Lincoln came back to mind. This reading rekindled my interest in the Lincoln assassination in a new way, aside from choosing a selection for this book. I began reading with one purpose in mind and discovered another purpose in the process. One reading almost always leads to many more readings. I needed to read more after rereading this passage.

On the need to reread history, consider the judgment of an editor about the high quality of historian John Erickson's history of the Red Army titled *The Soviet High Command: A Military–Political History* (New York: St. Martin's Press, 1962), and his other books: "They really merit three or four readings. In fact, the fifth or sixth reading will produce new judgments on the part of a reader. In other words, his books have to be studied" (*New York Times*, March 19, 2002). There is no short cut to reading history well. Rereading a text carefully is as important a tool for doing history as reading it for the first time. Each reading produces virtually a new text and new understanding.

Task: Photocopy a page from a history book you have read recently. Mark the passages that (1) provide information, (2) seem worth quoting in your own work, and (3) provide interpretation of the subject. Remember that defacing books is not a good idea. Taking good notes on your reading is a better one.

8.3 Taking Notes

Taking notes carefully and keeping them in order are essential tools in all historical research. How can you learn to take good notes? Good question! Some famous writers and historians have found themselves accused of plagiarism because they failed to take careful notes or to check those notes against the sources before publishing their own work (see section 10.4 on page 86).

Taking good notes begins with the historian's principle of *selectivity*. You cannot write everything down that is germane to your topic and your research. Copying everything down is as hopeless a task as trying to remember everything without taking notes at all. Learn to select what is important from what is merely interesting or informative as you read. Take notes on your reading.

Learn to *paraphrase* (say in different words) or *summarize* (say more briefly) the words of other authors in order to capture their meaning in brief without borrowing their language. A paraphrase normally uses about the same number of your words to convey the words of another person. A summary normally reduces the words of another to fewer words of your own.

Remember to put quotation marks around any phrase, sentence, or paragraph that is not your own words, but those of another author. If you do not do this, you may well return to your notes in a few days, weeks, months, or years and come to believe that you yourself wrote words that, in fact, originated with another person. Failing to use quotation marks properly while taking notes can easily lead to plagiarism allegations later.

When copying down the words of another, do not edit or correct the prose. You can later indicate any errors or misspellings by putting the correct entry in [brackets] in your later paraphrase, summary, or citation.

Keep a full citation (author's complete name, title, place of publication, publisher, and year of publication) for all books. The same goes for articles and archives. Keep each citation on a separate card in a file that can later serve as your bibliography. Then use a shorthand note (Smith 277) to refer briefly to the source and page number on every note card you use that is taken from that source.

Keep notes on separate note cards. (I prefer four-by-six-inch cards for convenience, since three-by-five-inch cards do not seem to hold enough words, and five-by-eight-inch cards can waste a lot of space and trees unless you have a lot of words to put on them.) You can then use these cards to organize and reorganize your material as you go along. A good card file in the end can lead easily to an outline or first draft of your paper. And you can always reorder the cards as you modify your topic or your argument.

Task: Take notes on this section of *The Historian's Toolbox* by listing the main points about good note-taking. Which points seem familiar? Which are new?

8.4 How to Write a Good History Paper

Writing clear and concise prose in ordinary language is a fundamental tool of any historian. How exactly can you learn to write a good history paper, or a good paper in any class? Individuals surely vary in their writing and research abilities. But the following suggestions may help you find your own voice and skills as you do history:

1   Choose an interesting topic that you think is important. Get excited about it. Read quickly and widely. The topic should not be too large (the Civil War), nor too small (the rifle pits at Fort Fischer in 1864), but just right (Fort Fischer during the Civil War and the naval blockade of the South by the North). The topic should be feasible: there should be sufficient primary and secondary sources on the topic, but not so many that you could not possibly get through them in the time allotted. (On primary and secondary sources, see Chapter 9.) If the topic is significant, there should be some secondary sources by other historians on the same topic.

2   Ask a good question that you may be able to answer. (How effective was the Union naval blockade of Fort Fischer during the Civil War?) The question might ask how or why an event happened (causation, explanation). It might ask what the consequences were of a particular event. It might discuss the intellectual origins of a particular idea. It might ask what the cultural context of an event was. It might ask whether or not an individual was responsible for a certain act. It might ask about the social history of a political event or quantify broad trends in a society at a particular time.

3   Research the topic and compile a bibliography of primary and secondary sources you have consulted or will consult. Search and research the topic. Read through books and articles more than once as you learn more. Identify the key primary sources that tell directly about the topic, as well as the secondary sources that argue about issues or questions related to the topic. Use one four-by-six note card for each item, with a brief comment or annotation on its usefulness. Include or exclude items from the bibliography as you research the topic. Consult your college or local library and use the Web to search the catalogues of other libraries. Expand your bibliography as you look through the bibliographies at the back of your secondary sources. Remember to write down complete citations for each entry.

4   Take notes carefully and selectively as you read. Be neither a human Xerox machine nor a master of total recall. Learn to be selective about what you write down. Make sure that you put quotation marks around the words of other speakers or writers so you can cite them accurately and fairly later on. Use a system of note cards whose order can be reshuffled and rearranged at will. If helpful, use colored or tabbed cards to separate the file topically. Indicate dates on each card for putting in chronological order. Indicate on each card in abbreviated form your source, which you have in full on a separate card. As you progress, you should take fewer and more significant notes. Accuracy and thoroughness will pay off later.

5   Investigate the historiography of your topic, that is, how historians' interpretations of it have developed and changed. Who has written what on the topic? When? What are the major issues and arguments about? How have they framed the topic and the question, or questions? How has each secondary source used and taken account of (or taken issue with) previous sources? What different schools of thought on the topic or question exist? Read quickly and widely at first, then more selectively and carefully again … and again. Think about reframing your initial question (and even topic) as you learn more.

6   Develop your own argument about the topic that answers a question. Your argument should make a good point and support that point with evidence. Does your argument fill a gap in the existing literature on the topic by providing new facts? Does it support an existing interpretation or argument that you think is more convincing than other interpretations? Does your argument represent a new interpretation of the topic? Does it employ a new method to look at an old topic? In any event, in this critical stage you situate your topic and your argument within existing historiography. Do not forget that you need to tell an interesting story

(narrative), in addition to arguing a case, or solving a puzzle, or answering a question. At its root, history is story.

7 Write a complete outline of your paper. The outline is the skeleton of a story and argument you will flesh out in your paper. A sentence outline is best (each entry is a complete sentence) because it forces you to think about each point you are making as you develop the paper. Use the outline to define the topic once again, to reframe the question, and to structure the answer in a logical and persuasive way. A page or two should do it. Do not forget to give the paper a title—the title challenges you to think about what to tell your mother you are doing and even to persuade her to read the paper. Reread the outline several times. Does it make sense? Should it be reordered before you start writing?

8 Write a first draft of your paper. Then consider writing a second and third (computers are wonderful for editing and moving paragraphs). Get all your ideas and information down on paper, even if the draft seems too long—you can always go back and shorten it, as you probably should. Brevity counts. So does logic. Start writing any-where—beginning, middle, end—that you feel most knowledgeable and comfortable. You can rewrite, abbreviate, and reorganize later. Let your ideas flow. Strive for clarity, precision, and accessibility even at this stage—your readers (audience) have probably not been spending the last week, or month, or year studying this topic. Think about the readers and how they might respond to every word you write. Be empathetic—put yourself in the reader's place.

9 Write a final draft. Make the language of the paper sing. Reduce the earlier drafts by writing more concisely and less redundantly. Use short words and short sentences. Start each paragraph with a strong lead sentence. Avoid the passive voice (use "Trump defeated Hilary" rather than "Hilary was defeated by Trump"), split infinitives, jargon, ill-defined terms, long words, misplaced antecedents, and poor grammar. Use proper citation and style as indicated by the instructor, the depart-ment, or the publisher. Make everything consistent. Use footnotes (or parenthetical citations within the text) to cite your sources. Add a selective bibliography that identifies your major sources and the major secondary literature.

10 Proofread the entire paper from beginning to end at least once. Do not trust your computer's spellcheck program. Look up strange or apparently misspelled words in a dictionary. Fix grammatical and syntactical errors. Break up long sentences. Fix split infinitives. Check that the page numbers are in order. Is this a paper you are proud of? Would you want it published? Shared? You're all done? On time? Congratulations! You are a historian.

For a more in-depth approach to doing history, see William K. Storey, *Writing History: A Guide for Students*, 2nd ed. (Cambridge, MA: Harvard University Press, 2003). "Writing history," Storey notes, "is about making decisions." At every point, historians must decide what to read, what to note, what to write about, and what to ignore.

Task: Make a checklist of the above suggestions that you normally follow when writing a history paper. Which might you want to incorporate in your next paper that you had not considered? What other suggestions can you think of? After you complete the paper, go back to your checklist and see what you did and did not use in the final version.

9 Sources and Evidence

History is, among other things, an argument based on sources and evidence that support that argument. Historians are not free to tell a story or make up an argument without supporting evidence. Evidence includes primary and secondary written sources (mainly documents) and nonwritten sources—maps, artifacts, images, quantitative data, fossils, and genetic DNA evidence. The evidence of the sources is the raw material of history and the historian's most valuable tool. Historians should not argue or narrate beyond what the evidence discovered demonstrates is the approximate truth about the past. History is nonfiction, not fiction. It is imaginative, but not imagined. It is constructed, but not invented.

9.1 Primary and Secondary Sources

Primary and secondary sources are the crucial tools of the historian. A primary source is a document, image, or artifact that provides evidence about the past. It is an original piece of evidence discovered or created contemporaneously with the event under discussion. A direct quote from a document is classified as a primary source. A secondary source is a book, article, film, or museum that displays primary sources selectively in order to interpret the past. The two passages below related to the Wannsee Protocol provide a good example of the distinction between a primary and a secondary source. The Wannsee Protocol was the account written during World War II by Adolf Eichmann, who was present at a conference held on January 20, 1942, in the Berlin suburb of Wannsee to discuss the "final solution" of the "Jewish question." The original document, written in German, is in the Archives of the Foreign Office of the Federal Republic of Germany, and a translation is reprinted in A. Grobman, D. Landes, and S. Milton, eds., *Genocide: Critical Issues of the Holocaust* (Los Angeles: Simon Wiesenthal Center, 1983, 442–449). The first passage below is an excerpt from the Wannsee Protocol. It is a primary source. The second passage is an excerpt from Michael Shermer and Alex Grobman, *Denying History: Who Says the Holocaust Never Happened and Why Do They Say It?* (Berkeley: University of California Press, 2000). It is a secondary source, a book about the history of Holocaust denial.

Primary Source: The Wannsee Protocol (1942)

Under appropriate direction the Jews are to be utilized for work in the East in an expedient manner in the course of the final solution. In large (labor) columns, with the sexes separated, Jews capable of work will be moved into these areas as they build roads, during which a large proportion will no doubt drop out through natural reduction.

The remnant that eventually remains will require suitable treatment; because it will without doubt represent the most resistant part, it consists of a natural selection [*naturliche Auslese*] that could, on its release, become the germ-cell of a new Jewish revival. (Witness the experience of history.)

Secondary Source: Denying History: Who Says the Holocaust Never Happened and Why Do They Say It? (2000)

The "evacuation of the Jews" Eichmann describes cannot mean simple deportation to live elsewhere, since the Nazis had already been deporting Jews to the east, and Eichmann indicates this was inadequate. Instead, he outlines a new solution. Shipment to the east will mean, for those who can work, work until death, and (as we know from other sources) for those who cannot work, immediate death. What about those who can work and do not succumb to death? "*The remnant that eventually remains will require suitable treatment.*" Suitable treatment can only mean murder. Why? Eichmann explains that a natural selection (*naturliche Auslese*) in the Darwinian sense will make these Jews the most resistant (to death by exhaustion), meaning they will be the fittest—the youngest, healthiest, smartest, etc. Should this population of naturally selected Jews survive, they might (Eichmann fears) "become the germ-cell of a new Jewish revival." History, Eichmann points out, supports this theory of social Darwinism (Illustrations 9.1–9.5).

Summary

In sum, the Wannsee Protocol is a *primary source*. It provides a direct description of an event by a participant and eyewitness who wrote down what he heard and saw. The book *Denying History* is a *secondary source*, the work of two historians telling the story of Holocaust denial using documents such as the Wannsee Protocol. In the case shown above, we have a secondary source interpreting and commenting directly on a primary source.

Task: Reread the secondary source selection. Which comments seem supported by the words in the primary source? Which comments seem speculative and go beyond what is demonstrated in the primary source?

L a n d	Zahl
A. Altreich	131.800
Ostmark	43.700
Ostgebiete	420.000
Generalgouvernement	2.284.000
Bialystok	400.000
Protektorat Böhmen und Mähren	74.200
Estland — judenfrei —	
Lettland	3.500
Litauen	34.000
Belgien	43.000
Dänemark	5.600
Frankreich / Besetztes Gebiet	165.000
Unbesetztes Gebiet	700.000
Griechenland	69.600
Niederlande	160.800
Norwegen	1.300
B. Bulgarien	48.000
England	330.000
Finnland	2.300
Irland	4.000
Italien einschl. Sardinien	58.000
Albanien	200
Kroatien	40.000
Portugal	3.000
Rumänien einschl. Bessarabien	342.000
Schweden	8.000
Schweiz	18.000
Serbien	10.000
Slowakei	88.000
Spanien	6.000
Türkei (europ. Teil)	55.500
Ungarn	742.800
UdSSR	5.000.000
Ukraine 2.994.684	
Weißrußland aus- schl. Bialystok 446.484	
Zusammen: über	11.000.000

Illustration 9.1 Wannsee Protocol, January 20, 1942

How does a secondary source utilize a notorious primary source? The Wannsee Protocol of January 20, 1942, lists the number of Jews in various parts of Europe slated for the "final solution." (*House of the Wannsee Conference, Memorial, and Educational Site*: www.ghwk.de/Seite6.jpg)

9.2 Documents

The main type of primary source historians use is a document. A document is a written piece of evidence from the past. Historians use documents as the basis for putting together a narrative or analysis of past events. Documents provide historians with clues and information but must be used carefully and selectively. The same care and selection should be applied to images and artifacts also used as historical evidence.

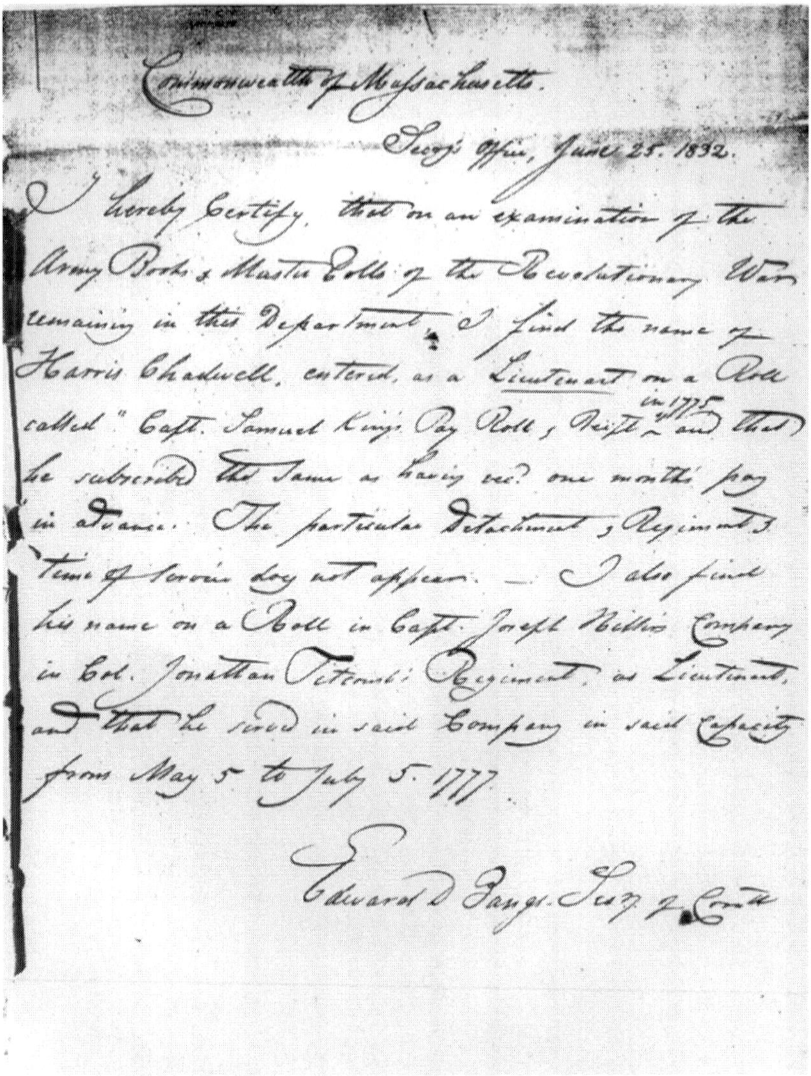

Commonwealth of Massachusetts.

Secy's Office, June 25. 1832.

I hereby Certify, that on an examination of the Army Books & Muster Rolls of the Revolutionary War remaining in this Department, I find the name of Harris Chadwell, entered, as a Lieutenant on a Roll called "Capt. Samuel King's Pay Roll, Regt in 1775 and that he subscribed the same as having recd one month's pay in advance. The particular Detachment, Regiment & time of service does not appear. — I also find his name on a Roll in Capt. Joseph Miller's Company in Col. Jonathan Titcomb's Regiment, as Lieutenant, and that he served in said Company in said Capacity from May 5 to July 5. 1777.

Edward D Bangs. Secy of Comth

Illustration 9.2 Military Pension Application of Harris Chadwell, Lynn, Massachusetts, June 25, 1832

A document is the basic tool of historical evidence: The Military Pension Application of my Revolutionary War ancestor, Harris Chadwell, of Lynn, Massachusetts, dated June 25, 1832. Chadwell, then 86 years old, had fought at the battles of Lexington and Concord in 1775, or at least taken a few shots at redcoats before throwing his uniform in a pond. What are some of the facts the document provides? (*National Archives*)

Illustration 9.3 Map of the Americas, c. 1540

Sebastian Munster's map of the Americas, 1540. Is it accurate? (*Cumming Collection, Davidson College Library.*)

A Revolutionary War Ancestor's Pension Application (1832)

My great-great-great-great-grandfather, Harris Chadwell (1746–1834) of Lynn, Massachusetts, was a soldier in the Continental Army during the American Revolution. He was part of a militia unit from Lynn, which joined the "minutemen" at Lexington and Concord in 1775. He in fact fired at British soldiers with his musket and then, fearing that he would be captured, threw his uniform shirt in a convenient pond and ran. In 1832, at the age of eighty-six, after telling (and undoubtedly improving) stories about his Revolutionary War exploits and adventures in local taverns for fifty years, he decided to apply for a pension offered by the U.S. government for surviving veterans of that war. This is a copy (or facsimile) of my ancestor's verification from the Commonwealth of Massachusetts that his name did indeed appear on a military list of Continental Army officers and soldiers in 1775. The original document of which this is a copy may be found in the National Archives in Washington, DC. If you want to verify the existence of this document, you could write (as I did) to National Archives and Records Administration, 7th and Pennsylvania Avenue NW, Washington, DC, 20408.

This document could be used for several purposes: in a biography of my ancestor, Harris Chadwell; a Chadwell genealogy; a history of the battles

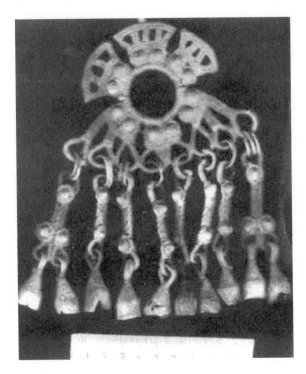

Illustration 9.4 Woman's Bronze Burial Decoration, Moscow Region, Fifth to Eighth
         Century

Artifacts of old Moscow: A woman's bronze burial decoration from the Moscow region, fifth to
eighth century. Does it look Russian? (www.dlc.fi/~kokov/mesher/object7.jpg)

at Concord and Lexington during the Revolutionary War; a history of the
Continental Army; a history of the Lynn militia; a history of Revolutionary War pensions and pensioners; and so forth.

Did he get his pension? Other documents suggest that he did. He died
two years later, duly rewarded by his town and his country for what he
may—and may not—have done during the war.

Task: List some other historical purposes or arguments for which this
document might provide useful evidence. What does this document tell
us? How reliable is it? Is there any reason to doubt it? Might there be
errors in the document? What does the document leave out?

9.3 Maps

How can maps be historical tools? An old map used long ago would certainly
constitute a primary source, providing direct evidence of how people saw the
world at that time. But a later map would most likely constitute a *secondary*

Illustration 9.5 Dead Confederate Soldier in Devil's Den, Gettysburg, July 6, 1863

Images can be deceiving: Alexander Gardner's photograph of a dead Confederate soldier in Devil's Den, Gettysburg, July 6, 1863. Was the body moved from somewhere else? *(Library of Congress)*

source, showing how a later historian wanted to construct or illustrate the past. We discover maps used in the past for various purposes, but we construct maps that help us explain that past.

Sebastian Munster's Map of the Americas, c. 1540

A sixteenth-century map of the Americas by a German scholar named Sebastian Munster provides an excellent and rare example of a historical map. Munster (1489–1552) was, together with Abraham Ortelius and Gerardus Mercator, one of the great cartographers of the age of discovery. He was also a mathematician, a professor of Hebrew, and (briefly) a monk. Munster's map is a woodcut originally published in his edition of Ptolemy's *Geographia* (Basel, 1540). Called "Die Nüw Welt" ("The New World"), it was the best-known and most widely circulated map of the Americas of his day, the standard map until Ortelius's map of the Americas (1570) appeared. Munster's map has many obvious mistakes. It incorrectly shows a northwest passage to India and an inland sea, suggested by Verrazano's voyage of 1524 that nearly separates North America at the Outer Banks of North Carolina. This misconception made people think that they could easily find a route across North America to the wealthy Spice Islands in the East. Munster also catered to European fascination with "cannibals" by drawing them in what is now Brazil.

But Munster got a lot of things right. Florida, Cuba, and the general shape of the continents—despite their distortions—are easily recognizable. Munster was the first European mapmaker to show the recently discovered Western Hemisphere, the first to name the Pacific Ocean *(Mare Pacificum)*, one of the first to depict Japan *(Zipangri)* on a map, and the first to show North and South America linked by land (Central America).

The Munster map is the oldest map in the William P. Cumming Map Collection at Davidson College in Davidson, North Carolina. The Cumming collection of 48 early maps offers the best set of maps of the American southeast in the world. For an introduction to the collection, see *The William P. Cumming Map Collection* (Davidson, NC: Davidson College, 1993). On the possibilities (often ignored) for historians to utilize maps in their research and writing, see Mark Monmonier, *Mapping It Out: Expository Cartography for the Humanities and Social Sciences* (Chicago: University of Chicago Press, 1993).

Ancient maps such as Munster's helped transform how Europeans envisioned their world, showing both its vast size and the existence of continents previously unknown to them. Though vastly different in subject, they are comparable in effect to contemporary images of distant solar systems, galaxies, and nebulae. These modern images help us picture the immensity of the universe much as Munster's map helped people picture the immensity of the planet. This sixteenth-century map is thus a key historical document that opens a window on people's knowledge and understanding of the world at a specific moment in time.

Task: Look closely at Munster's map. What other misconceptions can you see? What else looks correct? Compare it with a modern map of the Americas. How are they similar? How do they differ? What region did Munster portray most accurately? What does this reveal about the origins and goals of European exploration of the Americas? Why might Munster have put in the northwest passage? What does the map tell you about European conceptions and misconceptions about the New World?

9.4 Artifacts

An artifact is an object made by humans that is of anthropological or archaeological interest. How can old artifacts provide tools for studying the past? How do we interpret them? Do artifacts ever change our view of what happened? Where does history leave off and archaeology begin?

Digging Ancient Moscow

In recent decades, Russian archaeologists have engaged in constant excavations around the sprawling city of Moscow in hopes of learning more about the city's past. Tradition, based on an entry in the major document of old Russia, the so-called *Chronicle of Bygone Years*, dates the founding of the city in the year 1147. Thus, in 1997, the city celebrated its 850th anniversary with great pomp and circumstance, including even more intense archaeological digging. This digging yielded a trove of artifacts, including jewelry, shoes, ash and residue, and other items from ancient Moscow. These newly unearthed objects have become part of the historical record; like documents, they are primary sources that provide clues for understanding the past. Here are some of the new findings archaeologists and historians have developed based on recently discovered Muscovite artifacts:

- Hoards of silver jewelry buried beneath the ground suggest an attempt to save valuables before the Mongol invasion of the city in 1238.
- Remains of shoes tell archaeologists that men and women in sixteenth-century Moscow were taller than we thought, averaging some five-feet six-inches in height, and remaining about the same until the eighteenth century.
- Ash and residue reveal the effects of a fire that burned the city to the ground in 1493 and a wooden house dating from before 1300.
- Monasteries previously unknown existed in the area around the large estates of Muscovite aristocracy from the thirteenth century on.
- The kremlin (fortification) at the city center was originally built in the twelfth century with oak walls, replaced by stone 40 years later.
- Archaeologists unearthed the first birchbark document ever found in Moscow. (Such documents were common around Novgorod, where the soil was waterlogged, not dry and oxidized, thus preserving the documents.)

Earlier excavations of the Kazan cathedral on Red Square, constructed in 1636, unearthed original chapels, steps, and bell tower foundations. These discoveries enabled modern builders to reconstruct the cathedral faithfully in 1993. For more on these findings, see L.A. Beliaev and A.G. Veksler, "The Archaeology of Medieval Russia: Recent Explorations (1980–1990s)," *Rossiiskaia arkheologiia* 3 (1996): 106–133.

Task: Look carefully at the bracelet illustrated here, one of the many artifacts found in Moscow. Dating from the fifth to eighth century, it is a burial bracelet worn by a woman. What can you conclude about ancient Moscow from this example? What evidence is there that this is Russian? What does the existence of a burial bracelet suggest about the people who lived there? How do artifacts resemble, and differ from, other documents and primary sources?

9.5 Images

How can images help us understand the past? When is an image a primary source? When is it secondary? We all know that photographs, sketches, graphics, paintings, and films can help us "be there" in the past. They can provide evidence of past history in ways that words on the printed page simply cannot describe. They can also help us interpret the past in new ways by letting us see things visually rather than in our imagination based on our reading.

But images—like words and maps and other items—can be deceptive. Image makers can be highly selective in what they choose to portray. And images can distort unless we know what lies behind them. An image may be worth a thousand words, yet seeing may mean believing what is not necessarily true.

Sharpshooter's Home or Photographer's Studio?

The American Civil War (1861–1865) was one of the first conflicts to be photographed (the Crimean War in 1853–1856 was another). Developed in the 1830s, photography was a new medium that allowed people far from the battlefront to visualize the bloody reality of war. Intrepid photographers like Mathew Brady and Alexander Gardner carried their heavy equipment from battle to battle to shoot pictures, which they then developed and displayed to those on the home front. Most were accurate portrayals of soldiers and war scenes—but how could viewers know for sure? Consider the case of the famous photograph taken by Alexander Gardner after the three-day Battle of Gettysburg (July 1–3, 1863), the major turning point in the war that left tens of thousands of men dead in a small Pennsylvania town and stopped the Confederate advance into the North. Gardner's photograph shows a dead Confederate soldier in the impressive cluster of boulders known by the locals as "Devil's Den." Devil's Den is a great hiding place and directly faces Little Round Top, another rocky hill made famous by the bloody battle that occurred there. Gardner, a Scot and a former assistant of Mathew Brady, had established his own studio in Washington, DC, by 1863 and hired away two of Brady's assistants, Timothy O'Sullivan and James Gibson.

Gardner and his assistants took several photographs of the battlefield on July 6, when the scene of carnage had changed very little from the days of the battle itself. They were preoccupied with dead bodies as evidence of the horrors of war. In his caption for the photograph, Gardner wrote that "the sharpshooter had evidently been wounded in the head by a fragment of a shell which had exploded over him, and had laid down upon his blanket to await death." Gardner then speculated on the soldier's mental condition as he prepared for death: "Was he delirious with agony, or did death come slowly to his relief, while memories of home grew dearer as the field of carnage faded before him?" He also remembered that when he revisited the battlefield on November 19, in connection with Lincoln's Gettysburg Address and the dedication of a federal cemetery, he discovered that "the musket, rusted by many storms, still leaned against the rock, and the skeleton of the soldier still lay undisturbed within the mouldering uniform."

It is a striking and powerful image. But historians have argued that Gardner's account of the famous photograph was not quite accurate. Other photographs suggest that this particular soldier had died elsewhere on the battlefield and that his body had been dragged some forty yards into Devil's Den for a dramatic photograph opportunity (or "photo op," as it is called today). The rifle leaning against the rocks was not the Sharps rifle used by "sharpshooters" at all, but a common infantry weapon of the period. The soldier was an infantryman, not a sharpshooter at all. There are six photographs of the body, but no log whose entries might tell us in what order Gardner took them.

The idea that this photograph was staged is now so common that tour guides at Gettysburg routinely tell the story of its staging to tourists. The National Park Service display at Devil's Den does the same thing. Revisionism has now become the conventional wisdom.

In 1975, William Frassanito, in his book *Gettysburg: A Journey in Time*, showed several photographs of the same soldier taken in different locations as much as seventy-five yards apart. He suggested that there were photographic advantages to moving a body up the hill to get a more visually exciting composition among the rocks. The photographers had even placed a knapsack under the head to prop it up. The photographer was probably not Gardner, but his assistant, Timothy O'Sullivan. At the cemetery dedication in November, photographers even got Union soldiers to "play dead" as staged bodies in Devil's Den once more.

But was the photograph staged? Perhaps the revisionists are wrong. Perhaps there really was a dead Confederate sharpshooter among the boulders. Other historians cite the eyewitness account of Captain August P. Martin of the Union Army artillery in the *Gettysburg Compiler* of October 24, 1899. Martin was stationed on Little Round Top:

> Among the interesting incidents that occurred on Little Round Top was the summary way in which a sharpshooter was disposed of in the rear of Devil's Den. He had concealed himself behind a stone wall between two boulders and for a long time we were annoyed by shots from that direction, one of which actually combed my hair over my left ear and passed through the shoulder of a man a little taller than

myself who was standing behind me for a cover. At last we were able to locate the spot, by the use of a field glass, from whence the shots came by little puffs of smoke that preceded the whizzing of the bullets that passed by our heads. We then loaded one of our guns with a percussion shell, taking careful and accurate aim. When the shot was fired the shell struck and exploded on the face of one of the boulders. We supposed the shot had frightened him away, as we were no longer troubled with shots from that location. When the battle was ended we rode over to the Devil's Den and found behind the wall a dead Confederate soldier lying upon his back and, so far as we could see, did not have a mark upon his body, and from that fact became convinced that he was killed by the concussion of the shell when it exploded on the face of the boulder.

So perhaps the body was in Devil's Den after all. Perhaps Gardner the photographer never had to move him at all. The debate goes on. Students interested in photographs of Gettysburg should consult William A. Frassanito, *Gettysburg: A Journey in Time* (New York: Scribner's, 1975). For a broader study, see William F. Thompson, *The Image of War: The Pictorial Reporting of the American Civil War* (Baton Rouge: Louisiana State University Press, 1959). The best account of the sharpshooter debate, from 1865 to the present, is "The Lore of the Sharpshooter" in Gary E. Edelman and Timothy H. Smith, *Devil's Den: A History and a Guide* (Gettysburg, PA: Thomas Publications, 1997).

Task: New evidence can complicate, rather than simplify, a situation, making it more difficult to verify a fact or explain the larger significance of an event. In using photographs as tools for understanding the past, what questions must historians ask of them? How might the goal of taking a poignant picture affect its "accuracy" as a document? Look carefully at Gardner's photograph. What evidence can help you decide whether the body was placed in position or not? What else do you see of any historical significance? When examining photographs, what clues might suggest that the picture was staged? In what ways, if at all, does a staged photograph—such as a president performing a certain activity—diminish its accuracy?

9.6 Cliometrics: Using Statistics to Prove a Point

Numbers are powerful tools. But how and when should historians use them? When should historians count and not count? *Cliometrics* is an amusing term used to describe the use of quantitative data (numbers, census data, election results, graphs, etc.) in the study of history. Historians often must ask the question "How much?" as well as "How?" and "Why?" For a time in the 1970s, many historians became fascinated with computers and numbers as a way of asking and answering historical questions. Quantitative history is now simply one of many tools available to the historian. Political party historians and economic historians are particularly interested in "hard data" or numbers to do their work.

The Black Population of Colonial America

In Peter Kolchin's fine book *American Slavery 1619–1877*, he needed to convey something about the relative number of black slaves in the colonies before the American Revolution. Although the numbers of blacks, or slaves, may only be approximate, he decided to discuss the matter in the course of his text and to provide a table at the back of his book so the reader could also draw conclusions from the data available. How does the historian's narrative relate to his quantitative data? Are narrative and data consistent? How does he use other evidence to bolster his argument?

Throughout most of the seventeenth century, indentured servants filled the bulk of the colonies' labor needs. Although a Dutch captain sold 20 Africans in Virginia in 1619, and small numbers of blacks trickled into the mainland colonies over the following decades, until the 1680s the non-Indian population of the British mainland colonies remained overwhelmingly white. So long as a ready supply of indentured labor continued to exist, colonists saw little reason to go to the expense and bother of importing large numbers of Africans, who, unlike English laborers, had to undergo prolonged adjustment to alien conditions— strange masters had unusual customs and spoke an unintelligible language—before becoming productive members of the work force. Equally important, because the Portuguese and Dutch dominated the African slave trade until the British triumph in the Anglo-Dutch war of 1664–1667, the English colonists found slaves expensive and hard to obtain.

Beginning in the 1680s, however, the mainland colonies underwent a massive shift from indentured to slave labor. Some simple statistics drove home the point. Between 1680 and 1750, the estimated proportion of blacks in the population increased from 7 percent to 44 percent in Virginia and from 17 percent to 61 percent in South Carolina [see Table 9.1]. "They import so many Negros hither," wrote one Virginia planter, William H. Byrd II, in 1736, "that I fear this Colony will some time or other be confirmed by the Name of New Guinea."

This shift, which has been documented most carefully for the Chesapeake colonies, was the product of a fundamental change in the relative supply of indentured servants and slaves, in the face of escalating colonial demand for labor. Because servants were held only temporarily and then freed, a rapidly growing colonial population required an equally rapid growth in the number of indentured immigrants for servants to remain a constant proportion of the population. Between 1650 and 1700, the population of Virginia more than tripled; if indentured servants were to continue providing the bulk of the agricultural labor force, servant immigration would have had to triple, or come close to tripling, too.

From Peter Kolchin, *American Slavery, 1619–1877* (New York: Hill and Wang, 1993), 10–11 and Table 1 (here Table 9.1).

Task: Take a look at Table 9.1. Are the numbers here consistent with Kolchin's narrative? Are the terms and definitions used in the text and table consistent as well? Is the author selecting some data and omitting others? What other or different conclusions can you draw from the table that are not mentioned in the narrative?

9.7 Genetic Evidence

Recent technology has created a new type of evidence for historians to use in exploring the past. This evidence is genetic and is based on the DNA that exists in every human being. Because genetic material is passed on from one generation to another, historians can make strong links between people today and their ancient ancestors. By examining chromosomes, scientists can help answer questions that have long intrigued historians. DNA evidence has recently added a whole new dimension to

Table 9.1 Estimates of Blacks as a Percentage of the Population, by Colony, 1680–1770

	1680	1700	1720	1750	1770
Delaware	5.5	5.5	13.2	5.3	5.2
Maryland	9.0	10.9	18.9	30.8	31.5
Virginia	6.9	28.9	30.3	43.9	42.0
North Carolina	3.9	3.9	14.1	25.7	35.3
South Carolina	16.7	42.8	70.4	60.9	60.5
Georgia	—	—	—	19.2	45.2
Totals					
North	2.3	3.6	5.2	4.8	4.4
South	5.7	21.1	27.7	38.0	39.7
Thirteen Colonies	4.6	11.1	14.8	20.2	21.4

Source: Computed from *Historical Statistics of the United States: Colonial Times to 1957* (Washington, DC: 1960). Taken from Peter Kolchin, *American Slavery, 1619–1877* (New York: Hill and Wang, 1993), 240.

Table 9.2 Genetic Chart of Jefferson's and Hemings' Ancestries

A	Ancestry	B	Bi-allelic Markers	Microsatellite STRs	Minisatellite MSY1
	-Peter—Pres. Thomas Jefferson				
	—129–135———J41		0000001	15.12.4.11.3.9.11.10.15.13.7	(3)5.(1)14.(3)32(4)16
Thomas—	—16–112–120———				
Jefferson	—130–136———J42		0000001	15.12.4.11.3.9.11.10.15.13.7	(3)5.(1)14.(3)32(4)16
	-Field——— -J13–J21–J31–J37–J43———J47		0000001	15.12.4.11.3.9.11.10.15.13.7	
(3)5.(1)14.(3)32(4)16					
	-J6———				
	-J14–J23–J33–J39—— -J46–J49		0000001	15.12.4.11.3.9.11.10.15.13.7	(3)5.(1)14.(3)32.(4)16
	-J46–J50		0000001	15.12.4.11.3.9.11.10.**16**.13.7	(3)5.(1)14.(3)32.(4)16
Sally	Easton-H10–H15–H17———————H210000001			15.12.4.11.3.9.11.10.15.13.7	
Hemings	(3)5.(1)14.(3)32.(4)16				
	-Thomas-C6–C11–C19–C23———————C27		0000011	14.12..5.12.3.10.11.1013.13.7	
	(1)17.(3)36.(4)21				
John———	-Dabney-C8–C13–C21–C26———————C29		0000011	14.12.5.**11**.3.10.11.10.13.13.7	
Carr	(1)17.(3)**37**.(4)21				
	-Overton-C7–C12–C20–C24–C28–C30———C31		0000011	14.12.5.12.3.10.11.10.13.7	
	(1)17.(3)36.(4)21				
	-W8–W27——— -W40–W55		0000011	14.12.5.11.3.10.11.13.13.7	(1)16.(3)27.(4)21
	-W41–W56		0000011	14.12.5.11.3.10.11.13.13.7	(1)16.(3)27.(4)21
	—Lewis—				
	-W57–W69		0000011	14.12.5.11.3.10.11.13.13.7	(1)16.(3)27.(4)21
Thomas	-W9–W28—-W42–				
Woodson———					
-W58–W80 **1110001** 17.12.**6**.11.3.11.**8.10.11.**14.6			(0?)1.(3e)3.(1a)11.		
(3a) 30.(4a)14.(4)2					
—James———W12—W30—W46———W61			0000011	14.12.5.11.3.10.11.13.13.7	(1)16.(3)**28**.(4)**20**

Note: **[For genetics students only!]** Chart shows the male-line ancestry and haplotypes of participants. A = ancestry numbers correspond to reference numbers and names in more detailed genealogical data for each family. B = haplotypes. Entries in bold highlight deviations from the usual patterns for the group of descendants. **Bi-allelic markers**: order of loci: YAP-SRYm*299 sY81–1.1.Y22g-Tat-92R7-SRYm1532. 0, ancestral state; 1, derived state. **Microsatellite short tandem repeats (STRs)**. Order of loci: 19–388-389A-389B-389C-389D-390–391-392-393-dx-ys156y. The number of repeats at each locus is shown. **Mitnisatellite MSY1.** Each number in brackets represents the sequence type of the repeat unit; the number after it is the number of units with this sequence type. For example, J41 has 5 units of sequence type 3, 14 units of sequence type 1, 32 units of sequence type 3, and 16 units of sequence type 4. *Source: Nature*, Vol. 397, November 5, 1998, 27.

the old debate about the relationship between President Thomas Jefferson and his slave, Sally Hemings (see Table 9.2 on page 77). Similar evidence has shown conclusively that the woman who died recently in the United States who had claimed to be Anastasia—the daughter of Tsar Nicholas II of Russia—was not related to the Russian royal family, which was machine-gunned to death in August 1918 after the Bolshevik Revolution. Less sensationally, but more significantly, genetics has replaced linguistics as the tool of choice in measuring the origins of, and links among, various ethnic groups and peoples.

Welsh and Basques, Relatively Speaking

Historians have long wondered how different groups in Europe are related to each other. Because ancient records are scarce, historians have relied on linguistic evidence—that is, if the language of two geographically distinct groups share similar elements—grammar, structure, sounds—the groups are probably related. Conversely, if they do *not* share such elements, chances are they are *not* related. The Basques of northern Spain and the Welsh of Wales are two distinct groups with their own separate languages. Because these languages have little in common, historians long believed there were few links between the two groups. The Basques had been assumed, on the basis of this linguistic evidence, to be an offshoot of European aborigines from several thousand years ago. The Welsh presumably were related to the Celts, an ancient people that spread northward across Europe as far as Spain, Ireland, and Romania.

But genetic evidence tells a different story. In the 1990s, scientists collected saliva samples from children in Wales, England, Italy, Germany, and Spain. After examining the DNA in these samples, geneticists discovered something astonishing. A Y chromosome, very rare in England, Italy, and Germany, was common in Wales, suggesting separate origins. More interesting, the Welsh Y chromosome matched Basque genes in northern Spain. Thus, the Welsh and Basques have a close biological link. DNA evidence has established a clear line of descent from common ancestors in these two separate peoples. Linguistic evidence suggested separation. Genetic evidence proves a connection.

Independently, geneticists at University College, London, were studying the population of the Orkney Islands off Scotland, where neither Anglo-Saxons nor Romans ever settled. Celtic-speaking Picts who had lived there undisturbed until the arrival of the Vikings around 800 spoke the Norse language until the eighteenth century. Genetic evidence (Y chromosomes of Orkney men) suggested an Orkney link with the Norwegians, hardly surprising.

But other genetic markers resembled those found in Welsh and Irish men, suggesting a common origin. Where? Again, geneticists compared their evidence with DNA from the Basques and, to their surprise, found the same genetic signature. Yet their study of mitochondrial DNA among women links them with northern Europe, not the Basques. Presumably females from the continent were captured, purchased, or traded and ultimately swamped the earlier genetic influences on the maternal side. So genetic evidence is an important tool and is revising history as we watch. (For more on these recent genetic discoveries, see *National Geographic*, June 2001; *New York Times*, April 10, 2001.)

Thomas Jefferson and Sally Hemings—What's My Line?

In 1776, Thomas Jefferson (1743–1826) drafted the Declaration of Independence. He later served as minister to France and secretary of state. As one of the leaders of the emerging Democratic-Republican Party in the 1790s, he served as vice president under John Adams from 1797 to 1801 and as president of the United States from 1801 to 1809. He has long been recognized as one of the towering figures of the Revolutionary generation.

In 1772, Jefferson married Martha Wayles and took her to live at Monticello, his mountaintop home in Virginia. They had six children, only two of whom survived into adulthood, and Martha died in 1782. Jefferson never remarried. Like all wealthy southern plantation owners, Jefferson owned many slaves. One of them was Sally Hemings (1773–1835), about whom little is known. She left no letters or records, no images of herself. There are four known descriptions of what she looked like; she was probably light-skinned. Jefferson never mentioned her in his records. She was a nursemaid and companion to Jefferson's daughter Maria, lady's maid to daughters Martha and Maria, and chambermaid and seamstress in the household. She accompanied Jefferson for more than two years in Paris and lived most of her life at Monticello. She had several children who were light-skinned:

Harriet, born 1795, died in infancy
Beverly, born 1798
Unnamed daughter, born 1799, died in infancy
Harriet, born 1801
Madison, born 1805
Eston, born 1808

Jefferson freed her surviving children—Beverly and Harriet in 1822, Madison and Eston in 1826—by his wills. He never freed Sally.

Rumors that Jefferson and Hemings had a long-standing sexual relationship abounded during their lifetimes. James T. Callender, a disappointed office seeker who wanted Jefferson to appoint him postmaster in Richmond, Virginia, printed the rumors in the *Richmond Recorder*, a Federalist newspaper, in September 1802. Jefferson "keeps and for many years has kept, as his concubine, one of his slaves," Callender charged. "Her name is Sally. The name of her eldest son is Tom. His features are said to bear a striking though sable resemblance to those of the president himself." Hemings and Jefferson "had several children," Callender wrote. "There is not an individual in the neighborhood of Charlottesville who does not believe the story."

Jefferson was a Republican. His Federalist opponents immediately pounced on the rumors and published them frequently in newspapers throughout the country. Enemies mocked him in print and in verse. The following lines, to the tune of "Yankee Doodle," appeared in the *Boston Gazette* and *Philadelphia Port Folio*:

> Of all the damsels on the green,
> On mountain or in valley,
> A lass so luscious ne'er was seen,
> As Monticellian Sally ...
> When press'd by loads of state affairs
> I seek to sport and dally
> The sweetest solace of my cares
> Is in the lap of Sally.

Jefferson's supporters denounced the rumours and the president himself refused to respond to them. His daughter Martha denied them as well, as did her children. Despite these denials, the stories persisted until Jefferson's death in 1826. They resurfaced in 1873 when 68 year-old Madison Hemings, Sally's child, said in an interview that his mother had told him that Jefferson was his father (and the father of his siblings Beverly, Harriet, and Eston). Another former slave at Monticello, Israel Jefferson, agreed.

And there the matter rested for many years. In the twentieth century, two prominent historians, Dumas Malone and Merrill Peterson, published massive biographies of Jefferson. After examining his voluminous private papers, they both repudiated the rumors for lack of evidence. Malone's biography ran to six volumes. Malone doubted the Jefferson-Hemings relationship because it was out of character for Jefferson. Another biographer, Fawn Brodie, however, provided circumstantial evidence of a Jefferson-Hemings affair. She showed that Jefferson was in residence at Monticello nine months prior to the birth of each of Sally Hemings's children and that she bore no children at times that he was not living there.

In 1997, historian Joseph Ellis raised two questions about this subject. First, Hemings's last two children were born after Callender made the issue public in 1802—how could Jefferson as president have continued their relationship following such publicity? Second, neither John Adams nor Alexander Hamilton, Jefferson's political rivals, believed the gossip—

would they not have used any real evidence politically if they had? Having read all the available evidence and biographies, Ellis considered the case not proven one way or the other.

In 1998, Dr. Eugene Foster and a group of geneticists conducted a DNA study on Jefferson and Hemings descendants. Thomas Jefferson himself had no sons who sired children. But his uncle, Field Jefferson, did. The study took Y-chromosomal DNA samples from five male-line descendants of Field Jefferson, from two male descendants of Eston Hemings, and from other relatives. The study showed that there was indeed a genetic link between Jefferson and Hemings descendants. Human Y chromosomes are carried from father to son, so that all paternally related males have the identical Y chromosome. Foster's study concluded that a male with the Jefferson Y chromosome was the father of Eston Hemings, born in 1808, Sally's seventh and last child. The male-line descendants of Thomas Woodson, Sally's oldest son, did not match the DNA from the Jefferson line. Eston's DNA did. But there were 25 adult male Jeffersons living in Virginia within 20 miles of Monticello at the time—which one was the father? No one can know for sure, but the authors of the study concluded that Thomas Jefferson was most probably Eston Hemings's father. In January 2000, the Thomas Jefferson Foundation concurred, based on its own staff research. The foundation even suggested a high probability that Jefferson fathered six of Sally's children.

Other historians argue that Jefferson and Sally Hemings did not have any personal relationship at all. Some believe that the most likely father of Hemings's children was Jefferson's younger brother Randolph (1755–1815). So DNA as a tool may have narrowed the possibilities, but does not yet provide a definitive answer.

Whether Thomas Jefferson fathered children by Sally Hemings or not matters a great deal to their descendants, who belong to various family organizations. It also complicates our picture of Jefferson, the author of the Declaration of Independence who wrote that "all men are created equal," the plantation owner who owned slaves and believed blacks were inferior to whites, and the likely intimate companion of an African-American woman for close to forty years. The genetic evidence adds another layer of texture to the explosive and long-running issues of race relations, slavery, and interracial marriage in American history.

If you want to take the plunge into the murky waters of the Hemings-Jefferson controversy, see Joseph Ellis, *American Sphinx: The Character of Thomas Jefferson* (New York: Alfred A. Knopf, 1997), 216–219 and 303–307. Then look at Anne Gordon-Reed, *Thomas Jefferson and Sally Hemings: An American Controversy* (Charlottesville: University of Virginia Press, 1997). A more recent account is Peter S. Onuf and Jan E. Lewis, eds., *Sally Hemings and Thomas Jefferson: History, Memory, and Civic Culture* (Charlottesville: University of Virginia Press, 1999). You may also wish to look at the DNA study in the November 5, 1998, issue of *Nature*.

The biographies by Malone and Peterson also offer valuable perspectives, as does Fawn Brodie's *Thomas Jefferson: An Intimate History* (New York: W.W. Norton, 1974).

Task: Write down some possible conclusions if it were proven true that Thomas Jefferson fathered children by his slave, Sally Hemings. What other examples of the use of genetic evidence for historical purposes can you find? Does genetic evidence seem reliable? What are its limits? What other kinds of evidence might be used to test its validity? What other historical controversies might genetic evidence help resolve?

10 Credit and Acknowledgment

Historians depend on their primary sources and the secondary work of other historians in order to do their work. They do not work in isolation. They must learn to credit and acknowledge the work of others so that another historian can repeat and validate (or invalidate) their work by examining the original sources that they used. The tools of acknowledgment include footnotes, bibliography, and quotation marks around the words of another person. The work of a good historian should be transparent to, and repeatable by, any other historian. Crediting and acknowledging sources are professional and ethical responsibilities for all historians. If they use or quote sources without quotation marks or other acknowledgment, they may be accused of engaging in plagiarism or fraud.

10.1 Notes

Why do historians insist on diverting the reader's attention with those nagging footnotes at the bottom of the page? Why have endnotes at the back of the book? Footnotes and endnotes are powerful tools of the historian, although students and readers often find them annoying. Footnotes or endnotes (or parenthetical citations within the text) are essential for two reasons: (1) the note acknowledges the source, or sources, from which the historian got information, evidence, or a quotation, enabling the reader to go to the original source to verify its accuracy or applicability; and (2) the note permits the historian to carry on a second level of discourse with the reader that would otherwise break up the text. Notes do not close off, but open up, discussion and further research. Notes, like footprints, tell the reader where the historian has been and where the reader might go for further information or interpretation.

The following example shows how a historian uses an extended footnote both to acknowledge her sources and to converse with the reader about the work of two prominent historians. The author is Suzanne Desan. Her article on "Crowds, Community, and Ritual in the Work of E.P. Thompson and Natalie Davis" appeared in Lynn Hunt, ed., *The New Cultural History* (Berkeley: University of California Press, 1989), 47–71.

> "By staking out new issues and methods of inquiry, E.P. Thompson and Natalie Davis have had a tremendous impact on European history, and both well deserve their outstanding reputations. No one can now work on the Reformation without reading Davis or study the Industrial Revolution without perusing Thompson. Davis's work has widened the focus of Reformation studies beyond the theological issues toward the social history of the Reformation and the examination of popular religion. Although her writing fits within the context of the Annales school, with its turn towards grassroots history and the *histoire des mentalités*, her work also complements the French approach by making greater use of symbolic anthropology and by emphasizing the crucial determining role of cultural rather than climatological, geographic, or socioeconomic factors."[1]

Task: Look at the footnote. Which parts acknowledge sources? Which parts engage the reader in a conversation? Which make specific suggestions? What might the eager reader do in response to the footnote?

10.2 Bibliography

How can a bibliography be a useful tool for doing history? A bibliography is a written list of books, journal articles, or unpublished archival materials employed in the course of researching and writing a historical monograph, essay, or paper. Bibliographies normally list each entry alphabetically by the author's last name (Appleby, Joyce, under A, for example). You should keep a working bibliography on note cards as you do your research. The entry for each source used should be complete. You can then use a shorthand reference to each source at the bottom of any note card with information or text drawn from that source (Appleby 254, for example). A bibliography is a kind of blueprint for doing history, a schematic drawing of where you or other historians have been or where you or they intend to go.

The following conventions will help you keep a working bibliography, but please use your instructor's style manual for precise format.

Styling Your Bibliography

Books

Give full last name, first name, and middle name or initial of the author as it appears on the title page. Provide full book title, including subtitle, if any (in *italics* if you are typing). Indicate edition, if not the first. Show city of publication, publishing company, and year of publication.

Periodical Articles

Give full last name, first name, and middle name or initial of the author. Give full article title and subtitle, if any, inside quotation marks. Add full title of periodical (magazine, journal, newspaper, etc.) in italics, volume and issue number of the periodical, with month/day/year of publication in parentheses, and page numbers of the article.

Unpublished Materials

Provide full name of the archive or manuscript collection, city and state location, box number, file number, and pages if indicated.

Websites

Indicate author, editor, or translator, title and subject, and Internet address in the format www.xxxxxxxxxx.xxx. Also note the date you visited the website (in parentheses).

Types of Bibliographies

A bibliography may be selected, complete, or annotated. A *selected* bibliography, the shortest form of bibliography, lists only the most frequently consulted or significant works used in your research. A *complete* bibliography lists all works used in your research, even if not actually cited by you in your text. An *annotated* bibliography appends a phrase or sentence to each entry indicating its nature and value to you in your research. The most common form of annotated bibliography is a bibliographical essay that discusses entries in a narrative or analytical context.

A Selective, Annotated Bibliography

The following brief selection from "Note on Bibliographical Literature" comes from Benjamin Quarles, *Black Abolitionists* (New York: Oxford University Press, 1969), 251–252. Notice that it is selective, annotated, and almost historiographic. The author omits the publisher, using only city, state, and date to identify the publication. More complete publishing data as suggested in *The Chicago Manual of Style*, 15th edition, might make it easier for the reader to locate the book in question.

"All students of the abolitionist movement are indebted to Dwight L. Dumond for his comprehensive *A Bibliography of Antislavery in America*. Dumond's entries are not annotated, but many of them, notably the pamphlets, bear lengthy, descriptive titles. A few items have escaped Dumond's ccareful attention, particularly if the conventions held by Negroes be considered of abolitionist kidney [temperament or background]. A model for the other states, the excellent *New Jersey and the Negro: A Bibliography, 1715–1966* (New Jersey Library Association, Trenton, 1967), includes a number of citations dealing with the slavery controversy, many of them relating to matters by no means confined to New Jersey. Louis Filler's thoroughly researched *The Crusade against Slavery* (New York, 1960) has a highly useful annotated bibliography designed for both the scholar and the general reader. In the fine essay on sources in his *North of Slavery: The Free Negro in the United States, 1790–1860*, Leon L. Litwack devotes one heading to white abolitionists and another to black abolitionists, in the latter emphasizing the significant role of the antebellum Negro conventions. Two works which do not list a separate bibliography but whose footnote entries are richly suggestive are Larry Gara, *The Liberty Line: The Legend of the Underground Railroad* (Lexington, Kentucky, 1961) and Charles H. Wesley, *Neglected History: Essays in Negro History by a College President* (Wilberforce, Ohio, 1965), Chapters 3, 4, 5 ..."

Notice how this bibliographical essay is selective in what it describes, descriptive of a field of study, critical of secondary sources, and suggestive of further reading. The essay shows what Quarles himself has read and what you might want to read yourself if you are interested in black abolitionists.

Bibliographies and bibliographical essays are very important tools in the reading and writing of history. They show at a glance which particular works a historian has consulted on a given topic and therefore how complete and up-to-date the research may be. Historians often begin consulting a specialized book in their field by looking first at the bibliography. You may want to do this as well.

Task: Re-read the selection from Quarles. How many different types of sources does he list? What issues does he raise about the topic of black abolitionists?

10.3 Acknowledging Sources and Avoiding Plagiarism

In all your historical work, what tools will you need to acknowledge your sources and the work of others while producing work that is truly your own? How can you avoid the sin of plagiarism? And what is plagiarism?

Plagiarism means stealing and representing another's words or ideas as your own. These words or ideas may be few or many—a phrase, a paragraph, or several pages—but the principle is the same. Plagiarism, intentional or unintentional, is theft; it may be considered a form of lying (about one's sources) and cheating (failing to observe the ethical rules of scholarship). You need to learn to acknowledge and cite all sources properly, using quotation marks around (or indenting as a block quote) words not your own. Use footnotes, endnotes, or parenthetical citations to acknowledge the words or ideas of another. Do not plagiarize.

Consider the following paragraph from Donald Kagan, Steven Ozment, and Frank M. Turner, *The Western Heritage*, Brief Edition (Upper Saddle River, NJ: Prentice Hall, 1999), 99.

> In 36 B.C.E. Antony attacked Parthia, and the result was disastrous. His soldiers' faith in him was further undercut when Octavian mounted a propaganda campaign that convinced them that Antony had fallen under the spell of Egypt's queen, Cleopatra. By 32 B.C.E. all pretense of cooperation came to an end. Lepidus had already been shoved aside, and at Actium in western Greece in 31 B.C.E. Octavian defeated Antony.

In this example, if you use the entire paragraph in your own paper *without* indenting or quotation marks ("") around the paragraph (and without reference to Kagan, Ozment, and Turner 1999, 99), then you are plagiarizing from the book. If you use the entire paragraph *with* quotation marks around it and proper citation, you are not plagiarizing but neither are you writing anything in your own words. Even though you have not plagiarized and have indicated your sources, a paper with nothing but quoted paragraphs from other people is not yours either.

But these are extremes. Plagiarism is usually partial, a few words here and there, or a few sentences, or a few paragraphs. Following are two versions based on the passage from Kagan, Ozment, and Turner. Which version is plagiarized and which is paraphrased? Or are both plagiarized or both paraphrased? What is your evidence for your decision?

> *Version 1.* The Battle of Actium (31 B.C.E.) was a major turning point in the history of Rome. We know that Antony suffered a major defeat when he took his armies into Parthia around 36 B.C.E. His great rival Octavian then undermined Antony's authority by spreading the rumor among his troops that Antony was in love with Cleopatra. Antony and Octavian completely ceased to have any kind of alliance shortly before they engaged each other at Actium. Even

before Antony had lost the war to Octavian, Lepidus had been "shoved aside," according to one modern account, and Octavian had triumphed. (See Kagan 1999, 99.)

Version 2. Antony attacked Parthia around 36 B.C.E. The result was disastrous. Octavian mounted a big propaganda campaign that undermined Antony's soldiers' faith in him and showed them that Antony was spellbound by Cleopatra, the queen of Egypt. By around 32 B.C.E., cooperation between Antony and Octavian was at an end. They had shoved aside Lepidus and Octavian beat Antony at Actium in 31 B.C.E.

If you still do not get the idea, there are plenty of learned scholars to help you. Begin by checking out (and reading) the Bates College website on plagiarism, www.bates.edu/pubs/plagiarism. Then try the essay by Van E. Hillier, "Acknowledging Sources and Avoiding Plagiarism," which you can find on the Duke University website, http://uwp.duke.edu/sources.html. There is a particularly good discussion in "Recognizing Plagiarism and Acknowledging Sources," in *The New St. Martin's Handbook* by Andrea Lunsford and Robert Connors (Boston: Bedford/St. Martin's, 1999), 494–497. Another good discussion is "Managing Information; Avoiding Plagiarism," in *The Bedford Handbook*, 5th ed., by Diana Hacker (Boston: Bedford Books, 1998), section 48, 554–562.

I hope that this brief example will help you understand how to acknowledge your sources and avoid plagiarism. In your own work, begin with your note taking. Quotation marks are your best tools. Put quotation marks around the words of others from the very beginning as you are taking notes. Then you will not think the words were your own when you review those notes. Work on developing your own arguments in your own words so you do not need to depend on the words and ideas of others. Trying to research and write a paper that is simply a compilation of the work of others is a dangerous step in the direction of plagiarism. Before you write a paper, think it through and outline it in your own words. Please do not hesitate to speak with your instructor at any time about acknowledging sources correctly and avoiding plagiarism.

Over the years I have encountered plagiarism many times among students, faculty, journalists, and politicians. Most plagiarists plead ignorance or lack of intent. But plagiarism is a serious matter in the eyes of most historians and faculty generally. You want to avoid plagiarism at all costs. The goal is to produce work that is original and truly your own, work in which you can take great pride. Your instructors and other historians stand ready to help you achieve that goal. Don't plagiarize!

Task: Try to paraphrase or summarize the Kagan paragraph quoted above in a way that (1) plagiarizes by using some of the words, phrases, or even sentences of the paragraph while following closely its structure, and without quotation marks or source acknowledgement; and (2) does *not* plagiarize by reorganizing, rethinking, or properly citing words, phrases, and sentences in the paragraph with reference to Kagan 1999, 99. Try both approaches and see if you can succeed in both failing and succeeding to plagiarize.

10.4 Professional Plagiarism: How Not to Do History

Could a professional historian ever plagiarize the work of other people? Astonishingly enough, even professional historians do on occasion plagiarize the work of others. In the case of two prominent writers and historians, Stephen Ambrose and Doris Kearns Goodwin, they claim innocence because others took notes for them or otherwise assisted in their work. Both have produced popular, well-written histories at a prodigious rate. Both let research assistants do much of their work. The result is sloppy research and even plagiarism. But the result is also very profitable.

The idea that one could become rich and famous by pirating the work of others is hardly new. Back in 1976, Alex Haley, the author of *Roots*, a genealogical autobiography of his African background that became a famous television series and won him the Pulitzer Prize in 1977, committed plagiarism. Haley borrowed more than eighty passages from a 1967 novel titled *The African* by Hal Courlander without attribution. Haley used these passages to concoct the fictional story of his own African ancestors whom, in fact, he did not know much about. Courlander settled out of court with Haley in December 1978.

Stephen Ambrose is the prolific prize-winning author of many histories and biographies, including *The Wild Blue Yonder* (New York: Simon & Schuster, 2001), which tells the story of the United States Air Force during World War II in graphic detail. After his phenomenally popular earlier book *D Day: June 6, 1944* (New York: Simon & Schuster, 1994), carefully timed for the event's fiftieth anniversary, Ambrose formed a corporation (Ambrose and Ambrose) with his five grown sons in order to produce even more history at a faster rate. They took on jobs as his research assistants, visiting libraries, reading books, taking notes, and interviewing participants in the events described. His team made mistakes.

Sharp-eyed critics soon noticed that *Wild Blue* borrowed words and phrases from Thomas Childers, *The Wings of Morning* (New York: Perseus Books, 1995) and from two other books on air force history, Wesley Frank Craven and James L. Cate, *The Army Air Forces in World War II* (Chicago: University of Chicago Press, 1949) and Michael S. Sherry, *The Rise of American Air Power* (New Haven: Yale University Press, 1975).

Ambrose often did not put quotation marks around the words of these other authors. He used phrases and even entire sentences verbatim without proper attribution. And he borrowed heavily from the language and logical structure as well (Illustration 10.1).

For example, Childers wrote: "No amount of practice could have prepared them for what they encountered. B-24's, glittering like mica, were popping up out of the clouds all over the sky."

Ambrose wrote: "No amount of practice could have prepared the [pilot and the crew] for what they encountered [—] B-24's, glittering like mica, were popping up out of the clouds [over here, over there, everywhere]."

When confronted with accusations, Ambrose denied that he had plagiarized. He claimed that there was "no effort to deceive." "I tell stories," he argued; "I don't discuss my documents." "I wish I had put the quotation marks in, but I didn't," he added. "I am not out there stealing other people's writings. If I am writing up a passage and it is a story I want to tell and this story fits and a part of it is from other people's writing, I just type it up that way and put it in a footnote. I just want to know where the hell it came from." Huh? Ambrose still did not get the message that borrowing the exact words of other writers is unacceptable without proper quotation and attribution.

How could they? Professional Plagiarism: Historian Stephen Ambrose and philosopher George Santayana write on … in identical prose. *(Kevin Siers/ Reprinted with special permission of North American Syndicate).*

Illustration 10.1 Cartoon of Historian Stephen Ambrose and Philosopher George Santayana

Sherry was most generous and understanding. In an interview, he said merely that Ambrose had engaged in "sloppiness, or plagiarism, or some combination of the two." For Ambrose, the exciting and dramatic story came first. The careful and critical use of sources with correct attribution was a time-consuming nuisance.

Doris Kearns Goodwin is a popular historian and biographer of the Kennedy and Johnson families and the American presidency. In her 1987 book *The Fitzgeralds and the Kennedys* (New York: Simon & Schuster), Goodwin borrowed entire passages and sentences word for word from Lynne McTaggart's biography, *Kathleen Kennedy: Her Life and Times* (New York: Dell, 1983). When McTaggart threatened to sue for copyright infringement, Goodwin settled out of court. Simon & Schuster in 1987 paid off McTaggart and destroyed all copies of its inventory of Goodwin's book. (The publishing company plans to correct errors and republish the book, of course, thereby making more money.)

McTaggart wrote recently that she was "shocked to read passage after passage of my own book embedded in hers." "In my case," she said, "whether Ms. Goodwin had used footnotes or even quotation marks around the passages taken from my book would not have mattered. (Some passages were credited to me in footnotes.) It was the sheer volume of appropriation—thousands of my exact or nearly exact words—that supported my copyright infringement claim" (letter to *New York Times*, March 16, 2002.)

But Goodwin also failed to place quotation marks around sentences taken from Hank Searls, *The Lost Prince: Young Joe, the Forgotten Kennedy* (New York: New American Library, 1969), and his *Rose Kennedy: Times to Remember* (New York: Doubleday, 1974). She explained that the problem was in her handwritten notes from years earlier, which she failed to check. "I should have had the books in front of me," she added, with respect to McTaggart's book. "I failed to provide quotation marks for phrases that I had taken verbatim having assumed that these phrases, drawn from my notes, were my words, not hers ... I wrote everything in longhand in those days, including the notes I took on secondary sources ... Drawing on my notes, I did not realize that in some cases they constituted a close paraphrase of the original work." Again, Goodwin seems to miss the point. Unintentional theft is still theft.

These cases of plagiarism all vary in intent and method. Alex Haley borrowed passages without attribution from a novel in order to describe an ancestor that never existed. Stephen Ambrose (or his research assistants) borrowed passages without attribution from various air force histories and added his own style for flavoring. Doris Kearns Goodwin used passages without attribution ostensibly because she (or her team) took notes without using quotation marks in the first place. Haley, Ambrose, and Goodwin have many things in common: they write well, they employ others to do their research, they produce large amounts of prose, they make large amounts of money, and they plagiarize. They have admitted their plagiarism with varying degrees of candor. They write popular history for a mass audience, and they are very poor practitioners of the professional historian's trade.

Haley, Ambrose, and Goodwin got caught doing what any college student of history is constantly reminded to avoid: they plagiarized. As writers, they are imaginative and even compelling. As historians, they are not worthy of emulation.

If you wish to find out more about professional plagiarism, see David D. Kirkpatrick's articles on Ambrose in the *New York Times*, January 5, 2013, and 25, 2002. Also Paul Gray, "Other People's Words," *Smithsonian* 32: 12 (March 2002): 102–103. On Goodwin, see *Time*, February 4, 2002, and Gray, "Other People's Words," 103. On Haley, see Philip Nobile, *The Village Voice*, February 23, 1993.

Task: Look again at the examples of Haley, Ambrose, and Goodwin. Exactly how are they plagiarizing? How do they differ from, or resemble, each other in the way they have failed to acknowledge sources properly? See Chapter 19 regarding the Internet.

Notes

1 In recent years, numerous Annalistes have shifted their point of emphasis and analysis away from long-term socioeconomic factors and toward cultural elements. On some level, the turn toward *mentalités* has even undermined the original Annales position that the critical factors were social and economic rather than cultural. See Lynn Hunt, "French History in the Last Twenty Years: The Rise and Fall of the *Annales Paradigm*," *Journal of Contemporary History* 21 (1986): 209–224, esp. p. 217. On the history of the Annales school, see Traian Stoianovich, *French Historical Method: The Annales Paradigm* (Ithaca, NY: Cornell University Press, 1976).

11 Narrative and Explanation

History involves both telling a story and explaining how, or why, events occurred as they did. Historians narrate and explain the past in ordinary language of their own day—language that changes over time. They normally follow a sequence of events in chronological order. But historians may also start with the end, rather than the beginning, of the story to achieve dramatic effect. (I began my biography of newspaper editor Horace Greeley with the story of his funeral.) After all, historians already know the outcome of the story they intend to tell, unlike the actual historical participants in the events being narrated. Historians must try to explain what caused the events in their story—the reasons why events turned out the way that they did—without ignoring the free choices made by historical actors at the time.

11.1 The Language of the Historian

Language is a tool for writing. What kind of language should you expect to encounter as you read history? What kind of language should you use when you write history? Historians tend to write in ordinary language that ordinary people can read and understand. This is certainly a charm and virtue of the craft of history. Most people cannot pick up an issue of a scientific or social science journal and begin to understand the esoteric, technical, often quantitative and complex language and assumptions of the discipline. History is different. Most people can read and understand most history.

Historians try to write in a language that both captures the spirit of the historical period, event, or character and that appeals to a contemporary audience. The language of the historian is normally simple, direct, and comprehensible, however complex the evidence or argument may be. Most people can read and enjoy history because it uses ordinary language. Using ordinary language well is therefore one of the historian's most important tools. They abhor jargon.

Paul Revere and the New England Village

Language changes over time. Two historians separated by more than a century may well describe the same event but in a different language. Consider the well-known "midnight ride" of Boston silversmith Paul Revere on April 18, 1775, to warn the citizens, especially armed "minutemen," of the area around Boston that "redcoats"—British soldiers—were going to march on the nearby towns of Lexington and Concord to seize stores of arms and ammunition hidden by American patriots. Friends rowed Revere across the Charles River in a boat around 10 p.m. He then mounted a horse and rode west to Lexington, Lincoln, and Concord. Revere and his friend William Dawes were only two of dozens of riders out that night. But Paul Revere's midnight ride is part of American folklore. Inventor Thomas Edison even made a film about it as early as 1914.

Below are two different accounts of Paul Revere's ride, one written by mid-nineteenth-century historian George Bancroft, one written by late twentieth-century historian David Hackett Fischer. How do they differ? How are they similar? How is their language different? Similar? What does each emphasize? What facts do they present? Can you tell which was written by Bancroft and which by Fischer? How do their approaches differ? What clues reveal the era in which each account was written?

Here is the solution: Account 1 is by Bancroft, from his massive *History of the United States from the Discovery of the American Continent*, 9 vols. (Boston: Little, Brown 1857–1866) vol. 7, 289–291. Account 2 is by Fischer from *Paul Revere's Ride* (New York: Oxford University Press, 1994, 130), an entire monograph devoted to the story. Bancroft writes a flowing narrative in plain English. According to Bancroft, two dispatch riders, Paul Revere and William Dawes, rode off about 10 p.m. to sound the alarm. He then describes how British officers finally seized Revere and Dawes when they got as far as Lincoln, then took them back to Lexington and released them.

Account 1

"Revere stopped only to engage a friend to raise the concerted signals, and five minutes before the sentinels received the order to prevent it, two friends rowed him past the Somerset man of war across the Charles River. All was still, as suited the hour. The ship was winding with the young flood; the waning moon just peered above a clear horizon; while from a couple of lanterns in the tower of the North Church, the beacon streamed to the neighboring towns, as fast as light could travel ....

Express messengers and the call of minute-men spread widely the alarm. How children trembled as they were scared out of sleep by the cries! How wives with heaving breasts, bravely seconded their husbands; how the countrymen, forced suddenly to arm, without the guides or counselors, took instant counsel of their courage. The mighty chorus of voices rose from the scattered farmhouses, and as it were from the very ashes of the dead. Come forth, champions of liberty; now free your country; protect your sons and daughters, your wives and homesteads; rescue the houses of the God of your fathers, the franchises handed down from your ancestors. Now all is at stake; the battle is for all."

Account 2

"Two miles beyond Lexington Green, they entered the town of Lincoln, a new community that had been created only twenty years before. Paul Revere reckoned they had come 'about half way from Lexington to Concord.' Here the Great Road curved westward through open fields and pastures, interspersed with patches of swamp and woodland. Very near the boundary between Lincoln and Lexington, the road ran past a little cluster of farmsteads, three or four of them, a few hundred feet apart. Each house was set only a few feet from the north edge of the highway, facing south toward the warmth of the sun, according to the Yankee custom. All were occupied by families called Nelson. This pattern of settlement was typical of old New England. It was the custom for sons to settle close to their father's land, while the daughters moved away. As a consequence, many town centers in Massachusetts were surrounded by small hamlets of households with the same surname."

Bancroft's language is dramatic, charged with emotion and patriotism, part of the long narrative of American history, full of details about the time and the weather, imagining the response of women and children to the alarm. The citizens of Boston are "champions of liberty." Their resistance to British domination is God-given and ancestral. This is nationalist, narrative history at its nineteenth-century best. Fischer writes from a different, more modern perspective, reminding readers that "the saga of the midnight ride is one of many shared memories that make Americans one people, diverse as we may be." He notes that professional historians have largely ignored the ride as too patriotic, too "politically incorrect," the narrative about a "dead white male on horseback." Many contemporary historians have abandoned the study of individuals and events for social history, culture, and material artifacts. Fischer seeks to retell the story of Paul Revere's ride using the language of social history, as well as telling the story of one individual.

Notice how Fischer switches from the story of Paul Revere sounding the alarm to the story of New England town settlement and society. All of a sudden we find ourselves not simply in Lincoln, but in a typical New

England town, learning about land settlement, family life, and farm building patterns. We have moved from Bancroft's patriotic story of one "great man" to a glimpse into New England society and culture.

In the end, Fischer gives us the most complete and authoritative study of Paul Revere's ride ever written. We learn that Revere and Dawes were only two of dozens of alarm riders out that night in a well-organized effort to alert the countryside. We learn that people did not shout "The British are coming," because they were virtually all British citizens at the time; instead, they shouted, "The redcoats are out." And we learn about artifacts —Revere's saddlebags and eyeglasses, firearms and field guns, houses and churches, and about how society was organized, and about the mythical interpretations of Revere's ride as exemplified in Henry Wadsworth Longfellow's famous poem, "The Midnight Ride of Paul Revere" (1863) and the painting by William Robinson Leigh. Drawing on the language and research of his fellow historians, Fischer gives us quite a new and equally dramatic story of Paul Revere's ride with less emphasis on patriotism and more on historical contingency. What if Revere and Dawes had never gotten across the Charles River that night? Would American history have been different (Illustration 11.1)?

Both Bancroft and Fischer describe Revere's ride in clear, flowing prose using the ordinary language of their day. But individual liberty and national pride in the first account have given way to social history and micro-historical detail in the second account. Ordinary language and historical technique have both changed dramatically in the past century and a half.

The language of the historian changes over time, along with the language of the culture in which the historian resides. Historians today would not use the phrase "great men" so beloved of nineteenth-century historians. They try to write in a language that is gender-neutral, race-neutral, and objective. They emphasize social structure more than individual human agency. Historical language tends to follow social and cultural norms. The example of Paul Revere's famous ride, and his role as part of a committee of dispatch riders to small New England towns that famous night, alert us to the changing language and thinking of historians over time. Historians use ordinary language, but ordinary language changes.

Task: What are the merits of the two different accounts of the same event presented by Bancroft and Fischer? Which account seems more effective to you? Why? Look closely at William Robinson Leigh's painting of Paul Revere's ride. Does the painting reflect the language of Bancroft, or Fischer, or both, or neither? Why? Do you see a lone rider or a New England town at first glance?

11.2 Chronology

A chronology lists events over time in order. What kind of tool is a chronology? How can a chronology help you organize your material when you write a paper? Doing a chronology can be a very helpful intermediate step in researching and writing your history paper, especially in producing a narrative. Keep a chronology as you take notes on cards. Keep notes in chronological order (you may wish to reorder them as your ideas develop). After doing some of your research, do a chronology to help you order events and see possible patterns. A good chronology can be a great help when you come to do the first draft of your paper. A chronology also helps as a reference point during both the research and writing process.

Illustration 11.1 The Midnight Ride of Paul Revere

"Great patriot" or "dead white male on a horse"? *The Midnight Ride of Paul Revere by* William Robinson Leigh suggests visually the changing language of historians over time. (*Library of Congress*)

Illustration 11.2 Margaret Fuller, 1846

The only known photograph taken of Margaret Fuller, 1846. (*The Granger Collection, New York*)

The Life of Margaret Fuller

As an example, consider a brief chronology of the life of Margaret Fuller (1810–1850), a pioneer literary critic, writer, and journalist, colleague of Ralph Waldo Emerson, and author of *Woman in the Nineteenth Century*. The chronology is taken from Mary Kelley, ed., *The Portable Margaret Fuller* (New York: Penguin, 1994) (Illustration 11.2).

Notice how the historian limits her entries to the most significant events (I have reduced the entries even further). We know a great deal about Margaret Fuller's life. These are only a few of her most notable activities, publications, and travels. Any chronology is highly selective and excludes many events, including events that could give context to the life.

The last entry can hardly convey the sadness and grief with which Margaret Fuller's many friends responded to her tragic and untimely death with Osoli and their infant son.

If you were to write a biography of Fuller, this chronology would constitute a helpful reference tool. Chronology reminds you what happened when and in what order. But it is only a chronology—a list of highlights and milestones—not a narrative or a biography. You need to connect the dots, so to speak, and develop an argument to make chronology come alive in a significant way. This example is simplistic because it begins with the subject's birth and ends with her death. When you should begin and end a chronology is usually much more complex.

Chronology is a limited but important tool that you can use to do history. It is the skeleton on which narrative and interpretation will put flesh. You will find chronology helpful both in organizing your notes and in beginning to write.

Task: Write a brief chronology of your own life. What events should you include? What should you exclude? Why? What does the chronology reveal about your life? What does it not reveal?

Chronology

1810 Sarah Margaret Fuller is born in Cambridgeport, Massachusetts, on May 23.

1824 Begins a year as a student at Miss Prescott's Young Ladies' Seminary in Groton, Massachusetts

1825 Returns to Cambridge, Massachusetts.

1833 Moves to Groton, Massachusetts, with family and tutors her younger siblings Richard, Arthur, and Lloyd. Translates Goethe's *Torquato Tasso*.

1836 Begins teaching at Bronson Alcott's Temple School in Boston.

1837 Moves to Providence, Rhode Island, to teach at the Greene Street School.

1838 Resigns position at the Greene Street School.

1839 Publishes her translation of Eckermann's *Conversations with Goethe*. Continues research on a biography of Goethe. Agrees to edit newly founded Transcendentalist periodical *Dial*. Begins series of classes, or "Conversations," for adult women.

1840 Begins "Autobiographical Sketch." Edits *Dial* from July until July of 1842.

1842 Publishes "Bettine Brentano and Her Friend Gunderode" in *Dial*.

1844 Concludes final series of "Conversations." Publishes *Summer on the Lakes, during 1843*. Moves to New York City and begins literary editorship of Horace Greeley's *New-York Daily Tribune*.

1845 Publishes *Woman in the Nineteenth Century*.
1846 Resigns literary editorship and accepts position as foreign correspondent for the *New-York Daily Tribune*. Sails for Europe with Marcus and Rebecca Spring. Publishes first dispatch in *New-York Daily Tribune* on September 24. Travels in England, Scotland, and France.
1847 Leaves France for Italy in February. Arrives in Rome and meets Giovanni Angelo Ossoli in April. Travels in northern Italy and Switzerland from July to October. Begins residence in Rome in October.
1848 Angelo Ossoli is born in Rieti on September 5. Pellegrino Rossi is assassinated and Pope Pius IX flees from Rome in November.
1849 Roman Republic is proclaimed in February. Siege of Rome by the French begins in April. France invades Rome and restores the pope to power in June. Fuller, Ossoli, and their son, Angelo, move to Florence in November.
1850 Publishes her final dispatch in *New-York Daily Tribune* on February 13. Sails for the United States with Ossoli and Angelo on May 17. Dies in shipwreck off Fire Island on July 19.

11.3 Narrative

Telling a story or writing a narrative is one of the historian's most essential tools. Narrative moves beyond chronology. It selects, explains, and interprets events even while it sets them in some chronological order. How can you write a good narrative while keeping sight of your overall argument? Narratives are normally true stories of historical events in chronological sequence. They may be long or short, but they should not be isolated from the argument, thesis, or main point of your paper. Your paper should be neither entirely narrative nor analytic, but a creative combination of both approaches.

Pickett's Charge at Gettysburg

As an example, consider the problem facing James McPherson, the premier historian of the Civil War. In his prize-winning book *Battle Cry of Freedom: The Civil War Era*, he covered not only the war itself, but also the decades leading up to that "irrepressible conflict." When he came to the Battle of Gettysburg (July 1–3, 1863), the major turning point in the war, he had to deal in brief with a topic on which dozens, if not hundreds, of books have been written. Even covering Pickett's famous charge against the Union batteries was a challenge. He could

Illustration 11.3 The Aftermath of Pickett's Charge at Gettysburg, July 4, 1863
After Pickett's charge: How do you write a narrative when most of the participants are dead?
(*Library of Congress*)

have written hundreds of pages; he gave himself two (Illustration 11.3). Somehow, he had to make the narrative significant and dramatic, infusing it with meaning, while keeping it short. The result is above. Did he succeed?

Somehow, the historian here uses narrative as a tool to convey the "sound and fury" of combat along with the visual images of terrain and men at arms, the training of soldiers, the struggle between the industrial North and the agrarian South, and the romance and reality of battle. The narrative is spare and concise, yet rich in meaning and implication. It is tense, dramatic, and detailed. Anyone who has walked the ground and seen the monuments to the so-called high-water mark of the Confederacy understands what McPherson has accomplished. We should all write narrative history so well.

With Pickett's fresh division as a spearhead, therefore, [Confederate general Robert E.] Lee would send three divisions preceded by an artillery barrage against that weakened center on July 3 [1863]. [Confederate general J.E.B.] Stuart would circle around the Union rear and [Union general Richard] Ewell would assail the right flank to clamp the pincers when Pickett broke through the front. With proper coordination and leadership, his invincible troops could not fail.

Across the way a midnight council of Union generals resolved to stay and fight it out. With prescience, [Union general George] Meade told the general commanding his center that "if Lee attacks to-morrow, it will be in *your front*" At first light, however, fighting broke out at the extreme right of the Union line, along the base of Culp's Hill. Units of the Federal 12th Corps, which had been shifted to the left the previous day, came back during the night and attacked at dawn to regain their abandoned trenches now occupied by the rebels. In a seven-hour firefight they succeeded, and thus dimmed Lee's chances for turning the Union right simultaneously with the planned piercing of the center.

While this was going on, [Confederate general James] Longstreet once more urged Lee to maneuver around Meade's left. Again Lee refused, and ordered Longstreet to attack the Union center with Pick-ett's division and two of Hill's—fewer than 15,000 men to advance three-quarters of a mile across open fields and assault dug-in infantry supported by ample artillery. "General Lee," Longstreet later reported himself to have said, "there never was a body of fifteen thousand men who could make that attack successfully."

In this mood, Longstreet ordered a concentration of Confederate artillery—some 150 guns—for the largest southern bombardment of the war, to soften up the enemy at the point of attack. At 1:07 p.m. Longstreet's guns shattered the uneasy silence that had followed the morning's fight on the Union right. For almost two hours an artillery duel among nearly 300 guns filled the Pennsylvania countryside with an ear-splitting roar heard as far away as Pittsburgh. Despite this sound and fury, the Union infantry lying behind stone walls and breastworks suffered little, for the rebel aim was high.

Pickett's all-Virginia division waited with nervous impatience to go in and get it over with. Thirty-eight years old, George Pickett had graduated last in the same West Point class as [former Union general] George McClellan (who graduated second) ... . With his long hair worn in ringlets and his face adorned by a drooping mustache and goatee, Pickett looked like a cross between a Cavalier dandy and riverboat gambler. He affected the romantic style of Sir Walter Scott's heroes and was eager to win everlasting glory at Gettysburg.

Finally, about 3:00 p.m., Longstreet reluctantly ordered the attack. The Confederate bombardment seemed to have disabled the enemy's artillery; it was now or never. With parade-ground precision, Pickett's three brigades moved out joined by six more from Hill's division on their left and two others in reserve. It was a magnificent mile-wide spectacle, a picture-book view of war that participants on both sides remembered with awe until their dying moment—which for many came within the next hour. Pickett's charge represented the

Confederate war effort in microcosm: matchless valor, apparent initial success, and ultimate disaster. As the gray infantry poured across the gently undulating farmland with seemingly irresistible force, northern artillery suddenly erupted in a savage cascade, sending shot and shell among the southern regiments and changing to canister as they kept coming … . Yankee infantry behind stone walls opened up at 200 yards while Vermont, Ohio, and New York regiments on the left and right swung out to rake both flanks of the attacking force. The southern assault collapsed under this unbearable pressure from front and flanks. Two or three hundred Virginians and Tennesseans with General Lewis A. Armistead breached the first Union line, where Armistead was mortally wounded with his hand on a Yankee cannon and his followers fell like leaves in an autumn wind. In half an hour it was all over. Of the 14,000 Confederates who had gone forward, scarcely half returned. Pickett's own division lost two-thirds of its men; his three brigadiers and all thirteen colonels were killed or wounded.

Notice, however, that the established facts about Pickett's charge are few. We do not know the exact number of Confederate soldiers involved in the charge at all. Most soldiers at Gettysburg were not involved in the charge. Most of those involved were killed. The survivors lived to tell their stories, to memorialize the past, and to share memories at the subsequent reunions of Gettysburg veterans, North and South. Narrative can often raise more questions than it answers. What questions does this narrative of Pickett's charge suggest to you?

If you want to see how Pickett's charge—this brief but significant event—has been continually reexamined and reinvented ever since July 3, 1863, read Carol Reardon, *Pickett's Charge in History and Memory* (Chapel Hill: University of North Carolina Press, 1997). The account here is reprinted with permission of Oxford University Press from James McPherson, *Battle Cry of Freedom: The Civil War Era* (New York: Oxford University Press, 1988), 661–662.

If you wish to see and hear a re-enactment of Pickett's Charge, watch the film *Gettysburg*. If you wish to experience a *simulation* of Pickett's Charge, play one of the online board games by that name.

Task: Write your own brief narrative of Pickett's charge using only the information provided by McPherson in his account of this famous event. How is your narrative distinct from McPherson's? What did you include? What did you leave out?

11.4 Argument

Argument is another important tool of the historian. How is history an argument, as well as a story? Like lawyers, historians argue a case before their peers, that is, other historians. The logic of a good argument lies beneath the surface of any good work of history. In your papers, you will want to develop an argument based upon the evidence you discover and construct to tell your story. You will need to persuade the reader that your conclusion follows from your premises, your evidence, and your argument. Like a lawyer, you will go through a discovery phase of gathering your evidence. Unlike a lawyer, you do not have to satisfy a client.

An argument is an attempt to support a conclusion with reasons and evidence. An argument is not an assertion, nor is it an opinion, nor is it simply part of a dispute. Not all arguments are equal. Some are more persuasive than others. An argument begins with premises, reliable statements giving reasons. A conclusion is a final statement. Arguments may be based on (1) examples and evidence; (2) analogies (not very persuasive among historians); (3) authority (e.g., your sources). You will want to show how your argument fits into the historiography of other historians writing on your subject and how it relates to their arguments.

Watch out for fallacies when engaged in an argument. For example, do not generalize on the basis of incomplete or insufficient evidence. Do not overlook alternative explanations. Avoid confusing the correlation of two events with the causation of one event by the other. For a good introduction to the nature of argument, which also specifies various fallacies, see Anthony Weston, *A Rulebook for Arguments*, 2nd ed. (Indianapolis: Hackett, 1992).

"'Little Women' Who Helped Make This Great War"

Arguments may appear in a paragraph, a chapter, or a book. Here is a brief example of an argument from Glenna Matthews, "'Little Women' Who Helped Make This Great War," in *Why the Civil War Came*, ed. Gabor S. Boritt, (New York: Oxford University Press, 1996), 44:

> The abolitionist women's willingness to attend notorious trials involving the status of African-Americans attempting to attain their freedom in Northern courts provided another means for shaping public opinion [*premise*]. In effect, such women risked their reputations for respectability in order to dramatize their support of oppressed people. Says the legal historian Paul Finkelman: [*authority*] "As spectators women abolitionists unnerved proslavery jurists and lawyers. In this role they were effective because their very presence in the courtroom challenged the prevailing role of women." But the women went further. Finkelman describes how "the Boston Female Anti-Slavery Society initiated litigation on behalf of the cause." For

example, [*evidence*] in 1836 they were "spark-plugs" in bringing to
the courts the case of Med, a six-year-old slave girl who had come
to Boston with her owner[12] [*footnote to work cited as authority*].

By means both dramatic and subtle, then, abolitionist women undertook
to shape public opinion in the years preceding the war. [*Conclusion.*]

Please note that arguments are rarely so clear and present as in this
example. Try to find some yourself as you read. Check their logic. Check
your own logic too.

Task: Write down an argument about a historical event of your own
choosing. Make sure that the argument contains evidence, reasons, and
a conclusion. Are you persuaded? Will your readers be persuaded as well?

11.5 Causation

Causes are the tools of historical explanation. How do causes help to
explain the past? A cause is something that produces an effect, action, or
event. The force of gravity, for example, causes a ball to roll down an
inclined plane. Historians use causation to explain why, or how, an event
happened. Since history involves the study of change over time, causes
must precede events chronologically. Historians often distinguish between
necessary and sufficient causes. A *necessary* cause is a cause that had to
happen if the caused event were ever to occur. Without that cause, the
event would not have happened. A *sufficient* cause is a cause that led to the
event only because the necessary causes were already present at the time.

For example, historians trying to explain why the Civil War occurred must
first make clear which event, or trend, they are explaining: (1) the sectional
division between North and South, the states that fought each other in the war;
(2) the secession of southern states in 1860 and 1861; or (3) the outbreak of the
war itself in April 1861. Assuming they want to explain the actual outbreak of
war, historians would consider the following necessary causes (or conditions).
Without these necessary causes, the war would not have occurred:

1 Slavery: the institution of slavery in the South made the cultivation of
   cotton and tobacco crops economically profitable. Slavery employed
   unpaid labor, which competed with free wage labor in the North.
   Abolitionists considered slavery immoral and evil. They wanted to
   abolish it as soon as possible. Southerners felt threatened economically
   and socially by northern intervention and abolition of slavery. The
   United States was divided into free and slave states.
2 States' rights: the doctrine that the United States was formed as
   a compact among individual states, any one of which could nullify

that compact if it decided that the federal government interfered too much in the state's internal affairs.

3   Sectionalism: North and South had many disagreements and divisions apart from slavery, especially about the many tariffs imposed by Northern manufacturers on goods purchased in the South. In addition, the sections had distinct agricultural and industrial economies, different value systems, and different ways of life.

4   Cultural differences and perceptions: Many people in the North and the South came to believe hostile stereotypes about each other. Politicians stereotyped the sections as Southern "slavocracy" or Northern "black Republicans." Southern honor confronted Yankee ingenuity. In this case, what people believed was happening before the Civil War came to be as important as what did actually happen.

Given these *necessary causes* for a civil war between North and South, what constituted a *sufficient* cause for war? Many people had been predicting a civil war for decades. In 1858, New York senator William H. Seward referred to the sectional controversy as an "irrepressible conflict between opposing and enduring forces." Earlier in the century, several states had threatened to secede from the Union (e.g., New England in the Hartford Convention of 1814, and South Carolina in the nullification crisis of 1832). There had been bloody slave revolts (Nat Turner in Virginia in 1831) and dramatic attempts to incite a slave rebellion (John Brown in 1859). There had been moments of crisis such as the Mexican War of 1846–1848 and the Kansas-Nebraska Act of 1854. But a series of compromises, notably the Missouri Compromise of 1820 and the Compromise of 1850, had headed off conflict, so that various possible causes of a civil war turned out to be insufficient.

But the tensions and sectional divisions always existed, especially in the 1840s and 1850s. What finally sparked the Civil War? *Sufficient* causes for the war included (1) the election of Abraham Lincoln in 1860 because he was the first candidate of a political party resolved to stop the spread of slavery to become president; (2) the secession of southern states from the Union in late 1860 and early 1861 because it dissolved the Union with the North; (3) the resupplying of, and firing upon, Fort Sumter in Charleston Harbor in April 1861, because these were viewed as acts of war by either South or North. These causes would not have been sufficient to produce civil war unless they combined with the already existing *necessary* causes listed above.

Historians who accept the conventional wisdom that the Civil War became, after a point, an "irrepressible conflict" tend to emphasize necessary causes. In their view, the war was inevitable: it could be delayed but not postponed. Other historians reject the conventional wisdom in favor of the view that a few historical actors—militant abolitionists who condemned slavery, "fire-eating" southerners who denounced abolitionists, and "bungling politicians" who failed to resolve the dispute peacefully—brought on the Civil War by their actions. In this view, the war was not at all inevitable, but could have been avoided had a few leaders acted differently and sought compromise instead of conflict.

Historians also distinguish between monocausal (slavery) and multi-causal (sectionalism, the tariff, western expansion, slavery, perceptions) explanations of the Civil War. Most historians take a multi-causal approach, admitting the existence of more than one possible cause of any given event.

A good examination of the topic of causation is Kenneth M. Stampp, ed., *The Causes of the Civil War* (New York: Simon & Schuster, 1959), which includes both primary and secondary sources. A more recent interpretation of the causes of the Civil War puts evangelical Christianity at the heart of political party divisions North and South that led to the war. See David Goldfield, *America Aflame* (New York: Bloomsbury Press, 2011).

Task: Write a sentence in which you attribute the Civil War to a single cause. Now write another sentence in which you attribute the war to many different causes. Which sentence seems more persuasive to you? Why? How would you go about demonstrating your point? What evidence would you look for?

11.6 The Reasons Why

Explanation is a powerful tool of the historian. Explaining why, or how, events happened the way that they did is central to the historian's craft. Explaining an event means providing evidence of the reasons why that event happened. But what constitutes a good explanation? Exactly what is being explained?

Explaining the Mann Gulch Fire of August 5, 1949

One of the best examples I know of how to explain a historical (and natural) event is contained in writer Norman Maclean's famous book titled *Young Men and Fire*. Published by the University of Chicago Press in 1992, after Maclean's death, the book tells the story of 18 young smoke jumpers, most of whom perished trying to extinguish a forest fire in rugged Mann Gulch along the Missouri River north of Helena, Montana, in the hot, dry summer of 1949. A master craftsman who knew the area from his own youth, Maclean tells not only a tragic story in a compelling manner, but also the parallel story of how he, as a historian and writer, tried to find out what actually happened. He asks many questions and employs a number of techniques to help explain why, and how, a forest fire blew up and young men died terribly of burns and asphyxiation in a fire.

What Happened?

Maclean is a great storyteller. He describes the young smoke jumpers in loving detail, their training, their barroom brawls, their self-confident sense of immortality, their jump from a noisy, bouncing airplane into a fire from 2,000 feet, in high winds and at a temperature of ninety-seven degrees. He tells how a brush fire became spot fires, then crown fires at the tops of trees, then a "blow-up" of a fast-moving inferno.

What Is the Evidence?

Maclean soon discovers that the official Forest Service report of the incident conceals as much as it reveals. He conducts interviews; he visits the archives to examine documents. He gathers data about wind and temperature from the old weather reports. He finds maps and photographs. He reads about the science of fires.

What Was It Like?

Maclean knew Montana from his youth. He had fought fires himself. Several decades later, he returns to the scene of the fire, where only charred ash and crosses marking deaths remain. He climbs the gulch, retraces old routes with survivors and witnesses, and pores over old records and pictures. He tries to imagine what it was like to be 18 and scared and jumping into a conflagration. He remembers his wife, dying of emphysema, gasping for oxygen.

Why Did Some Survive and Others Perish?

Maclean interviews two survivors of the fire, Walter Rumsey and Robert Sallee, to discover how they made it out alive. They were the youngest members of the crew (at 18), but had plenty of experience. He concludes that they had advantages of strength and speed, but also some good luck. He also examines the chain of recruiting, training, and decisions by the Forest Service that brought the men into that fire that day and led most to their untimely death.

Why Did the Fire Blow Up?

Here Maclean turns to science. He visits a fire science laboratory. He learns about many different types of fires. He reads about winds and wind currents in mountainous terrain, updrafts and downdrafts. He maps the wind currents on the day of the fire. He plots the velocity of the fire against the time of death of men found with melted watches on their bodies. He graphs annual fire statistics to see the impact of the introduction of smoke jumpers into fire- fighting. He cross-checks the location of every cross on the hillside to establish who died where and when.

How Did Three Men Escape?

Interviews showed that Rumsey and Sallee had somehow found their way uphill and sideways to a ridge of rock formations along the top of the gulch. They located crevices and squeezed through to safety. A third man died of his burns after making it through. Maclean learns how the foreman, Wag Dodge, used an old Native American technique of lighting a backfire in the grass around him so that the main fire leapfrogged over him. Dodge alone survived in the gulch.

Did the Backfire Save Lives or Kill Young Men?

When the father of one of the men killed in the fire sued the Forest Service, he argued in court that Wag Dodge's backfire may have saved Wag Dodge, but the backfire killed his son when it became a branch of the main fire. Maclean used fire science and evidence from the melted watches to argue that the main fire, not the escape fire, finally caught up with the other men as they raced uphill pursued by a roaring fire fanned by 20 mile-an-hour dry winds.

What Does It All Mean?

Maclean was a Presbyterian, and he inserts tragedy and Christian motifs into his story at every turn. The footrace ahead of a rampaging fire becomes a passage through "stations of the cross." He considers the smoke jumpers' religious denominations. He imagines their conversations with God. And he compares the deaths of young men with the death of his wife. The story gets personal and more meaningful. It becomes tragedy and redemption as well as history. It truly moves the reader.

Conclusion

Norman Maclean was a writer and not a historian. Yet he employs virtually every known technique of historical research and writing to make the past come alive as he tries to discover, reconstruct and explain the events of August 5, 1949. Because of his empathy and understanding, the story of a footrace by young men against fire becomes a story of life against death. And because he writes better than most historians, we are grateful for the story of a story waiting all these years to be told, discovered, and constructed. Maclean's book is terrific history and great writing. You should read it.

Task: List all the different events to be explained in this example. Then list the different kinds of explanations tested or used by Maclean in his research and writing. How does breaking an event down into several smaller events affect the kind of evidence needed to explain those events? What type of evidence did Maclean employ? Could a similar history be written about the California wildfires of summer 2019?

12 Interpretation

12.1 Reviewing History

Peer review—the process of having historians familiar with the topic of a work comment critically on the work's value—is a powerful tool for maintaining quality control among historians. Historians regularly review the work of other historians in a wide variety of historical journals and periodicals, before and after publication. This complex process of peer review, which originated in the sciences, is widely used to check on the quality of research and writing. Often the review in advance of publication is "blind," that is, the name of the reviewer is not revealed to the author. The review of a published book or article normally indicates the name of the reviewer.

A book review in a scholarly journal helps keep all publishing historians honest. It informs potential readers of the merit of a particular book or historical monograph. It summarizes in brief the argument of a work of history. And it offers criticism regarding the weaknesses of the book's evidence, style of argument, or conclusions. Book reviews help other historians understand new developments in complex fields of inquiry. They can help you understand both the quality of the book under review and the debate over issues considered in that book. A book review is a powerful tool when you do not have the time or the ability to read the book itself. It tells you what one historian thinks of the work of another. Reading book reviews will deepen and strengthen your research as you try to incorporate a vast amount of material into your work.

Bellesiles's Arming America

In 2000, historian Michael A. Bellesiles published a controversial book titled *Arming America: The Origins of a National Gun Culture* (New York: Alfred A. Knopf, 2000). In it, he tried to show that the myth of an armed and effective patriotic American militia ready to fight the British at a minute's notice was not true to history. The second amendment of the U.S. Constitution guarantees the right to bear arms to support a "well-regulated militia." Militias were generally poorly armed, poorly trained, drunk, and ineffectively using muskets that were inaccurate, dangerous, and often useless. Few colonists possessed guns, according to Bellesiles's reading of wills and probate records; not until after the Civil War did gun ownership become widespread. *Arming America* gained enormous attention because it attacked the basis of contemporary American gun culture and by implication the National Rifle Association (the country's largest gun owner's organization and political lobby) and the assumed right to bear arms as an American founding tradition. The book won the Organization of American Historians' prestigious Bancroft Prize for American history in 2000. However, the book quickly achieved notoriety because questions were raised about the quality of the scholarship.

There were many critical, and even hostile, reviews of Bellesiles's book. In the article "Of Arms and Men: *Arming America* and Military History," in *William and Mary Quarterly*, 3rd ser., 59: 1 (January 2002): 217–222, military historian Ira D. Gruber charged that Bellesiles had "undertaken to use the past to reform the present" (217). In summarizing the book for the reader, Gruber observed that Bellesiles had generally minimized the importance of guns, militias, and warfare in the colonial and early national periods of American history. Poorly trained and armed militias were never very effective at fighting, according to Bellesiles, and peace, not war, was the normal condition of American society until 1861.

Following this brief synopsis, Gruber criticized Bellesiles's use of evidence and his argument. Gruber claimed that Bellesiles exaggerated the weakness and inaccuracy of muskets with respect to rifles, the role of bayonets, and the firepower available. Regarding militias, Gruber argued that Bellesiles "uses evidence in a partial or imprecise way" (219). Most historians, Gruber wrote, agree that the militias were not very effective as fighting forces or very well armed. But regarding the numbers of guns per man, Bellesiles allegedly "shaped his figures to suit his argument" (220), in order to emphasize the weakness of the militias.

Peace, Gruber argued, was not at all the norm between 1607 and 1775, when there were various wars for one-third of the time. There were also numerous examples of internal white-on-white violence in America that Bellesiles ignored, being "inattentive to numbers and context" (220). Gruber added that Bellesiles underestimated the number of Americans who fought in the British army during the French and Indian War (1756–1763) and generally tried to "minimize the importance of guns, militias, and war in early America" while employing a "consistently biased reading of sources" and "careless uses of evidence and context" (222).

In "Guns, Gun Culture, and Homicide: The Relationship between Firearms, the Uses of Firearms, and Interpersonal Violence," in *William and Mary Quarterly*, 3rd ser., 59: 1 (January 2002): 223–240, historian Randolph Roth presented a more detailed critique, focusing largely on Bellesiles's use of probate records. These records, inventories of people's estates made after their death, included relatively few guns, according to Bellesiles, evidence that not many colonists possessed firearms. After he analyzed these records, Roth argued that Bellesiles "makes arithmetic mistakes" (228, 17n), "counted inaccurately"

(228), and was "biased" in his estimates (230). Roth cited several historians whose analysis of probate records revealed much higher figures of gun ownership. Roth also challenged Bellesiles's claim that whites rarely assaulted each other in the antebellum era. "Those claims are false," Roth wrote, and "every tally of homicides Bellesiles reports is either misleading or wrong" (234, 235).

Bellesiles took up the *Quarterly's* invitation to respond to these criticisms. In the same issue, he defended himself in a long essay titled "Exploring America's Gun Culture," 241–268. Bellesiles denied Gruber's charge that he had treated guns in American culture as "superfluous." He reiterated his claim that guns were "heavy, inaccurate, required constant care, and were subject to repeated misfiring" (258). Despite Gruber's criticism, the introduction of the bayonet made muskets more useful. Bellesiles admitted that his book was "tentative in its statistics" (260). But even if some statistics were incorrect, as Gruber claimed, "I do supply footnotes giving my sources" (261). "We sometimes seem to read the evidence differently," Bellesiles concluded, and "Gruber appears to have misunderstood my discussion of the mythology of the militia" (262).

Bellesiles also responded to Roth's careful dissection of his interpretation of probate records. He conceded a few errors in his statistics, but he downplayed their significance. The book "is not ... about probate records," he noted; "it is about the growth of an American fascination with firearms." The probate records represented only a minuscule part of his evidence: "fewer than five paragraphs in a 444-page book to address probate materials" (243). Bellesiles also challenged Roth's analysis of court documents relating to assaults and homicides, noting "I read some of those records differently than he" (253). Bellesiles's defense was compromised when a flood in his office destroyed many of his notes. Despite the various attacks on his scholarship, Bellesiles observed that the central part of his study—"the question of arms production" in early America—remained unchallenged:

> Why, if most Americans ... owned firearms (as my critics contend), did the government devote so much effort and money to promoting the manufacture and use of firearms? Where did the guns come from if they were widely dispersed throughout the population? Does it matter that the first gun manufacturers in North America were established by the federal government in the 1790s? Why was it necessary for the new United States government to place its first arms purchase in England? What does it mean that the federal government had to buy seven thousand English gunlocks in the 1790s so that United States gunmakers could make that many muskets? Why did the government repeatedly report during the first seventy years of the republic that there were not enough guns made in the United States to equip even the United States army?
>
> (257)

The dispute goes on. In part, different historians do indeed read the evidence in different ways, as Bellesiles states. But what makes the argument so high-pitched is that the historical topic of guns and militias is embedded in an ongoing political debate over gun control and the constitutional right to bear arms for individual citizens. As long as there is political disagreement, there will be historical disagreement as well. But the political disagreement mattered to historians less than the possibility that Bellesiles might have engaged in faulty, fraudulent, and unethical research. Peer review in this case revealed that some of the historian's facts were wrong and that he selected them to fit his argument, rather than letting his argument follow from his evidence. In April 2002, Emory University, where Bellesiles taught, even launched an investigation into whether or not he had engaged in "research misconduct." Historians charged that he had cited sources that did not exist, ignored sources that did not support his thesis, misquoted his sources, and made other errors. In October 2002, Bellesiles resigned. The Bancroft Prize committee revoked his award. But whether charges of fraud discredited his overall thesis remains a matter of debate.

Task: List the issues that seem to divide Bellesiles and his critics. How might you resolve those issues? What evidence would you need? How might you revise Bellesiles's argument to fit the evidence? How can historians' political tendencies shape their interpretation of history?

12.2 Historical Revision

Can historians finally agree on anything? Sometimes they cannot. History thrives on continuous revision of what historians believe is true about the past, the argument without end. Historians are normally critical of the conventional wisdom on any topic and often receptive to new interpretations that contradict or advance that wisdom. Revising the conventional wisdom is a common, and often exciting, part of doing history.

The Denmark Vesey Slave Conspiracy (1822)

Open any college textbook on American history and chances are you will find mention of Denmark Vesey. Unless it is a brand-new edition, you will probably learn that Vesey planned a major slave revolt in Charleston, South Carolina, in 1822. Vesey, a free black man who had won his freedom in a lottery, got his odd name because he had been born on the island of St. Thomas, then owned by Denmark. He was literate, a carpenter by trade, and well versed in the Bible and the Declaration of Independence. Inspired by the Haitian slave rebellion of 1791, which led to the abolition of slavery there and the establishment of the only free black republic in the world, and by the Missouri Compromise of 1820, which prohibited slavery in the northern part of the Louisiana Purchase (except for Missouri), Vesey allegedly planned a slave rebellion.

The plan was to set fire to the city of Charleston, kill all the whites, seize ships moored in Charleston Harbor, and sail off to freedom in Haiti. Had it come to pass, it could have been the largest slave revolt in American history. But an informer betrayed Vesey and the plan. 131 black men were rounded up and charged with complicity in the plot. After a secret trial, with testimony from more than 30 accused participants, Vesey and 34 slaves implicated in the conspiracy were hanged. These events were recounted in the official report of the trial. The conventional wisdom among most historians since 1822 was that Vesey had indeed conspired to lead a slave rebellion, indicative of the widespread desire for freedom by slaves in the South. Historian Douglas R. Egerton's critically acclaimed *He Shall Go Out Free: The Lives of Denmark Vesey* (Madison, WI: Madison House, 1999) examined and retold this gripping episode in American history.

But did the Vesey slave conspiracy really exist? In 1964, Richard C. Wade wrote an article suggesting that historians had exaggerated the conspiracy, which consisted of little more than "a few rumors" ("The Vesey Plot: A Reconsideration," *Journal of Southern History* 30 [1964]: 143–160). At a history conference held in Charleston in 2001, historian Michael P. Johnson went a step further, arguing that the rebellion was a hoax. Instead of a plan by blacks to kill whites—as long alleged—it was actually a plan by whites to kill blacks, drawn up for political gain by Charleston mayor James Hamilton Jr. Hamilton's plan, Johnson claimed, was to invent—and then "uncover"—a slave rebellion conspiracy, publicize its potential horrors, and blame the governor for failing to act. In the process, Hamilton hoped to advance his own career by emerging as the saviour of Charleston.

To arrive at this theory, Johnson examined not only the well-known official report of the trial, but the original trial transcript as well. This transcript, which was never published, exists in manuscript form in the South Carolina state archives. The transcript differs markedly from the official report. The official report, which was soon made available to the public, recounts testimony by Vesey. The trial transcript, however, makes no mention of any testimony by Vesey. The court proceedings were held in secret, closed to the public and the press, and the transcript provides no evidence that Vesey ever even went on trial. The transcript shows that the court, conducted by seven white magistrates, asked witnesses questions about a conspiracy, that the witnesses did not agree, and that they named several people besides Vesey as the leader. Despite these discrepancies, the magistrates decided that Vesey was the ringleader and pronounced him and others guilty. Johnson claimed that all the witnesses were tortured and forced to testify under threat, thereby making their statements unreliable. To bolster his argument, Johnson pointed out that after the magistrates rendered their verdict, the governor condemned the court for its "usurpation of authority, and a violation of Law." So did the governor's brother-in-law, U.S. Supreme

Court justice William Johnson Jr., who wrote an article for the *Charleston Courier* attacking the court for its many irregularities. But the executions went forward, and Mayor Hamilton, who claimed he had rescued Charleston from a threatened black slave revolt, was elected to Congress and then in 1830 to the governorship.

Several scholars promptly challenged Michael Johnson's revisionist account. They supported the conventional wisdom that there really was a slave conspiracy in Charleston. Historian Douglas Egerton and others argued that the torture and threats inflicted on the witnesses does not necessarily mean their testimony was untrue. Like Johnson, Egerton used both the official 1822 report and the handwritten documents in the South Carolina state archives. Another pointed out that Johnson had based his argument entirely on the trial transcript in the state archives, ignoring letters and other evidence that there was a slave conspiracy. On the other hand, some scholars praised Johnson's detective work and challenged his critics. "The truly daunting aspect of [his] extraordinary tour de force," wrote Philip Morgan, "is the complicity of historians in accepting the corrupt verdict of a kangaroo court."

Ultimately, the controversy over the Vesey conspiracy may be less a matter of fact than of interpretation. As historian Thomas J. Davis observed,

> in the Vesey affair, as elsewhere, the conspiracy charge and criticism may too easily distract the historian from inquiring into more fundamental questions. The historian's conspiracy question is not usually about conspiracy, not legally. The trial courts and legal system of the day answered the legal question. Was there really a conspiracy? … were there plans for an insurrection, even when there was no insurrection? If so, were the plans credible? The questions return to perception.

Johnson published an article based on his findings in *William and Mary Quarterly*, the leading scholarly journal of early American history (Michael P. Johnson, "Denmark Vesey and His Co-Conspirators," *William and Mary Quarterly*, 3rd ser., 58 [October 2001]: 915–976). His critics responded in the following issue ("Forum: The Making of a Slave Conspiracy. Part 2," *William and Mary Quarterly*, 3rd ser., 59 [January 2002]: 135–216). As a result of Johnson's article and the ensuing historical debate, textbooks will likely be revised in the coming years.

The furor over the Vesey affair shows no signs of abating and has achieved attention beyond the usual circle of historians. After many years of lobbying by black leaders, the city of Charleston approved construction of a monument to honor Denmark Vesey as a freedom fighter. A group of local whites opposed the monument because Vesey had promoted "genocide." Now it is not clear what role Vesey actually played in the affair. Was he a rebel who planned a slave revolt? Or was he simply the victim of a white supremacist plot? The questions remain unanswered for the moment.

The interested reader may find the story summarized in brief by Jon Wiener, "Denmark Vesey: A New Verdict," *Nation*, March 11, 2002, 21–24. The more interested reader will want to turn to *William and Mary Quarterly* or even the South Carolina state archives. See also Douglas R. Egerton, "Of Facts and Fables: New Light on the Denmark Vesey Affair," in the January 2004 issue of the *South Carolina Historical Magazine.*

Task: Design an imaginary research trip for yourself to South Carolina to decide whether Johnson or his critics are right. What kind of evidence would you look for? How could you prove your case? Are the documents from the South Carolina state archives available online?

12.3 Historiography

Historiography is a powerful tool to help you understand the context of your own work. What is historiography? Literally the word means the study of the writing of history. Historians generally use the term *historiography* to mean the history of how historians have dealt with a particular topic. In historiography, revision is a normal part of doing history—it is the ongoing debate by historians that reveals how views of the past have changed over time. Historians regularly read and criticize the work of their predecessors, testing that work against new evidence and new interpretations, seeing things from a different angle of vision, and then revising previous interpretations to produce their own. The conventional wisdom of one generation of historians becomes the revisionism of another generation. When many historians begin to revise their view of a complex series of past events, we speak of *revisionism*. Historical revisionism then may become the new conventional wisdom, subject to future revision, and so on. In communist and authoritarian countries, revisionism is a product of the party line, determined by present politics, not future historians.

In your own work, you should write a brief section on historiography for each of your papers. Historiography is really the only tool that can help you place your own work in the context of other historians and judge its originality as a contribution to knowledge. How does your own work compare with the work of others? What new contributions have you made to historical knowledge?

World War II

The historiographic battle over the history of World War II (1939–1945)—the epic conflict of the twentieth century—often seems as bitterly contested as the war itself. Those who fought and won that war on the Allied side, including the United States, the Soviet Union, France, and Britain, have one version of events. Those who lost—Germany, Japan, and Italy—have another. Even among the Allies, national histories are often in conflict. The "official" histories began even during the war and continue to proliferate.

Unofficial historians contest these histories. Nations apologize, or not, for what they did during the war. Historians argue about the origins of the war, collaboration and resistance, the outcome of particular battles, and the moral issues of war crimes and financial support for the enemy. The battle for history goes on.

Historiography generally changes over time because new generations of historians either discover new evidence or develop new interpretations because of changing times and perspectives. In the case of World War II, the historiography of wartime intelligence developed out of new evidence, and the historiography of the atomic bomb because of changing times.

How much did intelligence matter? Code-breaking and intelligence became an area of controversy among historians only because of new evidence. Until 1974, few knew that the British and the Americans had broken the German and Japanese military codes and were regularly reading enemy communications "traffic," code-named "Ultra" for the Germans and "Magic" for the Japanese. But in 1974, the 30-year limits imposed by the British Official Secrets Act began to expire and wartime code breakers began to tell their story in memoirs and interviews. Thousands of British scholars and cryptographers (many of them women, the so-called Bletchley Girls) had worked secretly at Bletchley Park, north of London, deciphering the languages of the German Enigma machine, which set and changed codes daily. Their stories of breaking enemy codes provided a wealth of new information that historians could use to reinterpret many aspects of the war. Thousands of decoded enemy battle plans were published and analyzed by historians.

Knowing enemy plans in advance of a battle clearly provides a significant advantage. But how much of an advantage? New evidence showed that British Prime Minister Winston Churchill shared Ultra-decoded information with Soviet leader Joseph Stalin in advance of the German invasion of the Soviet Union in 1941, but Stalin simply ignored it as British disinformation. Did U.S. president Franklin D. Roosevelt know in advance that the Japanese were going to attack Pearl Harbor? Did Churchill know in advance that the Germans were going to bomb Coventry? Did they protect such secrets simply in order to prevent the enemies from knowing that their codes were broken? How important were decoded enemy intelligence reports in battles where thousands of men and machines clashed? The answers to such questions have created a veritable industry of books on intelligence and espionage during World War II, along with an army of critics who argue that men, weapons, and industrial materials won the war, not intelligence.

Declassified intelligence information from World War II gave historians access to previously secret evidence that was significant in understanding the actions of wartime leaders and the success or failure of entire armies and navies in battle. After 1974, no historian could ignore the history of intelligence in writing a history of any aspect of the war.

Why did the United States decide to drop two atomic bombs on Japanese cities? The decision to use the atomic bomb on Hiroshima and Nagasaki in August 1945 was particularly controversial. Historians began to revise and rewrite the history of the atomic bomb not so much because of new evidence as because of a changing political climate during the Cold War.

The conventional wisdom among historians after World War II followed the official history of the Manhattan Project to build the atomic bomb. That is, the decision by U.S. president Harry S Truman to use the atomic bomb was necessary to compel Japan to surrender and thereby save countless American and Japanese lives in the planned Allied invasion of the Japanese homeland. After years of effort, scientists secretly detonated the first plutonium bomb at Alamogordo, New Mexico, on July 16, 1945. This secret test showed scientists that the bomb indeed worked: the $2 billion project was a success. But should the bomb be used on Japan? Some scientists urged in 1945 that a public test of the devastating weapon, with invited Japanese visitors, would lead Japan to surrender. But others argued that, even if successful, such a test would only impress the Japanese with America's apparent unwillingness to use the bomb against them; therefore, the only course for compelling Japan to surrender and ending the long, bloody war in the Pacific was to drop the bomb directly on Japan. A demonstration test simply would not do the job.

In the 1960s, the conventional wisdom gave way to revisionism among many scholars. A new generation of historians argued that the bombs were not really needed to ensure the surrender of an already destroyed Japan. Nuclear weapons were more useful as a form of "atomic diplomacy" intended to impress Stalin at the outset of the Cold War. In his book *Atomic Diplomacy* (New York: Simon & Schuster, 1965), Gar Alperovitz argued that the Soviet Union, not Japan, was President Truman's real target when he decided to use the bomb. Herbert Feis promptly responded with a defence of the conventional view in his book *The Atomic Bomb and the End of World War II* (Princeton: Princeton University Press, 1966). A decade later, Martin Sherwin provided a more balanced view in his *A World Destroyed: The Atomic Bomb and the Grand Alliance* (New York: Knopf, 1975). The debate continues in a post-Cold War age of deterrence.

What shaped the debate over the use of the atomic bomb was not so much new evidence, but a new context. In 1945, the Soviet Union and the United States were allies in the war against Japan. The Soviet Union had declared war on Japan a few days after American bombs dropped on Hiroshima and Nagasaki. But after 1945, the Soviet Union and the United States became adversaries in a new Cold War that included a race to build and deploy nuclear weapons and missiles. The United States developed secret war plans to drop atomic and then hydrogen bombs on Soviet cities, and the Soviet Union developed similar plans against the United States. The Cold War turned hot in Korea (1950–1953), then Vietnam, Afghanistan, and Iraq.

Historians therefore began to reinterpret the events of 1945 in the context of a much later Cold War. The fact that Truman had warned Stalin at the Potsdam conference in July 1945 of a powerful, new weapon in the hands of the United States was well known. The American president spoke of a "weapon of unusual destructive force" (Stalin's spies were already well informed about the Manhattan Project). Stalin said only that he was glad the weapon would be used against Japan. Now, in the 1960s, that well-known meeting became evidence for "revisionist" historians that Truman intended to drop the bomb not simply to end the war with Japan, but to impress Stalin with America's new nuclear power. It would also give the United States much greater authority in securing the peace, negotiating terms, and rebuilding Japan. Other evidence also seemed to fit such an interpretation. The times had changed, and so had historians. They divided between those who still believed that the bomb was dropped to end the war and save American lives, and those who believed that dropping the bomb was part of the Cold War, as well as part of the end of World War II. The entire debate became public in 1995 when the Smithsonian Museum in Washington, DC, launched a 50-year anniversary exhibit of the B-29 bomber *Enola Gay*, which had dropped the first bomb on Hiroshima. Revisionist historians wrote the script for the exhibit, criticizing use of the bomb. World War II veterans were outraged, and the exhibit was substantially modified to avoid further controversy. (On the exhibit and the response of historians, see Section 17.2.)

The examples of military intelligence and the decision to drop the atomic bomb during World War II illustrate that historiography changes over time both because of new evidence and because of new interpretation. Both evidence and interpretation are critical tools for the historian. But neither new evidence nor new interpretations will put an end to the historical arguments that make up historiography.

The historiography of World War II is enormous and controversial. The interested reader might well begin by looking at the brief historiographic survey by military historian John Keegan, *The Battle for History: Re-fighting World War II* (New York: Vintage Books, 1995).

Task: Make sure to include a section on historiography in your next paper. What are the arguments? On what issues do historians disagree? Which revisions in historiography are based on new evidence? On new interpretation? How does your own argument fit into the historiographical debate on your topic? Are you making a contribution to the study of your topic that will interest other historians?

12.4 Women's History: The Leo Frank Case

Women's history is one of the most significant new fields in the historical profession since World War II. The discipline of history had been traditionally a male preserve, with men often writing about men in male-dominated language. Male historians tended to focus on male-dominated domains, such as war, politics, and industry, and treated men as the motive force in history. Prompted by the emergence of the feminist movement in the 1960s and 1970s, an increasing number of women began to enter the historical profession. They challenged historians of both genders to study new aspects of history previously neglected—marriage, sexual relations, motherhood, sisterhood, working women, the legal status of women, property and inheritance, the women's movement itself, and the struggle for female suffrage. By the late twentieth century, women's history came of age. No longer was it possible for male historians to ignore or deny the significance of women in history. Women were increasingly important both as historians and as the subject of historical study. So were members of the LGBT movement.

Gender perspectives cast old issues in a new light and revised traditional approaches to the study of the past. Women's history flourished on the basis of both new evidence and a new perspective. By considering women and the issues of gender and sexual orientation, historians could achieve a more balanced and complete picture of historical events.

The Leo Frank case provides a fascinating example of how the perspective of women's history provides a tool that can help us understand a complex historical event in new ways. In the early 1900s, Leo Frank was supervisor of the National Pencil Factory in Atlanta, Georgia. Raised in the North as Jewish, he stood out in the largely Protestant South. In 1913, a 13 year-old white girl named Mary Phagan, who worked in the factory, was raped and murdered. Frank was accused of the crime and arrested. Both anti-Semitism and racism flourished in the growing South in the early twentieth century. The population of Atlanta had quadrupled between 1880 and 1910 as new people flocked to the city and its factories. Ironically, Jim Conley, a black custodian at the factory with a record of prior arrests, was suspected of the murder, but was absolved by the prosecutor, the jury, and public opinion eager to demonize a wealthy, white "Yankee Jew."

Frank's trial lasted four months. Although there was little evidence, a jury convicted him of the crime and sentenced him to death. Frank's lawyers appealed the decision all the way to the United States Supreme Court, which in April 1915 rejected the appeal. The governor of Georgia then commuted Frank's death sentence. On August 16, 1915, a mob broke into the work farm where Frank was held, seized him, and lynched him for a crime he had not committed. (Frank was posthumously declared innocent in 1985 by another governor of Georgia.)

Why had a Southern mob and Southern public opinion condemned a Jewish factory supervisor and ignored a black man who might well have committed the crime? For decades, historians viewed the case as a key example of how industrialization and urbanization of the agrarian South had unleashed dark forces of anti-Semitism and anti-capitalism that pitted rural populism against urban progressivism. In 1966, as the civil rights movement gathered force, historian Leonard Dinnerstein, in *The Leo Frank Case* (Athens: University of Georgia Press), looked at Frank in terms of his race (white), religion (Jewish), background (northern), and class (middle/upper). Dinnerstein produced a thorough study of the rape and murder, the legal response, and the popular outrage against Frank's alleged crime and lynching. Dinnerstein examined all the evidence in the case and emphasized that Frank was convicted by a Southern populist culture that hated him as a Yankee, an employer, and a Jew:

> Although the newspapers devoted a great deal of space to the murder, they did not sufficiently explain why the police and the populace could so easily accept the indictment against Frank. To understand this more fully, an examination of the social milieu in which the case unfolded is necessary. The keynote to much of Southern society was a commitment to tradition and an opposition to change. The Southern heritage, moreover, had nurtured a strong in-group loyalty that at times manifested itself as a paranoiac suspicion of outsiders. Leo Frank as a Northerner, an industrialist, and a Jew represented everything alien to that culture.
>
> (32)

In 1991, women's historian Nancy MacLean, in an article titled "The Leo Frank Case Reconsidered: Gender and Sexual Politics in the Making of Reactionary Populism" (*Journal of American History* 78: 3 [December 1991], 917–948), reconsidered the case from the perspective of gender, rather than race, religion, and class. She focused on the rape as well as on the murder of Mary Phagan, who to many symbolized the "flower of southern womanhood." MacLean examined the possibility that Phagan may have been sexually active—a possibility most Southerners at the time could not accept. She argued that "the furor over gender relations and sexuality fueled class hostilities and anti-Semitism" (920) in reactionary populism, a form of anti-elitism that stimulated the emergence of the second Ku Klux Klan in the South. MacLean focused less on Frank and more on Phagan as an attractive young female worker, a member of the First Christian Bible School, who was on her way to attend a Confederate Memorial Day parade when she was murdered. She was a perfect symbol capable of uniting a broad variety of social grievances and resentments:

> Gender analysis thus opens a new window on the Frank case and the social order that produced it. Through this window, we see more clearly how change and contestation, not stasis and consensus, constituted the very essence of early twentieth-century southern history. Economic development acted as a solvent on older relations of power and authority—between men and women and between parents and children as well as between workers and employers and blacks and

whites. The dissolution of the older sexual order produced losses as well as gains. The popular anxieties and resentments thereby created proved multivalent; they made class hostilities at once more volatile and more amenable to reactionary resolution. To observe these operations in the Frank case is to gain insight into the processes by which protean concerns about the family and sexuality may help tame and redirect popular opposition to a dominant social order. The inclusion of gender as a category of analysis is thus not an optional flourish, but a vital tool to uncover elements upon which both mobilization and outcome hinged.

(921)

MacLean did not deny the conventional wisdom of the Leo Frank case, but by examining it through the lens of women's history, she gave it new perspective and new meaning, emphasizing how different groups in southern society viewed the roles of women in a rapidly changing world. She emphasized Mary Phagan as much as Leo Frank. She looked at male control of females, the anxiety about young women's sexual activity, and the sexual power of employers over employees. She looked beyond anti-Semitism and class conflict to explore how gender roles and sexual jealousies helped create the fervor and hysteria that led to Frank's lynching. She showed how a case of a female sexual victim played into the hands of a conservative populism enraged by Yankee employers, Jewish success, and urban unrest. Women's history is thus a vital tool, providing historians with a valuable perspective for understanding and reinterpreting the past.

Task: Reread the paragraphs on the Leo Frank case by Dinnerstein in 1966 and MacLean in 1991. What similarities and differences do you see in how they approach the case? How does a women's history perspective change your view of what happened? Consider another historical event or case with which you are familiar. Can you make it look different by considering issues of gender that may have been ignored by the conventional wisdom? Are there examples of women who have been ignored? Can you enrich your own understanding by looking at events from the point of view of women, as well as men?

13 Speculation

13.1 Historical Speculation

Speculation means coming to a conclusion without sufficient evidence. But speculation can often be a helpful tool when deepening our understanding of the context or background of events or individuals. When does a historian have the right to speculate about the past without any direct evidence? Should historians speculate about the future, or about imaginary outcomes if historical events had turned out differently than they did? Most historians will refuse to do this. Some will speculate, often with imaginative and creative results. In general, however, you should avoid speculation, since your instructor is unlikely to share your creative impulses about the truth. If you must speculate, say clearly that you are doing so.

Will the Real Martin Guerre Please Get an Identity?

Consider the case of historian Natalie Zemon Davis's prize-winning book on sixteenth-century France, *The Return of Martin Guerre* (Cambridge, MA: Harvard University Press, 1983). Certain facts about the story of Martin Guerre are known and accepted. Guerre lived with his wife Bertrande in the Basque village of Artigat in the mountains between France and Spain. In 1548, he left Artigat to become a soldier. When Guerre failed to return over the next eight years, villagers assumed he had died. Then, in 1556, a man appeared in Artigat claiming to be Guerre. Bertrande accepted him into her bed as her rightful husband. But was he? Or was he an impostor named Arnaud du Tilh? Villagers were not sure. Over the next three years, tensions mounted between Guerre/du Tilh and Guerre's uncle, and when Bertrande and her alleged husband tried to claim an inheritance, many villagers became suspicious. A trial resulted at which many villagers testified, about half claiming the man was Guerre and half claiming he was an impostor.

The Return of Martin Guerre is a gripping story, and Davis is a brilliant and widely recognized historian. But she peppers the pages of her book with speculation. Consider the following statements (italics added):

- "The economic link of Artigat with nearby villages and burgs *would have been* apparent to the Daguerres at once" (10)—but was it?
- "Sanxi's wife *probably* continued to carry baskets of grain on her head" (14)—but did she?
- "The marriage contract of Bertrande and Martin has not survived but *we can assume* its content from numerous others that have" (17)—but can we?
- "The couple *must* have consulted a local wise woman more than once" (21)—but did they?
- "Among other things, *so one must surmise*, they decided to make the invented marriage last" (46)—why must one surmise this? On what evidence?
- On Protestantism: *"It is possible, even probable*, that the new Martin and Bertrande de Rols were becoming interested in the new religion" (48) —why is it possible or even probable?
- "They *must have been* among the one hundred and eighty witnesses heard before the case was through" (49)—but were they?
- "His two unmarried sisters *probably* moved back in with him, as would be expected in Basque custom" (51)—but did they?
- "The consuls of Artigat *undoubtedly* discussed the matter of Martin Guerre at many meetings in the spring and summer of 1559" (55)—but did they discuss the matter at all? If so, what records exist?

And on it goes. Davis speculates about what she does not know. Other historians took Davis to task for basing much of her history of the Martin Guerre story on a continuous series of *speculations*—informed as they were by her vast knowledge of time and place—rather than on the trial transcripts, court proceedings, church records, and other evidence. That evidence simply does not support her conclusion that the "new" Martin Guerre and his wife, Bertrande, conspired to deceive the court with an invented marriage. But she uses the tool of speculation to paint a rich portrait of village life in sixteenth-century France.

Speculation is easier when one assumes that facts exist only in the mind of the historian or as words in the text. The postmodern impulse is to tell marvelous stories about the past that might be true or are as close to the truth as we are likely to get. One history is as good as another, some postmodernists say. But can the historian imaginatively reconstruct the past on the basis of context but not text, imagination but not evidence? Most historians think not. Speculation belongs more to the realm of fiction than of fact, even when we recognize that the lines are often blurred and that the historian constructs, as well as discovers, the historical truth.

For a substantial critique of *The Return of Martin Guerre*, see Robert Finlay, "The Refashioning of Martin Guerre," *American Historical Review* 93 (June 1988): 552–571. Natalie Davis responded with her article "On the Lame" in the same issue, 572–603.

Task: Make a list of all the different kinds of evidence you might use to prove your own identity. What are the problems with each item in terms of making a persuasive case that you know who you are and can prove it? How would you go about proving or disproving another person's identity? How would this evidence differ from that available in the sixteenth century?

13.2 History as Fiction

Historical fiction can often be solidly grounded in the facts and the sources. Such novels as *Burr* by Gore Vidal and *Cold Mountain* by Charles Frazier vividly capture and re-create distant eras and historical figures. But imagined situations and characters are fiction, not fact. History depends on being a nonfictional enterprise. May a historian legitimately introduce a fictional account into a work of history? Most historians emphatically think not. Yet the tendency to do so may be strong, even among professional historians. Fiction can make fact more colorful, more dramatic, more meaningful, more plausible, more entertaining, and more convincing. But it is still fiction. What happens when a historian introduces a fiction into an account without footnoting any source or informing the reader that what is on the page is a useful fiction, not an accurate historical account?

The Soldier Who Never Was

In his book *Dead Certainties (Unwarranted Speculations)* (New York: Vintage, 1991, 3, 5–6) eminent historian Simon Schama introduces his story of British general James Wolfe during the French and Indian War with the following dramatic account:

> Anse du Foulon, Quebec, four a.m., September 13, 1759
>
>   Twas the darkness that did the trick, black as tar, that and the silence, though how the men contriv'd to clamber their way up the cliff with their musket and seventy rounds on their backs, I'm sure I don't know even though I saw it with my own eyes and did it myself before very long. We stood hushed on the muddy shore of the river, peering up at the volunteers. They looked like a pack of lizards unloosd on the rocks, though not so nimble, bellies hugging the cliff and their rumps wiggling with effort. We couldn't see much of 'em for they disappeared now and then into, the clumps of witherd cedar and spruce that hung on the side of the hill. But we could feel the squirming, pulling labour of it all ....
>   I had no sooner got to the very top and was rejoicing and taking good care not to look down behind me when our men gathered together amidst the tamaracks and the spruce. Before us were a group of tents, white in the first thin light of the coming dawn, and of a sudden a commotion and shouting broke forth. A Frenchy officer came flying

out in his nightshirt as we loosd off our first rounds and sent them running across the open fields towards the town leaving a few of their company shot or stuck with our bayonets wearing that surprisd look on their face as they lay there amidst the pine needles and brown grass.

And so on, and so on. This gripping firsthand account of scaling a cliff and encountering surprised French troops at Quebec is bold, graphic—and totally imagined by the historian. It is a work of fiction. There is no historical British soldier, no memoir, no document, no footnote, no source. If alert readers make their way to the end of the book, they discover a remarkable afterword in which Schama, the historian, tells us how he is doing history here:

> Though these stories may at times appear to observe the discursive conventions of history, they are in fact historical novellas, since some passages (the soldier with Wolfe's army, for example) are pure inventions, based, however, on what documents suggest. This is not to say, I should emphasize, that I scorn the boundary between fact and fiction. It is merely to imply that even in the most austere scholarly report from the archives, the inventive faculty—selecting, pruning, editing, commenting, interpreting, delivering judgments—is in full play ... Claims for historical knowledge must always be fatally circumscribed by the character and prejudices of its narrator.
>
> (322)

Schama goes on to a further disclaimer, observing that "this book is a work of the imagination that chronicles historical events." The soldier's description of the Battle of Quebec is "purely imagined fiction" that has been "constructed from a number of contemporary documents" (327).

Schama probably used an actual document, the journal of Captain John Knox about his campaigns in North America in 1757–1760, to construct his fictional account. Knox wrote that:

> this grand enterprise was conducted and executed with great good order and discretion; as fast as we landed, the boats put off for re-enforcements ... We lost no time here, but clambered up one of the steepest precipices that can be conceived, being almost a perpendicular, and of an incredible height. As soon as we gained the summit all was quiet, and not a shot was heard ... The general then detached the light troops to our left to rout the enemy from their battery, and to disable their guns, except they could be rendered serviceable to the party who were to remain there; and this service was soon performed.
>
> (See John Knox, *An Historical Journal of the Campaigns in North America for the Years 1757, 1758, 1759, and 1760*, ed. Arthur G. Doughty [Toronto: Champlain Society, 1914–1916], vol. 2, 94–101)

Why didn't Schama simply quote from Knox's real account? Probably he felt that the real account was too dull and nonspecific for his purposes, with the language of a report from an officer to his commander. It was much more fun to imagine the dramatic than to quote the prosaic.

So, the question becomes: when historians make up stories as imagined fictions, are they doing history? They probably are not. Schama is brilliantly re-creating a historical event with a nonexistent participant whose account is based on unnamed and uncited sources. Is it dramatic? Yes. Is it well informed by historical evidence? Probably. Is it good history? No. Is it fiction? Yes.

Schama has written many fine works of history. *Dead Certainties* is not one of them, although I imagine he had great fun speculating and imagining what might well have happened. History students have no such license except in a creative fiction class.

Task: Compare the accounts of Knox and Schama's imagined soldier. What does the fictional account add to the story? Was it necessary? Is it justified? How might the urge to tell a good story distort the truth?

13.3 Conspiracies

Speculation can lead historians to develop theories and ideas that help explain the past. Conspiracy theories especially have long been popular among general readers and students. Historians treat them sceptically: like all theories, they must be based on evidence and reality. Two of the most widely studied conspiracy theories in American history focus on the assassination of President Abraham Lincoln in 1865 and the assassination of President John F. Kennedy in 1963. Who really killed Lincoln? Who killed Kennedy? Was it a lone gunman acting independently or a group of individuals secretly conspiring together? Behind every controversial event seems to lurk a hidden plot, a clandestine plan designed by some fiendish group. Rather than advance wild-eyed theories—as film director Oliver Stone did in his 1990 movie *JFK*, which relied heavily on discredited rumours—historians examine the evidence to determine what happened in a specific event, who was involved in it, and whether a conspiracy in fact existed.

Who Really Really Killed Lincoln?

On April 14, 1865, five days after the South surrendered, a well-known actor and Southern patriot named John Wilkes Booth climbed into President Lincoln's box seat at Ford's Theater in Washington, DC, and shot him with a small pistol. Booth then leaped to the stage, injuring his leg, limped from the theater, got on a horse, and rode off in the night to southern Virginia, despite a number of federal patrols and closed escape routes. A doctor named Samuel Mudd treated his broken leg. A few days later Booth was cornered by federal troops in a Virginia barn and shot. Sergeant Boston Corbett most likely killed him. Booth's body was delivered to the Washington Arsenal, where it was secretly buried. Although Booth fired the gun that killed Lincoln, he did not act alone. Others had helped plan the assassination, including George Atzerodt, David Herold, Michael O'Laughlen, Lewis Powell, and Mary Surratt. They were quickly tried and convicted by a military tribunal and then hanged. The tribunal gave long prison sentences to Mudd, Ed Spangler, and Samuel Arnold, who were all pardoned by President Andrew Johnson in 1869. Mary Surratt's son John received a civil trial in 1867, but got off because of a hung jury, and spent his days giving lectures about his mother and the assassination.

Such are the bare facts. But over the years these facts have come under scrutiny again and again in an effort to find deeper conspiracies that might have been behind the assassination. There was speculation immediately that Vice President Andrew Johnson was in on the plot because he succeeded to the presidency. There were rumours that Booth did not die, but had been sighted in Mexico, Italy, Turkey, China, and other parts of the world. In 1907, Finis L. Bates, in his book *The Escape and Suicide of John Wilkes Booth*, claimed that Booth had turned up as a drifter in Texas and Oklahoma before killing himself. The entrepreneurial Bates made a tidy sum renting "Booth's" mummified remains to carnivals for exhibition on into the 1930s.

As time went on, the conspiracy theories got bigger and better. Otto Eisenschiml, in his two books *Why Was Lincoln Murdered?* (Boston: Little, Brown, 1937) and *The Shadow of Lincoln's Death* (New York: Wilfred Funk, 1940), suggested that Secretary of War Edwin Stanton had masterminded the plot. After all, he asked, did not Stanton keep General Ulysses S. Grant from attending Ford's Theater that night? And why did Stanton not discipline the guard in Lincoln's box for neglect of duty? Others argued that the head of the National Detective Police, Lafayette Baker, or even Secretary of State William Seward (who was himself badly wounded in another attack that night) were involved.

In 1977, David Balsiger and Charles Sellier produced a book and movie, titled *The Lincoln Conspiracy*, in which they claimed that Booth was involved in a number of broad conspiracies by Maryland planters, Confederate secret service agents in Canada, Northern businessmen speculating on the cotton market, and radical Republicans wishing for a more brutal occupation of the defeated South under Reconstruction.

The most recent conspiracy theory involves the Confederate secret service, operating out of Montreal and other Canadian cities. In their book *Come Retribution: The Confederate Secret Service and the Assassination of Lincoln* (1988), William Tidwell, David Gaddy, and James Hall provide a wealth of circumstantial evidence that links Booth to shadowy agents of the Confederacy and to Confederate president Jefferson Davis personally. Didn't Booth smuggle quinine into the Confederacy from the North? Wasn't he in Montreal at the same hotel with Confederate agents in late 1864? Didn't he tell someone he knew the Confederate ciphers and codes? Tidwell and Gaddy both worked for the Central Intelligence Agency. They knew a good intelligence operation when they saw one, and this, they believed, was it.

Conspiracy theorists love assassination. They contend that a lone individual never could have carried out an assassination without a plot and lots of help. Every shred of evidence, the more circumstantial the better, becomes grist for the mill of conspiracy. The Lincoln assassination presents a superb example. After all, there was a conspiracy of sorts, as Booth acted in concert with several companions, one of whom assaulted Seward the same night. But how extensive was the conspiracy? Was anyone else—especially higher-ups or prominent individuals—involved? Here the trail grows cold as the evidence becomes murkier and murkier. Thus, the argument goes on and on without end. The case is never closed.

The Kennedy assassination is even murkier. Whereas no one doubts that Booth shot Lincoln, some dispute whether Lee Harvey Oswald actually shot Kennedy on November 22, 1963. Claims of additional gunmen—one lurking behind the mysterious "grassy knoll"—surfaced almost immediately, and conspiracy theorists have pointed the finger at numerous suspects who presumably wanted Kennedy dead, such as white supremacist extremists, Cuban leader Fidel Castro, and organized crime figures. Lack of evidence has never stopped people from speculating about who might have been involved in the Kennedy assassination, and the mystery has fueled an entire industry of books and movies (including Stone's *JFK*).

Ballistics evidence did not close the case. In 1977, the nuclear chemist Vincent Guinn employed neutron activation analysis (NAA) to examine bullets and bullet fragments from the rifle of Lee Harvey Oswald allegedly used in the Kennedy assassination, a 1940 Italian-made Mannlicher-Carcano M91 bolt-action weapon with a side-mounted Ordinance Optics 4 x 18 scope. The FBI had examined similar evidence in 1964. Guinn concluded that the "magic bullet" (CE399) found in both Kennedy and Connally's bodies and on a stretcher at Parkland Hospital matched perfectly samples from a box of Mannlicher-Carcano ammunition in their antimony concentration. Guinn's evidence convinced the House Select Committee on Assassinations (HSCA) that Oswald had in fact shot and killed JFK, but that a second shooter and a conspiracy to kill Kennedy were "probable." No ballistic evidence supported their conclusion, so the debate continued.

The Kennedy assassination literature divides between those who essentially accept the 1964 verdict of the Warren Commission that a lone gunman, Lee Harvey Oswald, shot and killed JFK in Dallas, and those who believe that more than one gunman was involved. Various investigators have argued that: (1) the CIA had copious files on Oswald long before he fired his shots; (2) President Lyndon Baines Johnson, Kennedy's successor was behind the shooting; (3) Oswald was actually trying to kill Governor Connally of Texas who, as Secretary of the Navy, had turned down Oswald's request for an honorable (not dishonorable) discharge from the Marines and instead killed the President he admired; (4) there is evidence of a crossfire that involved various international crime hit men who were in Dallas at the time; (5) mafia bosses Carlos Marcello (New Orleans) and Santos Trafficante (Tampa) planned to kill both Castro and Kennedy; they organized earlier attempts on JFK in Chicago and Tampa in 1963; (6) Oswald was involved in a plot to murder Fidel Castro while conducting cancer research in New Orleans under cover of the Reily Coffee Co.; (7) the KGB trained Oswald in Russia for assassination, but Oswald went rogue before he shot Kennedy. The case remains open, not closed, and arguments about the Kennedy assassination are likely to continue for many years.

Conspiracy theories flourish these days as political weapons. Donald J. Trump spent years supporting the false theory that President Barak Obama had been born in a foreign country and had destroyed his birth certificate (Obama was born in Hawaii, as his real birth certificate indicates). Trump ultimately abandoned this conspiracy theory in favor of many others sponsored by FOX News on television or by the *Enquirer* tabloid newspaper. He lives by conspiracy theories that contradict established facts and evidence. He considers journalists and historians to be purveyors of fake news out to get the malignant narcissist they despise. He combines the malice of Roy Cohn (Sen. Joseph McCarthy's attorney) and the entertaining satire of P.T. Barnum.

Conspiracy is not so much a tool as a theory. Conspiracy theories are often faulty or incomplete explanations, usually based on highly selective and sometimes discredited evidence. You should avoid assuming a conspiracy theory unless you have hard evidence to back it up. The best tool for testing conspiracy theories is evidence. Historians consider every piece of evidence to determine whether or not there are grounds for a conspiracy.

For a good introduction to the Lincoln assassination and its conspiracy theories, see Thomas R. Turner, *The Assassination of Abraham Lincoln* (Malabar, FL: Krieger, 1999). On the Kennedy assassination, see James W. Douglass, *JFK and the Unspeakable: Why He Died and Why It Matters* (New York: Simon and Schuster, 2008). On Vincent Guinn's ballistic analysis, see my book *The Forensic Historian: Using Science to Reexamine the Past* (Armonk, NY: M. E. Sharpe, 2013), 38–44.

Task: Dream up a conspiracy theory for some historical event of your own choosing. Then make a list of evidence that might support or contradict that theory. Is there sufficient evidence to prove that theory? To disprove it? Why do you think conspiracy theories are so popular?

13.4 Forgeries and Facsimiles

Conspiracy theories are one thing; outright fraud and forgeries are another. How do we know if something is genuine? How can we tell if a document or image in front of us is authentic? Could someone have fooled us by creating or copying a bogus document? History is replete with rogues who have forged and copied documents and images for fun and profit. A forgery is a document or image that pretends to be something it is not. A facsimile is a copy of a document or image that claims to be the original. Your best tool for detecting a forgery or a facsimile is your critical and sceptical approach to all historical sources.

Here are just a few examples:

Is a Document Genuine?

In the nineteenth century, a man named Robert Spring (born in 1813 in England) emigrated to America and opened a bookshop in Philadelphia. He soon found he could make more money forging documents associated with George Washington. He used a goose quill pen and mixed his own aged ink to forge Washington letters on paper that he cut out of the blank pages of old books. He then stained the paper with coffee grounds to make it appear even older and more authentic. He copied Washington's signature. His documents were usually very short (e.g., a pass through the army lines), and he changed individual names every time he wanted to sell another forgery. To this day, forged Washington documents turn up all over the world several times a year. The official editors of Washington's papers at the University of Virginia have collected over 150 Spring forgeries of documents signed by "Washington."

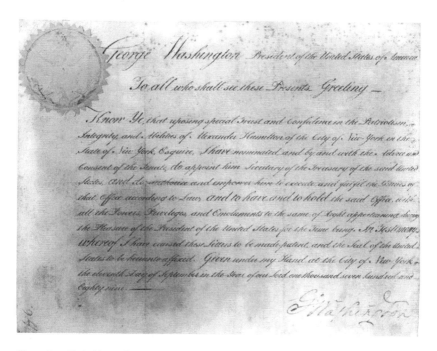

Illustration 13.1 Alexander Hamilton's Commission Letter as Treasury Secretary

A commission letter from George Washington to Alexander Hamilton: Is it authentic, or is it a forgery? How can you tell? *(Hamilton Papers, Library of Congress)*

How can you detect a forgery or authenticate a document? Detection and authentication are difficult (Illustration 13.1). Many documents can only be authenticated by using microscopes, by examining watermarks in the paper, and by chemically testing ink and paper.

Is a Collection of Documents Authentic?

In 1945, historians became excited about the appearance of a beautifully bound set of three volumes titled *The Horn Papers: Early Westward Movement on the Monongahela and Upper Ohio, 1735–1795*. The papers claimed to be the diaries, maps, court records, and other artifacts of Jacob Horn and his son Christopher from about 1735 to 1795. Supposedly the papers had been found in an old chest handed down through the Horn family for many generations. Historian Julian Boyd of Princeton University, suspecting a forgery, charged that they were "complete fabrications" in the *American Historical Review*, the journal of the American Historical Association, one of the most prominent historical organizations in the country. An investigating committee turned up bad copying of known documents, examples of then unknown words and phrases (e.g., "home front," "race hatred," and "frontier spirit,"), biographical inconsistencies, erroneous statements of fact, and internal discrepancies. The committee tested the ink and found that it dated no earlier than 1930! *The Horn Papers* became history in quite a different sense than their prankster editor, descendant W.H. Horn of Topeka, Kansas, intended. Horn never said why he forged the documents.

How Can Forgeries Influence History?

Anti-Semitism was widespread in Europe in the late nineteenth century. The *Protocols of the Elders of Zion* purported to reveal a secret meeting of Jewish elders in Prague planning to take over the world by establishing democracies, parliamentary government, banks, and other "insidious" institutions of modern society. Because the book preyed on ancient, widely held stereotypes of Jewish people, many Christians believed the text was authentic. The model for the forgery first appeared in France in *Dialogues in Hell between Machiavelli and Montesquieu* (1864), a book critical of Emperor Napoleon III by Maurice Joly. In 1903, a right-wing Russian Orthodox monk produced a Russian-language edition for anti-Semitic groups known as the Black Hundreds. Agents of the Russian secret police, the Okhrana, were also involved in creating and distributing the *Protocols* for the ill-educated conspiracy theorist, Tsar Nicholas II. The forgery migrated to Germany after World War I with some Russian émigrés and was published in English by the anti-Semitic automobile manufacturer Henry Ford in his *Dearborn [Michigan] Independent* in 1920. Adolf Hitler mentioned the *Protocols* in his anti-Semitic screed, *Mein Kampf* (1924).

In 2020, anti-Semitism is on the rise worldwide, from Europe and the U.S. to New Zealand. In the U.S., a "Unite the Right" rally in

Charlottesville, Virginia, featured the murder of a young woman by a neo-Nazi automobile driver, the injury of 19 demonstrators, Nazi swastika flags and tattoos, and a lukewarm tweet by President Trump that there were "fine people on both sides." At the Tree of Life synagogue shooting in Pittsburgh, Pennsylvania, in October 2018, bystanders shouted "All Jews must Die!"—11 did. Another attack occurred on the Chabad Poway Synagogue near San Diego, California, on April 27, 2019. Wealthy financiers like George Soros, a Hungarian Jew, became targets of those who believed in a global Jewish conspiracy. Both hate crimes and anti-Semitic incidents were increasing at an alarming rate around the world, fanned by the hateful rhetoric of authoritarian leaders.

The *Protocols* continued to carry their hateful message of Jewish conspiracies on line in cyberspace and internationally. Translations are readily available in Russia, the U.S., Britain, France, Germany, Pakistan, Syria, Iran, Iraq, Lebanon, and Palestine. Few editions ever indicate that the *Protocols* is in fact an historical forgery more than a century old.

The *Protocols* were not a forgery of any genuine document, but a fiction masquerading as an original document. Like *The Horn Papers*, they were a complete fabrication and exposed as such in 1936. Historians have long dismissed the *Protocols* as an anti-Semitic forgery. But some people, especially in the Middle East, still believe them with deadly results. Tragically, any anti-Semitic conspiracy theory continues to find fertile soil among hate groups and politicians in the United States and elsewhere.

Is a Newly Discovered Collection by a Well-Known Author Authentic?

Even the eminent British historian Hugh Trevor-Roper, a noted scholar of Adolf Hitler and German history, fell for this one. In 1983, the German magazine *Stern* boldly announced that it had found some 60 leather-bound volumes of Adolf Hitler's daily diary. Gerd Heidemann, a *Stern* reporter known for his interest in ex-Nazis and Nazi memorabilia, trumpeted this discovery as earth shaking. *Newsweek* ran selections from the diary. Historians sat on the edge of their chairs with eager anticipation. But careful analysis showed that the handwriting was an inept imitation of Hitler's own style, that the imitation leather did not match the elegant, real leather Hitler used at his own desk, and that all the events described in the diaries matched perfectly the entries in Max Domarus's *Hitler: Speeches and Proclamations, 1932–1945*, published in 1962–1963. In the end, the diaries turned out to have been a completely bogus creation of Konrad Kujau, a Stuttgart dealer in Nazi art and memorabilia. Trevor-Roper, who edited the diaries and vouched for their authenticity, was thoroughly embarrassed by the affair. Heidemann and Kujau served prison terms for fraud.

Using forensic science, experts quickly determined that the Hitler diaries were bogus. A German state chemist in Wiesbaden examined the paper and found that it was made after 1955. The bindings contained polyamide fibers also produced only after the war. Likewise, in England, Julius Grant, another chemist working for a paper company, labored for MI6 during the war producing edible paper, forgery-proof ration books, and paper that retained invisible writing. Later Grant demonstrated that Mussolini's supposed diaries were printed on paper made after 1956. Then he ran ultraviolet light tests on the Hitler diaries and agreed they were forgeries.

Historians were gullible in this one. So were handwriting experts who compared two sets of diary forgeries, which, quite naturally, matched each other. The chemists with their forensic tools knew from the start that the diaries were created by someone well after Hitler's death in 1945. The media circus that publisher Rupert Murdoch created around the Hitler diaries amplified everything. Gerd Heidemann learned about the forensic tests but told no one. Forensic history was less interesting that Nazi ideology and historical sensationalism. But Trevor-Roper was a sucker and the forensic scientists were right.

Likewise, the American chemist Walter McCrone used a light microscope to show that the famous "Vinland Map" at Yale University had twentieth-century ink with anatase, rather than the Indian ink made of soot and iron-gall commonly used in the 1400s when the map was allegedly made. McCrone also used Carbon-14 dating to show that the Shroud of Turin, supposedly used to wrap the body of Jesus after the crucifixion, was made in the fourteenth, not the first, century. Again, forensic science trumped religious and historical speculation.

If It Is a Forgery, Who Is the Forger?

Demonstrating a forgery often means identifying the forger. For centuries, the famous twelfth-century *Igor Tale* has stood as the only great piece of epic poetry from medieval Russia. Critics compare it to the *Song of Roland*. Books and seminars dealing with the *Igor Tale* abound. There has long been some scepticism about the work, whose original manuscript supposedly burned in a fire in Russia in the late eighteenth century. Just recently, Harvard historian Edward Keenan has apparently discovered the man who actually forged the eleventh-century Igor Tale, a Czech Slavic scholar working in Prague in the 1820s. If Keenan's argument survives the test of peer review successfully, he will have unmasked as a forgery one of the greatest and best-known examples of Russian literature. He will have achieved something quite remarkable.

These examples suggest that historians should approach all their sources with a critical eye. Your best tools for treating sources critically are a skepticism about authenticity and a knowledge of the origins of every source: its original location, author, owner, history, and context. In other words, be careful out there!

Task: Choose a primary source. Who wrote it? When? Where? Why? How can you be sure? Have other historians vouched for its authenticity?

Might it be a facsimile or a forgery? If so, who might have copied or forged it and why?

For Further Reading

On forgeries and facsimiles, including the Hitler diaries, see Kenneth W. Rendell, *Forging History: The Detection of Fake Letters and Documents* (Norman: University of Oklahoma Press, 1994), especially 106–123. Another useful book is Joe Nickell, *Detecting Forgery: Forensic Investigation of Documents* (Lexington: University Press of Kentucky, 1996; paperback edition 2005). On other specific examples, see Dorothy Twohig on the Washington forgeries, *Provenance: The Journal of the Society of Georgia Archivists* 1 (Spring 1983): 1–13; Arthur Pierce Middleton and Douglass Adair, "The Mystery of the Horn Papers," *William and Mary Quarterly*, 3rd ser., 4 (October 1947): 409–443; Norman R. Cohn, *Warrant for Genocide: The Myth of the Jewish World Conspiracy and the Protocols of the Elders of Zion* (New York: Harper and Row, 1967); B.W. Segel, *A Lie and a Libel: The History of the Protocols of the Elders of Zion*, trans. and ed. Richard S. Levey (Lincoln: University of Nebraska Press, 1995); Hadassa Ben-Itto, *The Lie That Wouldn't Die: The Protocols of the Elders of Zion* (London: Valentine Mitchell, 2005); Edward L. Keenan, *Joseph Dobrovsky and the Origins of the "Igor Tale"* (Cambridge, MA: Harvard University Press, 2003); Robert C. Williams, *The Forensic Historian: Using Science to Reexamine the Past* (Armonk, NY: M.E. Sharpe, 2013), 10–33.

13.5 Fiction as History

Some people, like Robert Spring, forged historical documents for money. Others, like the authors of the *Protocols of the Elders of Zion*, forged and fictionalized events to foment hatred. But sometimes the motivation for deception is not entirely clear. Take the case of one Benjamin Wilkomirski. In 1995, he published *Fragments: Memories of a Wartime Childhood* (New York: Schocken Books), a remarkable memoir of his childhood in the Nazi death camps during World War II. In it, he recounted a terrible story: a toddler rendered homeless when the Nazis destroyed the Riga ghetto in Latvia, he was separated from his family, deported to Poland, and somehow survived Auschwitz and other concentration camps. The book was well received and widely reviewed as an accurate and deeply touching recollection of the Holocaust. It was translated into 12 languages and made into three films and a play. For three years, Wilkomirski gave lectures and collected prizes for his memoirs. He told stories of unspeakable horror and brutality in the camps. He cried frequently in public. He seemed to epitomize the cruelties inflicted on innocent children in a world of evil.

Then, in 1998, another Holocaust survivor, Daniel Ganzfried, claimed fraud in a sensational article in the Zurich journal *Weltwoche*. Ganzfried charged that Wilkomirski was neither Jewish nor Latvian, but actually a Swiss Protestant named Bruno Dossekker, born on February 22, 1941, to an unmarried couple, Yvonne Berthe Grosjean and Rudolf Zehnder, who gave him up for adoption. (His mother later married Walter Max Rohr and died in 1981.) Bruno was raised by a series of foster parents, the last of whom Walter and Olga Dossekker legally adopted him in May 1945. (They died in 1985.) He spent the entire war not in the camps of Poland, but in Switzerland. He was simply a Swiss musician and instrument builder, married and the father of three children. His account of the Holocaust was a fictional biography, a novel, but not history.

Dossekker/Wilkomirski claimed in response that he had, in fact, survived the harrowing experiences of Auschwitz and other concentration camps in Poland. He admitted that his Swiss documents were authentic, but claimed that, like many Holocaust orphans, he received a new identity after the war. He said that he was born a Jew in Latvia in early 1939 and that his Swiss identity and birth date were legal fictions. "It was always the free choice of the reader to read my book as literature or to take it as a personal document," he added. "Nobody has to believe me." Wilkomirski then suffered a nervous breakdown and was hospitalized and put in seclusion for some six months.

Wilkomirski claimed that he did not arrive in Switzerland until late 1947. But Ganzfried found evidence that he had moved in with his foster parents in October 1945. When faced with such a contradiction, Wilkomirski brushed it aside.

Was the memoir a hoax? Was Wilkomirski a conscious liar? Or was he the victim of his own delusions of the past, gleaned from other Holocaust survivors? Was he fact or fiction? He himself did not care. Only memory mattered. At one level, he claimed objectivity: "I just happen to be a historian, too." At another level, he disavowed any belief in the validity of historical records: "No matter what they say, or what they constructed —legal or not legal, half-legal papers—this is all shit for me. I know that I can trust my memory. *Basta [Enough]*!" No wonder high school friends remembered him as a practiced, if occasional, liar.

But Wilkomirski persisted. He claimed to be practicing "interdisciplinary therapy" so that fact and fiction were intertwined in memory and could not ever be distinguished. The Holocaust existed as historical experience because he remembered it. Memory trumped evidence. To doubt the veracity of his account would be, in his view, to doubt the Holocaust.

Wilkomirski did not deny the Holocaust. He fictionalized it. Much of his book could have reflected his long-standing conversations with Holocaust survivors and his post-war visits to the camps. But even as fiction, Wilkomirski's stunning book raised questions about identity and memory in the recollection of historical experience. In fact, critics who admired the book suggested that the publisher simply reclassify it as fiction. As a work of fiction, his "memoirs" would be gripping enough. But his claim to have lived through the experience he knew only second-hand was false. He was neither historian nor primary source nor memoirist. Perhaps he was deluded by a "compelling fantasy." Perhaps he was a con man. He was, at any rate, a fiction writer posing as a nonfiction survivor, even though he himself may not have recognized the fact. Would you have suspected that he was making up his story?

How can one tell whether a memoir or autobiography written many years after the events portrayed is fiction or nonfiction, real or imagined? If the writer believes an account is true, is it valid, even if it contradicts some known evidence? How do our later memories vary from the events we remember shortly after they occurred?

The best tool available in confronting a historical account that may be fictional is a critical approach to all memoirs and autobiographies. Understand why and under what circumstances an individual wrote a memoir. Cross-check statements against other verifiable accounts of the same events. A memoir consistent with most other accounts is probably reliable.

On the Wilkomirski affair, see Philip Gourevitch, "The Memory Thief," in *The New Yorker*, June 14, 1999: 48–68. Daniel Ganzfried's charges appeared in *Die Weltwoche*, August 27, 1998. See also Dorrit Cohn, "Fictional versus Historical Lives: Borderlines and Borderline Cases," *Journal of Narrative Technique* 19: 1 (Winter 1989): 3–24. Most recently, see Blake Eskin, *A Life in Pieces: The Making and Unmaking of Benjamin Wilkomirski* (New York: W.W. Norton, 2002).

Task: What facts in Wilkomirski's story seem most likely to be true? False? What specific circumstances made it possible for him to invent a fictional past? Write an autobiographical paragraph recounting some event or experience in your life. Write a second paragraph inventing an event or experience in your life. Try to make each as real and believable as you can. Exchange these paragraphs with another student's paragraphs and see if each of you can determine which is real and which is fiction. How can you tell? What clues are there? How can we know if what we read is true or not?

13.6 Film as History: Fact or Fiction?

How does film re-enact, help us understand, and "get inside" a historical event? How does film distort the past by providing us with an entertaining illusion? Let's admit that film is a powerful tool for seeing and hearing history. It provides us with the sights and sounds of a recreated past that can have a powerful impact on us. Film can put us "there" in ways that the printed page simply can never accomplish. But it can also distort, falsify, or simply ignore historical truth. The following positive and negative examples of film and history should get you thinking about this topic.

Films Can Help the Historian Understand the Past

- *Films can help document the past.* Ken Burns is perhaps the best-known documentary filmmaker of our times. A documentary—the term itself dates back to 1935—is a work of art based on evidence and fact, generally a film or radio program. For the first documentaries in the early 1900s, many directors simply opened the camera lens and portrayed real life around them. More recently, they have tried to combine images and sounds from the past to bring us directly there. Burns has produced masterful films on U.S. National Parks, the Civil War, Prohibition, baseball, jazz, and the women's movement in the nineteenth century. He interviews both participants and historians on camera, reproduces old films and photographs, and lets us hear the music and sounds of a bygone era as recorded at the time. He makes history live for us in the present with loving attention to detail and historical accuracy. Documentaries aim to be true, but like any work of history are subject to bias, distortion, and interpretation.

- *Films can help us visualize the past.* The 1965 film *Dr. Zhivago*, with Omar Sharif and Julie Christie, tells the dramatic story of the Russian Revolution based on Nobel Prize winner Boris Pasternak's 1956 novel of the same name. Although based on a historical event and a specific era, there are numerous points where the film deviates from historical fact. (Even the opening scene of Zhivago's mother's funeral was shot in Spain.) But what the movie does remarkably well—far better than a work of history could—is to convey visually the many elements of symbolism in the novel. On the printed page, Pasternak is forced to show us frost-covered windows and shattered dreams in words. The film uses visual images to give us powerful insights into love, revolution, and history. It fictionalizes the past but vividly evokes another era, thus enhancing our understanding of history.

- *Films can help us understand mental states.* In the 2001 film *A Beautiful Mind*, based on the 1998 biography by Sylvia Nasar, we see the life and mind of the tormented Nobel Prize-winning economist and mathematician John Nash. Film critics have pointed out that the movie ignores or contradicts many of the facts of Nash's life described in the biography. Props are often from the wrong decade (his wife wears espadrille shoes not popular in America until the 1970s); the Nevada atomic bomb test shown to Nash in 1953 was not held until 1955; Nash gave no Nobel speech because he was ill at the time; mathematics is limited to a few drawings on a blackboard; and an insight into game theory is supposedly based on picking up a woman in a bar, rather than mathematics.

    Despite these inaccuracies and drawbacks, the film gets it right about Nash's disease, schizophrenia. The movie effectively conveys the results of insulin shock therapy and the visual patterns seen by a mind descending into madness. The portrait of Princeton University in the 1950s is remarkably true to life, even if some of the events are made up. The film conveys more realistically than a history book ever could the state of Nash's tormented mind, if not his life and work. It gets us inside his head as no book could.

Films Can Hinder Our Understanding of the Historical Past

- *Films can be based on bad history.* The 1990 movie *JFK* by director Oliver Stone provides great entertainment and feeds the paranoia of movie audiences who come to the theater prepared to believe in a conspiracy to assassinate President John F. Kennedy in 1963. In this case, Stone treats the long-discredited theories of a Dallas, Texas, assistant district attorney, Jim Garrison, as historically valid. The result is a conspiracy theory film that hints darkly at plots to kill President Kennedy by anti-Castro Cubans, Castro, the mob, and highly placed Americans in the CIA, FBI, and other agencies. In this case, a director takes bad history and turns it into a dramatic film that entertains only as a work of fiction.
- *Films can be anachronistic.* The 1998 film *Titanic* is a fictional love story set on the doomed ocean liner that sank on its maiden voyage in 1912. The ship, parts of which were rebuilt on a scale model, looks vivid on screen, and many scenes capture the splendor of the Edwardian era. And yet numerous details in the film are wrong. Claude Monet's painting of water lilies shown framed on the wall was not painted until 1923. In one scene viewers can glimpse a Roosevelt dime, which was not minted until 1950. The crown and torch on the Statue of Liberty are shown as lit at night, which did not occur until the 1950s. The color photograph of a diamond would have been impossible, since no color photography was used at the time. The Colt 1911 pistol used by one of the characters was limited to military use and would have been quite illegal for a civilian to carry. And so on.

Only in the decade after the film *Titanic* was made did forensic scientists discover that the rivets that held the steel plates together in the *Titanic's* hull had three or four times as much slag as expected, therefore less tensile strength. (Slag is a combination of iron, oxygen, and silicon called iron silicate.) The rivet theory helped historians understand finally why the great ship sank in 1912 after colliding with an iceberg off of Newfoundland. Forensic history again provided an answer to a real historical question: Why did the ship sink? But no one really wanted to see a film about defective rivets when they could see a Hollywood love story about a doomed Edwardian couple at sea.

- *Films can be historically inaccurate.* In the 1998 film *Saving Private Ryan*, director Steven Spielberg took on the epic topic of the Normandy invasion of Europe in June 1944 on D-day. The first half hour provides one of the most gripping, horrible, realistic views of battle ever created or replicated on film. And yet, as moving and convincing as the scene is, inaccuracies abound. The German Tiger tanks of a Panzer division used against American troops defending a bridgehead were not actually there on D-day. The village battle against the Nazi Panzer division Das Reich was also a mistake—the division was nowhere near Normandy at the time. The P-51 fighters used in the film as "tank busters" were actually used mainly for bomber escort service during the war. The antitank aircraft used at Normandy were Hawker Typhoons, and they were British, not American.

    Another war movie, *The Patriot* (2000), provides a dramatic view of the American Revolution in the Carolinas. It blends fact and fiction together in a powerful way. But why are those uniforms so clean? And why does the battlefield at Cowpens look nothing like the actual battlefield that I visited? The British Union Jack flag is actually the current one, not the one used in the eighteenth century, which did not have the diagonal red cross of St. Patrick. The British never burned a church with people in it, as they do in the film. The comment "Tell me about Ohio!" uttered by one of the characters makes no sense, since Ohio was not yet either a territory or a state. The Green Dragoons in the film inexplicably wear red uniforms, when in fact they wore (guess what!) green uniforms.

Whether accurate or inaccurate, film provides a powerful tool for conveying and understanding—or misunderstanding—history. Through film, we can imagine ourselves in another time and place. We understand the past visually and aurally. Past images and sounds in a film can supplement historical texts we have read. Films can also be primary sources that tell us about the time, place, and circumstances under which they were made. They are pieces of evidence about the director, the audience, and the culture that produced them and paid to see them.

Task: Choose any film you have seen recently that involves a historical event, person, or context. Make your own list of the ways in which that film helps you understand history. Then make another list of how that same film hinders your understanding of history. Was the film accurate? Did it increase or decrease your understanding of history? What are the differences between a documentary and a historical film? What are the merits and drawbacks of each? How does each shape our view of the past?

For Further Reading

For a good recent study of the way history becomes entertainment, see Peter C. Rollins, *Hollywood as Historian*, 2nd ed. (Lexington: University Press of Kentucky, 1998). A highly insightful look at the relationship between history and film is Siegfried Kracauer, *History: The Last Things before the Last* (New York: Oxford University Press, 1969). For a fascinating grocery list of nit-picking historical mistakes in a number of historical films, see the website www.nitpickers.com/movies.

Part III

The Relevance of History

14 Everyday History

14.1 Studying Ordinary People

Ordinary people, rather than extraordinary leaders and event makers, may sometimes provide a useful tool for understanding a society or culture. But how can historians study ordinary people? Who is ordinary? How do ordinary people reflect their society and their times? What sources exist to tell us about ordinary people? History today, especially social history, certainly involves the study of ordinary people, as well as "great" individuals. While we still enjoy our biographies of princesses and film stars, presidents and generals, we are equally fascinated by the lives and stories of so-called ordinary people. Most people, after all, do not so much affect history as reflect their society and their times. The problem is that ordinary people largely go unnoticed and rarely leave traces. One may read with delight, then, one account of an ordinary person who turns out to be quite extraordinary—Anna Buschler, a sixteenth-century German woman who conducted a lifelong struggle for justice within a court system run by and for men.

The Burgermeister's Daughter

Harvard historian Steven Ozment must have been elated when he discovered the court records of Anna Buschler (1496/8–1552), daughter of the burgermeister of the German town of Schwabisch Hall during the Protestant Reformation. Schwabisch Hall was an imperial city run by a council of 26 men drawn from the nobility and middle class of the surrounding region. As a young woman during the early 1520s, living in her father's house, Anna somehow managed to carry on two love affairs simultaneously with Erasmus Schenk, a young nobleman, and Daniel Treutwein, a cavalryman from the lower nobility. These affairs were recorded in some detail in Anna's letters to and from both men, letters found by her father in his own house and used in subsequent court proceedings. Anna worked for several years at the Schenk castle outside of town, while living in her parents' home (her mother had died in 1520). She refused to marry either of her lovers and soon became a local scandal and an embarrassment to her beleaguered father, Hermann Buschler, perhaps Hall's leading citizen.

By 1525, both Erasmus and Daniel had disappeared from Anna's life. By 1533, Erasmus, after a bout with syphilis, had married someone else and become a Lutheran. Anna now petitioned the Hall city council and the imperial supreme court for a share of her mother's inheritance and her father's estate so that she could live independently. As a dependent child and an unemployed single woman, she needed a male to represent her interests. Her father Hermann responded by petitioning the imperial ruling council for parental custody over his wayward daughter and a "mandate for surreptitious capture" so that he could bring her home after she escaped. Having retrieved Anna, Hermann kept her chained to an oak table for six months, a prisoner in her own home.

The tale that follows is bizarre. Anna succeeded in getting ever more inadequate portions of her father's money. He continued to try to disinherit her, on the grounds that she had rejected his proposed marriage arrangements in the past. After his death, in 1543, the town council ruled that she should get her fair share of the inheritance. But now her siblings took her to court. She was arrested, imprisoned, and then released. The whole affair dragged on in the courts in a competition between her father's last will and testament and her parents' marriage contract, which contradicted each other. Agreements with her siblings broke down in acrimony.

In the end, Ozment concludes that Anna Buschler's story makes her an ordinary "sign of the times," but also a hero. She was able for several decades to exert her legal rights in court despite the fact that she was a woman. The Schwabisch Hall city council continued to hear her case. She mirrors in a sense the broader upheavals in German society spawned by the Reformation, religious wars, and peasant revolts. (Ozment's links with these broader trends are sometimes tenuous.) Anna Buschler was her own success story, a story "stranger than fiction" and "truer than history."

Because of the legal paper trail left by Anna Buschler's lifelong dispute with her family over her inheritance, the historian was able to turn an "average," hitherto unknown woman into a remarkable person. The conventional wisdom that women were virtually without rights in the sixteenth century is revised, at least in this case. We discover in the end through the historical evidence that an apparently ordinary person was really quite extraordinary. Examining the lives of ordinary people can be a very useful tool for historians.

For the full story of Anna Buschler and her life, see Steven Ozment, *The Burgermeister's Daughter: Scandal in a Sixteenth-Century German Town* (New York: HarperCollins, 1996).

Task: Consider Anna Buschler again. What aspects of her life seem ordinary? Extraordinary? What might her life story tell us about her society? How does a biography of a generally unknown person differ from one of a famous person? What are the merits and advantages of each kind of history?

14.2 Everyone's a Historian

How does doing history resemble our everyday activities? In what sense are we all historians all the time? If so, what tools do we use in our daily round? Certainly the study of the past bears comparison with the study of our own past. Some even consider autobiography at the root of all history. Here are some random thoughts on how history is not some arcane academic enterprise, but a deep structure that underlies our own lives.

- *Memory*: You get up in the morning. In order to function, you need to remember daily routines, overdue bills, medical appointments, feeding the pets, and myriad other items. Alzheimer patients who have lost their memory have also lost their identity and their ability to function.
- *Evidence and records*: Did you pay that bill? Better look in your check book or in your Turbo Tax records on line. You should have a record of past checks written, as well as cancelled checks cashed, to provide you (or the IRS) with evidence that you did or did not pay that (deductible?) bill.
- *Chronology*: Just when was that second paper due in your history class? Better consult the syllabus for the course, which provides a chronology, or chronicle, of what assignments are due on what day and at what hour. (And whose birthday is it today anyway?)
- *Story*: All of us sit around the breakfast or dinner table every day and tell stories to our roommates or significant others of what we have recently (or distantly) done. Telling stories is at the root of history. We do it all the time.
- *Reading history*: Again, we do it all the time. Just consider the morning newspaper (or the *Washington Post* online) and the enormous amount of historical information that we read every day. How can we possibly remember all that history? We don't. We remember selectively.
- *Research*: You are involved in an accident. Thankfully no one was hurt, but there was considerable damage. Does your insurance company cover the damage? Better research your insurance policy and see just what all that fine print you never looked at actually says. Research into your policy will help you and the insurance company negotiate a reimbursable claim.
- *Argument*: Argument is a basic part of every discourse. You want to convince your instructor that you really deserve an incomplete in the course, an extension on the paper, or an excused absence for your early departure for break. You need to convince or persuade someone else that your case is valid.
- *Maps*: You are throwing the mother of all parties. You want everyone to get there. How? Have your friends go online and use Map Quest to figure out how to get to your party. Or e-mail the map to them. Or put the map up on your website or Facebook page.

- *Photographs*: You are spending time abroad and want a historical record of all those exotic places you just visited. How do you create that record? Perhaps with a diary, but definitely with a camera or camcorder. A photograph provides visual evidence that you really were there and had a great, or not so great, time.
- *Films*: Virtually every film you see has historical context embedded in it. Some films are based on historical events. Every film has a history of how it was made, who the stars were, how much it cost, how much it made at the box office, and what the film critics thought about its merits.
- *Events*: We live through, or witness, historical events daily, thanks to the miracle of the Internet and television worldwide news. Today's event is another attack by Iranian mines in international waters on oil shipping. The U.S. condemns it, Iran denies it. Clearly that attack has historical significance. What that significance will be, we do not yet know.
- *Networking*: You probably use Twitter, Facebook, or texting every day to communicate with your friends. Just remember that you are producing a warts-and-all historical profile of yourself that is transparent to the world. There is nothing private about your social networking, so be careful. The Russian trolls might be trolling.

Surely by now you get the idea. The tools in the historian's toolbox can be just as useful in living your life every day as they can be in doing, or enjoying, history. You are in some sense a historian every day of your life. History can certainly give you a valuable perspective on how to live your life, even when it does not appear to be directly relevant. You know and do more history than you realize. Understanding that you do may be yet another important tool.

Task: Write down what you did yesterday or last week. Then write down what evidence you might use to prove to a friend that you did what you did. You are doing history.

14.3 Local History. A Tale of Two Towns

Look around your own town and neighborhood. Observe your neighbours, views, and buildings. Where and when did your local history begin? How did your family get there? I have lived for years in two Maine towns with both similarities and differences. Recently I published histories of both of them. I learned that documents for local history were readily available but widely scattered in the archives of libraries and historical societies in both Maine and Massachusetts, of which Maine was a province until statehood in 1820.

Lovell (originally Lovewell's Town) was a western Maine town of around a thousand people, two libraries and no traffic light, incorporated by Massachusetts in 1800. My grandfather built a summer camp on Kezar Lake in 1920 (Illustration 14.1). John Lovewell was a scalp-hunter who was killed in battle by the Wabenaki Indians in Fryeburg in 1725. Boston-area

Illustration 14.1 The Center Lovell Inn, Built in the Nineteenth Century and Still Operating

settlers seeking cheap land and lower taxes migrated to western Maine after the American Revolution and founded the township of New Suncook, that later divided amicably into Lovell and Sweden. The Wabenaki occupied most of northern New England when the first English and French settlers arrived in the seventeenth century seeking land, furs, and fish. Ultimately the Wabenaki were either exterminated or driven north to Canada. Kezar Lake residents have included painter Eastman Johnson, singer Rudy Vallee, film maker Jonathan Demme, and horror writer Stephen King.

Both Lovell and adjacent Fryeburg had historical societies with extensive archives. So did Massachusetts and New Hampshire. They also had a significant number of local history buffs willing to share their knowledge of the subject. They presented a consistent picture of towns that had begun as trading posts dealing with the Wabenaki, moved on to logging the surrounding forest and then to hosting the seasonal migration of tourists, "sports," and people from away who help drive the Maine economy. Lovell's population peaked just before the Civil War and has yet to recover. Wool carding and dowel factories gave way to real estate for summer residents from away. Logs went by truck, not river, after the 1960s.

Topsham, to which we moved in 2013, was on Midcoast Maine along the Atlantic Ocean, founded around 1715 by English who had settled their differences with the French over fishing the North Atlantic at the Treaty of Utrecht. Topsham settlers also traded with the Wabenaki before logging their forests and then profiting from the tourist trade. Wabenaki names still predominate in Sagadahoc County along the Androscoggin

River, an area known to the natives as Pjepscot. Topsham's original purpose was to defend Brunswick from the Wabenaki, which its Ulster Scot settlers did with efficiency. Soon Topsham men began to build vessels along Merrymeeting Bay and shipbuilding became a major industry until taken over by neighboring Bath with its deep-water Kennebec River. Then came the French-Canadian mill workers, the Italian feldspar miners and the Boston mill-owners of Brunswick. Many Bowdoin College graduates remained in the area, as did the U.S. Navy veterans after World War II. Duck hunters and fishermen flew in from New York and San Francisco.

Lovell and Topsham share much in common. Wabenaki place names, arrowheads and petroglyphs still exist in Maine. Wood products remain a commercial part of Maine's economy. So do the tourists from away, winter and summer, especially Americans and Canadians.

Local history involved a constant search for local sources: archives, libraries, historical societies and residents with long memories. It was fascinating to explore your own neighbourhood as a historian, and to learn how small Maine towns were tied into a global economy. Consumer goods flowed in from Europe. Beaver furs, fish, lumber and apples went back across the Atlantic. Maine towns lived in a global economy where the price of lumber in Havana and Barbados, of ice in China, of apples in England had a direct effect on the locals. Topsham ships sailed the globe. Local history was not parochial but linked to world history. And the sources were all around you.

Task: Find a history of your own town if you can. Check out its primary sources and your local library and historical society. See if you can write an outline of a contemporary history of your town that brings the story up to date. Maybe someday you can actually write one yourself.

Further Reading

Robert C. Williams, *Lovewell's Town: From Howling Wilderness to Vacationland in Trust* (2007) and *Topsham, Maine: From the River to the Highlands* (2015).

15　Oral History

15.1　The Perils of Memory

In studying the relatively recent past, one of the most useful but problematic tools in the historian's employ is oral history, the interviewing of living subjects about their past experiences. There is in theory no better way to gain an understanding of events in living memory than to talk to the people who observed or participated in them. Unlike letters, diaries, audiotapes, memoranda, video, and other archival documents, people interviewed can be asked specific follow-up questions about their experiences and impressions, based on what the historian wishes to study or discover. Interviewing living historical participants can remind us of a crucial fact that underlies all good works of history: however strange and distant the past can seem at times, history is a tale of *real people*, with all the richness and subtlety that human reality entails. A participant observer was there!

But the practice of oral history also involves many pitfalls. For one, memory is a tricky thing. As fallible beings, we can often get confused about relatively innocuous events that happened as recently as this morning—for example, what we had for breakfast or what e-mails arrived in our inbox today—let alone events that occurred years or even decades ago. Even memories that were once extremely vivid can get confused and distorted over time (particularly when the person being questioned is getting on in years or the memories involve very important or emotionally charged events). As we all come to learn, the memory of an emotion accompanying an event—sadness, exhilaration, bewilderment—is often much more potent than the memory of the details involved.

Thus, the memories of people who experienced a past event will almost always be infused with feelings unknown to someone who was not alive during the time. (As our elders are invariably prone to say, "You had to be there.") For example, people's memories of the presidency of Lyndon Johnson will almost always be inflected by their feelings about the civil rights movement and the Vietnam War, two electric events that few Americans could remain dispassionate about at the time (or thereafter).

FDR and the 1930s recall the Depression. Trump's White House in 2019 is full of staff members who leak secrets, lie about events, or simply forget what happened. This is not necessarily a weakness of oral history—to the contrary, it is part of what makes oral history such a rich and useful tool for understanding the past. Still, this intensity of feeling is something that historians, who should try to maintain at least some neutrality and emotional distance from the story they are covering, must take into account when relying on oral histories to explain the past.

Complicating matters even further, several people can watch exactly the same occurrence take place and form very different impressions of it. Our own personal, individual experiences with the past very often resemble the parable of the blind men and the elephant, in which six blind men touch different parts of a pachyderm—a tusk, a trunk, a leg, a tail—and each insists that his impression of the elephant is the correct one. The Robert Muller hearings of July 2019 on Trump and the Russians revealed a wide gap between Democrats and Republicans as to what Muller said and what he meant. In a sense, they are all correct, but it is the historian's task to try to see and describe the whole elephant, not just the parts, after interviewing the blind men.

In short, memories are rooted in individual emotion and perspective. While they can illuminate the contours of earlier events and help to bridge the emotional gap between past and present, they rarely if ever tell the whole story, and therefore they should be used with caution.

Task: Ask about a parent's or grandparent's memory of an important or controversial historical event that the person lived through. How does the answer compare to what you might find, or have found, in a history textbook about that event? What are the strengths and weaknesses of each approach? Which do you find more involving? Which do you find more illuminating?

Second Task: Pick an event in your recent past, preferably one that you experienced with other students in the class. Think about how and what you remember about the event. How did it make you feel? What details of the experience come to mind? Now, interview one or two of your fellow students about the same event. How do your memories compare? Does everyone remember the same details?

15.2 Interviewees and Interviewers

Alas, the fallibility of memory is just the tip of the iceberg: when using or conducting an oral history interview, there are other important considerations a good historian must take into account. As we have seen, even if interviewees attempt to be dispassionate and detached about their recollections, certain distortions of memory or emotional prejudices will invariably leak into their testimony. These concerns become much more important if, as is often the case, the people being interviewed have a specific agenda in mind, such as promoting a particular historical interpretation or improving their own standing in history by enhancing or obscuring their role in a given set of circumstances. It is entirely possible, if not probable, that oral history interviewees—rather than attempting to be impartial—will instead subscribe to a variation on Winston Churchill's famous dictum: "History will be kind to me, for I intend to write it."

An excellent example of this danger, and how it can be successfully surmounted, is filmmaker Errol Morris's fascinating 2003 documentary *The Fog of War: Eleven Lessons from the Life of Robert McNamara*, which consists mostly of Morris's extensive interviews with McNamara, the U.S. secretary of defence during the Kennedy and Johnson administrations. Over the course of these interviews (as in his 2001 book *In Retrospect: The Tragedy and Lessons of Vietnam)*, McNamara—a brilliant, complex, and often frustrating individual —can be seen trying to rehabilitate his public image, which had been in eclipse since the Vietnam War. McNamara expertly parries and deflects Morris's questions about Vietnam to subjects he prefers to talk about. In response, Morris supplements his interviews with first-rate archival research and visual representations that enhance McNamara's explanations and cut through his occasional evasions (for example, falling dominoes on a map of Southeast Asia to evoke the domino theory and a candid epilogue in which McNamara admits that he does not want to talk about Vietnam). Since Morris is making a documentary film rather than writing a work of history, he can rely on visual cues and resources that are out of reach for most historians, who must convey meaning through words. Nevertheless, Morris's documentary illustrates how even as cagey and partisan an interviewee as Robert McNamara can still yield profound and important historical insights, if his answers are taken in perspective.

Few interview subjects that you meet are likely to be as explicitly tendentious as McNamara. But even so, the interviewee is only one half, albeit the more important half, of the process of oral history interviewing. The interviewer may be equally problematic. Political pollsters have recognized for years that the answers people give to a certain question depend a good deal on how that question is posed to them. The same is often true of oral history. More troubling still, if interviewers are not extremely careful, their implicit biases—racial, ethnic, sexual, class-based, political, or even historical—can very easily seep into and affect the entire interview.

The WPA Slave Narratives

During the Great Depression, the Federal Writers' Project, a subsidiary of President Franklin Roosevelt's Works Progress Administration (WPA), attempted to create work for unemployed writers, journalists, and historians by having them travel across the South to interview former slaves, many of whom—70 years after emancipation—were fast nearing the end of their lives. The WPA researchers conducted and transcribed interviews with more than 2,300 former slaves about their experiences before and after emancipation, thus providing subsequent generations of historians with a priceless resource for understanding the lives of African American slaves and freedmen in the Civil War and Reconstruction eras, including their perceptions of and responses to the daily indignities of that "peculiar institution," as John Calhoun and others called slavery.

Yet, for all their worth, the WPA slave narratives pose many significant problems for historians. To take just one example, consider the following passage from a 1937 interview with Charity Anderson, a 101-year-old (by her reckoning) former slave in Mobile, Alabama:

> My old Marster was a good man, he treated all his slaves kind, and took care of dem, he wanted to leave dem hisn chillun. It sho' was hard for us older uns to keep de little cullered chillun out ob de dinin' room whar ol marster ate, cause when dey would slip in and stan' by his cheer, when he finished eatin' he would fix a plate and gib dem and dey would set on de hearth and eat. But honey chile, all white folks warn 't good to dere slaves, cause I'se seen pore niggers almos' tore up by dogs, and whipped unmercifully, when dey did'nt do lack de white folks say. But thank God I had good white folks, dey sho' did trus' me to, I had charge of all de keys in the house and I waited on de Missy and de chillun. I laid out all dey clos' on Sat 'dy night on de cheers, and den Sund'y mawnings I'd pick up all de dirty clos,' they did'nt have to do a thing. And as for working in the field, my marster neber planted no cotton, I neber seed no cotton planted til' a'ter I was free.[1]

The most immediately evident characteristic of Anderson's account is the dialect in which it is written, which perhaps suggests to the reader a plausible manner of speaking for a 101-year-old woman who had been born and raised under slavery. Yet this dialect in fact tells us much more about the interviewers than it does about the former slaves, since it is uniform throughout all the WPA narratives and, as historian John Blassingame and others have noted, was ascribed even to African-Americans who spoke perfect English! Indeed, in his 1975 essay "Using the Testimony of Ex-Slaves: Approaches and Problems," Blassingame points out that the WPA narratives were altered in even more disturbing ways, including some that were "edited to delete references to cruel punishments, blacks serving in the Union Army, runaways, and blacks voting during Reconstruction."[2]

These lamentable revisions aside, the WPA narratives are also compromised by the often condescending attitude of the young, well-educated, and almost universally white interviewers—some of whom were even the grandchildren of the interviewees' former masters—toward their subjects, as well as the resulting patterns of deference and obfuscation that African Americans were accustomed to using in the presence of white people in the still overtly racist Jim Crow South. As Blassingame puts it:

The white staff of the WPA had mastered so little of the art and science of interviewing that many of them found it impossible to obtain trustworthy data from their informants. Many of the WPA interviewers consistently referred to their informants as darkeys, niggers, aunteys, mammas, and uncles. Reminiscent as these terms were of rigid plantation etiquette, they were not calculated to engender the trust of the blacks. Rather than being sensitive, the white interviewers failed to demonstrate respect for the blacks, ignored cues indicating a tendency toward ingratiation, and repeatedly refused to correct the informants' belief that the interviewer was trying to help them obtain [a] coveted pension. Not only did most of the whites lack empathy with the former slaves, they often phrased their questions in ways which indicated the answers they wanted.[3]

Despite these significant problems, Blassingame concedes, the WPA narratives "are incomparable sources" and "a rich source of information on black speech patterns." But, he warns, "uncritical use of the interviews will lead almost inevitably to a simplistic and distorted view of the plantation as a paternalistic institution where the chief feature of life was mutual love and respect between masters and slaves."[4]

If you want to peruse more of the WPA slave narratives, many of them are available online at either the Library of Congress website Born in Slavery: Slave Narratives from the Federal Writers' Project (http://memory.loc.gov/ammem/snhtml/snhome.html) or the online anthology of American slave narratives at the University of Virginia. Check them out at http://xroads.virginia.edu/~HYPER/wpa/wpahome.html.

Task: Consider Charity Anderson's discussion of her master and of white folks in general once more. How do you think Anderson's testimony may have been influenced by the race and ethnicity of her interviewer? In your opinion, how much does this complicate the use of Anderson's oral history, or of the WPA slave narratives in general, in understanding antebellum slavery?

15.3 Techniques of Oral History

One hopes that historians today have a better sense of their own partiality and biases than did many of the writers of the WPA seventy years ago. Nevertheless, when conducting an oral history, it is important to recognize how both your questions and your very presence may affect the answers you receive. You should choose and phrase your questions very carefully to allow for open-ended responses that will not seem dictated by you, while keeping a focus on your areas of inquiry. When in doubt, *listen* to your subject, and let the questions evolve organically from your conversation. In science labs, particularly those studying quantum mechanics, physicists speak of the observer effect—the idea that the act of observing something changes the observed. Keep the observer effect in mind as you conduct your own historical interviews!

Also, when interviewing people for your own historical project, it is important to be as candid and forthright as possible with your subjects. Let them know the purpose and format (paper, video, online article) of your intended study, as well as exactly what you intend to use their recollections for and how they will be used. Finally, make sure you come to a written agreement with your sources about the confidentiality of their interviews—let them know if their real names will be used in your final text, and, if so, be sure to obtain their permission before publishing any of their responses.

Task: Choose a family member or person in your community who you believe would make for an interesting oral history. Craft a series of questions for your interview and, after obtaining permission, interview your source about your chosen topics. Evaluate the process. Did some types of questions work better than others? Did your questions change once the interview process had begun? How might you have handled the interview differently?

Notes

1 "Interview with Charity Anderson, Mobile, AL," conducted by Ila B. Prine, Federal Writers' Project, Dist. 2, April 16, 1937, in *The American Slave*, supplement series 1, vol. 1: 14–15. Reprinted at American Slave Narratives: An On-line Anthology, University of Virginia (http://xroads.virginia. edu/~hyper/wpa/wpa home.html).
2 John W. Blassingame, "Using the Testimony of Ex-Slaves: Approaches and Problems," *Journal of Southern History* 41, no. 4 (November 1975): 485.
3 Ibid., 483.
4 Ibid., 490.

For Further Reading

To read excellent examples of oral history, see Studs Terkel, *The Good War: An Oral History of World War II* (New York: Pantheon Books, 1984) and *Hard Times: An Oral History of the Great Depression* (New York: Pantheon Books, 1970). To get a better sense of Terkel's methodology, visit this pioneering oral historian's official website at www.studsterkel.org, which includes audio excerpts of interviews conducted by Terkel for his various tomes. For more information and guidelines on how to conduct your own oral histories, see Valerie Yow, *Recording Oral History: A Guide for the Humanities and Social Sciences*, 2nd ed. (Walnut Creek, CA: AltaMira Press, 2005), or visit the website of the Oral History Association at www. dickinson.edu/oha/index.html.

16 Material Culture

16.1 Spirits in the Material World

As anthropologists and archaeologists like to remind us, and as some scholars—particularly in years gone by—have been prone to forget, remnants of the past also exist outside of the musty bound volumes of libraries and historical archives. For history, populated as it is with human beings who, like us, ate, drank, wore clothes, slept, and otherwise lived a day-to-day existence, is not only written on paper, but carved in wood, stitched in fabric, molded in clay, blown in glass, and hewn from stone. Americans today can often immediately recognize what period a film or TV show takes place in simply from the outfits worn by the actors, be they poodle skirts or bell-bottom trousers. So, too, historians have come to discover that the fashions, finery, furniture, tools, and architecture of earlier generations are as important to reconstructing the past as are letters, diaries, and legal documents.

Physical, man-made things, or artifacts, crafted and then left behind by previous generations, are often referred to as *material culture*. As the second half of this term implies, historians often study these artifacts not just as individual items, but also to explore broader questions about the culture and the people that made them.

Take, for example, a typical nineteenth-century American whalebone corset. On the one hand, it may seem merely a fashionable affectation of the times, one in a long series of corsets dating back 3,000 years to ancient Crete. Yet from this unwieldy, confining corset, which returned to the height of fashion in this period, we can learn much about the gender division of labour in the nineteenth century, the cult of domesticity and doctrine of separate spheres that increasingly isolated wealthy and middle-class white women from the world of work, the rise of conspicuous consumption in American cities, and the changing role of women in American society. (After all, it seems more than coincidence that the corset fell out of fashion in the 1920s, the age of the flapper, soon after women obtained the right to vote and started taking an increasingly active role in all facets of American life.) What is more, this corset also highlights the importance of the nineteenth-century whaling industry, which at its peak slaughtered 15,000 whales a year to obtain such products as lamp oil, soap, candles, perfume, and corsets.

Richard Bushman and the Refinement of America

An excellent example of the study of material culture and how it can be used to illuminate much broader corners of history than one might initially expect is Richard Bushman's 1992 book *The Refinement of America: Persons, Houses, Cities.* In this work, Bushman traces the rise of gentility in eighteenth-and nineteenth-century America through architecture, fashion, cutlery, etiquette books, and other elements of material culture, explaining how gentility, respectability, and "refinement," coupled with a growing ethos of consumerism, transformed American democracy in its first hundred years by smoothing social mobility while blurring class distinctions. "This book would never have been written," notes Bushman in his preface, if his time at the University of Delaware, home to the Center for Material Culture Studies (http://materi alculture.udel.edu), had not "started me thinking about material culture ... The faculty created an atmosphere congenial to the investigation of house furnishings, landscapes, and costumes, the materials historians frequently neglect."[1] Bushman wrote *The Refinement of America* "in the hopes of showing how ideals interacting with materials changed the American environment and reshaped American culture."[2]

In the passage below, Bushman discusses changing habits of eating in America over the course of the eighteenth century:

> The simpler mode of eating was long in disappearing. The studies of Plymouth, Massachusetts, inventories from 1660 to 1760 list very few plates. Since more than half of the inventories in most places show no knives or forks even in the eighteenth century, plates, which served primarily as surfaces for cutting, were unneeded. Food that required no cutting—porridge, mush, or the various pottages—could be eaten as easily from bowls or dishes with spoons. More commonly, then, people in poor households well into the eighteenth century probably ate their partially liquid meals from bowls with spoons, or perhaps in still more primitive ways ...
>
> These conditions changed through the eighteenth century as tables and chairs increased in frequency. By the end of the century both items were nearly as common as beds in more settled areas. By the middle of the century irregular seating and eating from bowls with spoons and fingers remained mainly as an image at the lower end of the refinement spectrum to which genteel dining could be compared. Gentility regulated dining as it did the body, including the wish to keep the food clean, separated from dirt and fingers. The growing spirit of refinement placed people on chairs at tables, gave each individual utensils, and put the food on platters and in

serving bowls. Bodies were placed before the food with knives and forks in hand, separating the person from tactile contact with the food, and on chairs that encouraged people to sit upright in the proper erect posture. Genteel aesthetic principles thus took over the process of dining in its entirety, and refined and exalted it.

The advance of regulated and refined dining can be measured through the proliferation of the tools that made it possible: tables and chairs, knives and forks, and porcelain plates and serving dishes. Dining accoutrements were added one by one, usually beginning with chairs that lifted people from the floor, and brought them to order around a table. Then rough plates of some kind, normally of pewter, were added and about the same time knives and forks to separate bodies from the food. Smooth porcelain serving dishes and plates, with their fine polished surfaces, usually came last.[3]

Bushman also examines architecture (the introduction of parlors and separate dining rooms, for example), fashion (the rise of silks and other smooth fabrics to replace coarse linens and cotton), and decorum (changes in conventions of letter-writing and conversation) to buttress his explanation of the rise of gentility and its consequences for American society. Bushman thus illustrates both the importance and the effectiveness of studying material culture to enhance our understanding of the past.

Task: Reread the excerpt from Bushman's *The Refinement of America*. What does Bushman use for his primary sources in this passage? What conclusions does he draw from them? In your opinion, is Bushman successful here in his stated purpose, to show "how ideals interacting with materials changed the American environment and reshaped American culture"?

16.2 Studying Material Culture

Richard Bushman dedicates *The Refinement of America* to "the curators of America's history museums," and for good reason. Historians can get enamoured by a relatively new technique of examining history and begin to think that they invented it. But, in fact, both museum curators—who must often deduce the provenance and historical background of artifacts on display solely from visual and tactile cues—and archaeologists and anthropologists studying oral, premodern societies have been studying material culture for decades, if not centuries. For archaeologists in particular, such elements of material culture as arrowheads, ancient tools, scraps of cloth, ceramic shards, and building foundations may well be the only sources available to study entire epochs of the prewriting past. For them, the study of material culture is not merely one technique of their discipline, but by necessity the central component of their toolbox (Illustration 16.1)!

It is therefore helpful to examine an artifact of material culture for historical study as if you were a museum curator or archaeologist. Here are some of the issues to consider:

- *Use*: What was the intended purpose for the artifact? Why was it made? Does the artifact show signs of its intended use? How often was it likely used?
- *Materials*: From what materials is the artifact made? How was it put together? What other materials could the artifact have been made from instead? Were the materials routinely available at the place the artifact was found, or were they probably rare or hard to find?
- *Craftsmanship*: Who probably designed and created this artifact? Was it made at home or in a factory? Does it show signs of craftsmanship? Is it a unique item, or was it mass-produced?
- *Ownership*: Who was the probable owner or user of this artifact? What was the owner's probable occupation or social standing? Does the artifact seem to be a necessary item or a luxury?
- *Decoration*: Does the artifact have any decorative flourishes or designs on it? Has it been painted or dyed? What might these decorations symbolize?

Illustration 16.1 Material Culture Artifacts in a Polish Museum

This museum in Poland is devoted entirely to Material Culture. (http://commons.wikimedia.org)

- *Context*: What other artifacts were found nearby? Do they seem to date from roughly the same age? Do they seem to share a common purpose with the artifact in question?

Task: Choose an object from your home at random—a cup, a shirt, a soda bottle, a piggy bank—and pretend you are an archaeologist from the far-flung future who has found this object over the course of an excavation. What does it tell you about the time in which it was made? Having determined its provenance, what broader questions of history might this artifact help to illuminate? How do the tools of archaeology and material culture compare with the tools of history?

For Further Reading

For another informative account of colonial America that uses the study of material culture as its primary methodology, see Laurel Thatcher Ulrich's *The Age of Homespun: Objects and Stories in the Creation of an American Myth* (New York: Alfred A. Knopf, 2001). For more general works on the uses of material culture in studying history, see Thomas Schlereth, ed., *Material Culture: A Research Guide* (Lawrence: University Press of Kansas, 1999); Thomas Schlereth, ed., *Material Culture Studies in America* (Walnut Creek, CA: AltaMira Press, 1995); and Henry Glassie, *Material Culture* (Bloomington: Indiana University Press, 1999). Excellent online resources include the University of Delaware's Center for Material Culture Studies (http://materialculture.udel.edu) and the Digital Library for the Decorative Arts and Material Culture at the University of Wisconsin-Madison (http://decorativearts.library.wisc.edu).

16.3 Provenance and Ownership: Tracing Stolen Art

Historians are often called upon to produce the history of an art object. That history is often known as the *provenance*, a chronological narrative of who owned that object, probably purchased (or stolen) from a previous owner and sold to a subsequent buyer. The question of ownership then becomes a question of law: who legally can claim ownership of an object in a court of law and on what grounds?

Historians try to establish a true account of an art object's history. Attorneys and lawyers try to establish the legal ownership of that art object for their client. In the case of Vincent Van Gogh's famous painting *Night Café* (1888) (Illustration 16.2), attorneys for a living claimant in Paris, Pierre Konowaloff, filed a lawsuit claiming title for the painting because it was purchased by Konowaloff's grandfather, a wealthy Moscow textile merchant named Ivan Morozov, in 1908 and taken by the Bolsheviks in 1918, along with Morozov's home and entire art collection. The Soviet government sold the painting to wealthy American art collector Stephen

C. Clark, heir to the Singer sewing machine fortune in 1933. Clark then bequeathed the painting to Yale University, his alma mater, which took title to *Night Café* in 1960 upon Clark's death. In 2002, a Paris court declared Konowaloff to be the sole living heir of Ivan Morozov. The legal question became: was Yale University or Pierre Konowaloff the rightful owner of the painting? Konowaloff took Yale to court to find out.

Yale sued pre-emptively in court to "quiet title" to *Night Café* in 2009. The courts ruled that Yale could keep the painting in its art gallery in 2014. Yale's attorneys argued successfully that under Act of State doctrine, any case that could limit the U.S. executive branch of government in its dealings with a foreign power could not be tried in a U.S. court. Konowaloff's attorneys argued that this was stolen art purchased by Stephen Clark from the Soviet government, which stole it from Morozov, and then received by Yale University. But Konowaloff's attorneys never got their day in court.

As a historian, my job was to research the history of this particular example of "material culture," a Van Gogh masterpiece worth an estimated $150 million on the art market if sold at auction. The story of the provenance of a painting was fascinating, but not enough to overcome a legal doctrine that barred any test in an American court. The attorneys on both sides wished to win the case for their client. I wanted to research

Illustration 16.2 Van Gogh's *Night Café* (1888)

and write the history of a painting. I did so as an independent historian. The lawyers were scrupulous about not leading the witness, even though they wished to win the case for their client.

Historians often provide lawyers with litigation support in the form of archival evidence, expert witness testimony, and narrative accounts of disputed objects or events. But the historian's purpose remains to give a true account of the past. If it proves useful to the lawyers, they are welcome to it. And the legal title to material culture objects is often at stake.

Task: Choose a familiar art object or artifact. Who owned it? When and where? How did it come to be located where it is now? Was it altered or sold? Now write down a brief history of the provenance of your object.

Notes

1 Richard Bushman, *The Refinement of America: Persons, Houses, Cities* (New York: Vintage Books, 1992), ix.
2 Ibid., xii.
3 Ibid., 75–76.

For Further Reading

Robert C. Williams, *Stealing Van Gogh: The Russian Collection, Soviet Confiscation, and American Reception of Night Café* (Overland Park, Kansas: The Heritage Consulting Group, 2015).

17 Public History

17.1 History beyond the Ivory Tower

While the ferocity with which historians can battle in journals and at academic conferences may suggest otherwise, most people in the historical profession understand that, for all the masterful work done by professional researchers every year, few people outside of academia really obtain their understanding of the past directly from articles, essays, and scholarly monographs. This is not to say that the work of academic historians is not important. To the contrary, the writing and publishing of good academic history will often have a trickle-down effect into the wider culture. One masterful synthesis—Eric Foner's splendid 1988 history of Reconstruction after the American Civil War, for example—can eventually transform the way an event is perceived across society. Still, most people's everyday contact with history comes not from college textbooks and academic lectures but through a host of other resources: museums and libraries, parks and monuments, television documentaries and online Web sites, walking tours, and genealogy archives.

These arenas and institutions where the study of the past flourishes—outside of the traditional college or university setting and often for public consumption—are often collectively referred to as public history. As Emma Wilmer, *emerita* editor of the Public History Resource Center (www.pub lichistory.org) describes it, "Public history is history, practically applied. It is based on the understanding that history is not taught solely in the classroom, but is learned in a variety of places, and in a variety of ways."[1] Graduates of doctoral programs in history are increasingly forsaking the usual teaching jobs in favor of employment in this burgeoning public history sector, where they can experience more interaction with non-professionals and help to shape and influence the shared public interpretation of the past. The many jobs that come under the rubric of public history include museum curators, archivists, tour guides, preservationists, park historians, historical consultants, documentary filmmakers, website creators, and even historical reenactors! Anyone who works to enhance laypeople's general knowledge of history or facilitate its popular understanding is doing public history. Indeed, even "private" historians can dabble in public history, particularly now that academic scholars can post their ideas and research in blogs or online journals at a moment's notice. (See Chapter 19.)

In many ways, public historians are the most important members of the historical profession. They bridge the gap between academic scholars and the community at large, transmitting ideas back and forth between the two. And as archivists, curators, and guides, they pave the way for all other historians to follow by organizing primary source archives into a coherent order and chronology. As all historians come to learn once they start visiting faraway collections under time constraints, archivists often know better than anyone else the contents and limitations of a given historical resource. Without public historians providing this crucial first step of interpretation, the task of academic scholars in writing history would become much more burdensome, if not impossible.

Task: Make a list of the ways that you have learned about history of late. Other than your courses and classes, what comes to mind? Have you been to a museum, taken a walking tour, or watched a history documentary recently? How did the approach taken toward history in that venue differ from the one used in class? How did it make textbook history come alive for you?

17.2 History and the Public

Because public history involves many more actors than just academic scholars, and because it often presupposes some degree of public consensus about the past, even on extremely controversial issues, the practice of public history poses distinct challenges for its practitioners.

In academic circles, when historians disagree, as they often do vociferously, they tend to have acquired much of the same information and to rely on a shared background of scholarship. (It is safe to say that all too many virulent academic feuds can be ascribed to what Sigmund Freud called the "narcissism of petty differences.") But the bones of contention can be much meatier in the field of public history, because diverse groups in society may hold radically different interpretations of past events. They may not even agree on the uses of history itself. While contemporary historians can generally agree that the central purpose of history is to broaden our understanding of the past, other groups believe that history should instil national pride, promote fidelity to certain common values or identities, raise collective self-esteem, or help atone for the sins and mistakes of the past. When these varied viewpoints collide in the public arena, the results can get particularly ugly, as well as informative.

The Enola Gay Controversy

A good example of the type of intense and bitter controversy that can erupt in the field of public history occurred in 1993 and 1994 at the Smithsonian's National Air and Space Museum. In commemoration of the 50th anniversary of the end of World War II, the museum planned an exhibit around the *Enola Gay*, the B-29 bomber that dropped an atomic bomb on Hiroshima on August 6, 1945. This exhibit was titled The Crossroads: The End of World War II, the Atomic Bomb, and the Cold War. "The primary goal of this exhibition," argued the Smithsonian's July 1993 planning document for the exhibit,

> will be to encourage visitors to undertake a thoughtful and balanced re-examination of these events in the light of the political and military factors leading to the decision to drop the bomb, the human suffering experienced by the people of Hiroshima and Nagasaki and the long-term implications of the events of August 6 and 9, 1945.[2]

After discussing the viciousness that characterized the Pacific theater of World War II, the rise of strategic and civilian bombing during the war, the building and delivery of the bomb to Japan, and President Harry Truman's final decision to use this unprecedented weapon, the exhibit would examine the considerable damage and lasting effects of the atomic bombings on Hiroshima and Nagasaki. According to the Smithsonian's planners, the exhibit, taken in total, "will embody one common wish: that nuclear weapons never be used in anger again."[3]

When made public, this proposed exhibition soon drew concerned and angry responses from many World War II veterans and organizations, particularly the Air Force Association and the American Legion. "The concept paper dwells, to the effective exclusion of all else, on the horrors of war," wrote retired USAF general Monroe Hatch to the Air and Space Museum's director, Martin Harwit:

> Once war begins, casualties are inevitable. It is less than honest to moralize about the casualties unless one also claims the war to be immoral, and I don't believe many people are ready to say that about World War II … Furthermore, the concept paper treats Japan and United States in the war as if their participation in the war were morally equivalent. If anything, incredibly, it gives the benefit of opinion to Japan, which was the aggressor. The revised concept plans for flashback segments, including a major one on the firebombing of Japan—emphasizing the casualties—but there is little mention of Pearl Harbor, except to characterize the American response as "vengeance." Japanese aggression and atrocities have no significant place in this account.[4]

Veterans, newspaper columnists and editorial boards, members of Congress, and even Paul Tibbets, the pilot of the *Enola Gay* (Illustration 17.1) in 1945, also decried what they perceived as an overemphasis on war atrocities and an imbalance against American veterans in the Smithsonian's exhibit.

Illustration 17.1 The Controversial *Enola Gay* Exhibit at the National Air and Space Museum

The Smithsonian exhibit of the B-29 that dropped the atomic bomb on Hiroshima in 1945 created enormous controversy. (http://commons.wikimedia.org)

The Smithsonian has become infected with the "bacterium of political correctness," wrote the *Boston Herald*, while the *Washington Times* accused the National Air and Space Museum of "distorting history." "My blood boils when revisionist historians … challenge the views of history of those who actually lived it," lamented a letter to the *San Diego Union-Tribune*, while, according to the American Legion, the proposed exhibit was guilty of "disseminating a deconstructed view of American history with the potential to undermine … our people's faith in our forefathers."[5]

But the public outcry was far from unanimous. Other writers and newspapers, as well as some Japanese citizens and many professional historians, came out in support of the Smithsonian's proposed exhibition. "History is often not pretty nor pleasant, but the only way we learn from it is if it is presented fully," opined the *Austin-American Statesman*. Author Kai Bird concurred in the *New York Times*: "The Smithsonian should display history with all its uncomfortable complications, and not feel-good national myths." Some people, such as *Newsday's* Robert Reno, saw the specter of censorship in the Air and Space Museum being "forced by a witless public controversy to revise its grim treatment of Hiroshima in ways that give greater emphasis to Japanese perfidy and American nobility of purpose. Maybe they'll bring in Disney people as consultants." Similarly, the Organization of American Historians passed a resolution stating that it "condemns threats by members of Congress and further deplores the removal of historical documents and revisions of interpretations of history for reasons outside the professional procedures and criteria by which museum exhibitions are created."[6]

Ultimately, after an internal review and several attempts to revise the exhibit to everyone's satisfaction, the Smithsonian decided to cancel the *Enola Gay* exhibition as originally planned. "I have concluded that we made a basic error in attempting to couple an historical treatment of the use of atomic weapons with the 50th anniversary commemoration of the end of the war," declared the secretary of the Smithsonian, I. Michael Heyman, in January 1995. Instead, Heyman proposed "a much simpler [exhibition], essentially a display, permitting the *Enola Gay* and its crew to speak for themselves."[7] This stripped-down exhibit finally premiered in June 1995, remaining (and drawing record crowds) until May 1998. But even this move by the Smithsonian did not completely stem the controversy. "I thought the Secretary showed considerable good judgment in deciding that the academics had overreached," remarked House majority leader Newt Gingrich of the decision, while Kai Bird found "the cave-in … a sad commentary on our collective inability as a nation to face our history."[8]

If you want to know more about the uproar over the Air and Space Museum's proposed *Enola Gay* exhibit, students at Lehigh University have created an informative, balanced website titled The *Enola Gay* Controversy (www.lehigh.edu/~ineng/enola). For more partisan overviews of the incident, see Kai Bird and Lawrence Lifshultz, eds., *Hiroshima's Shadow: Writings on the Denial of History and the Smithsonian Controversy* (Stony Creek, CT: Pamphleteer's Press, 1998) and the *Enola Gay* Archives at the Air Force Association website (www.afa.org/media/enolagay).

Task: Read over the paragraphs above. (You can read the full plan of the proposed *Enola Gay* exhibit at www.afa.org/media/enolagay/07–93.html.) With whom do you agree in the controversy? Do you think the Smithsonian ultimately made the right decision in canceling the originally proposed exhibition? Why or why not? What, in your opinion, is the appropriate response of a public historian to this type of controversy? Of an academic historian?

Notes

1 Jennifer Evans, "What Is Public History?" Public History Resource Center, May 8, 1999 (www.publichistory.org/what_is/definition.html).
2 "National Air and Space Museum Exhibition Planning Document: July 1993" republished by the Air Force Association at www.afa.org/media/enolagay/07–93. html.
3 Ibid.

4 Monroe W. Hatch Jr., "Letter to Martin Harwit, September 12, 1993," republished by Air Force Association at www.afa.org/media/enolagay/09–12–93. asp.
5 *Boston Herald*, August 31, 1994; *Washington Times*, August 21, 1994; *San Diego Union-Tribune*, October 16, 1994; *Washington Times*, October 14, 1994, all excerpted at Lehigh University's website on the *Enola Gay* controversy (www.lehigh.edu/~ineng/enola).
6 *Austin-American Statesman*, September 2, 1994; New York Times, October 9, 1994; *Newsday*, September 2, 1994; OAH resolution of October 13, 1994.
7 "Statement by I. Michael Heyman, January 30, 1995," republished at www.exploratorium.edu/nagasaki/Library/ArtHeyman.html.
8 "Smithsonian Exhibit of *Enola Gay*," *ABC World News Tonight*, January 30, 1995, transcript #5021–6; *Nation*, February 20, 1995, 224–225, excerpted at Lehigh University's website on the *Enola Gay* controversy (www.lehigh.edu/~ineng/enola).

For Further Reading

If you are interested in learning more about public history, there are a number of excellent websites, including those of the National Council on Public History (www.ncph.org) and the Public History Resource Center (www.publichistory.org). In addition, the American Historical Association has created a worthwhile list of public history links and resources (www.historians.org/info/public.cfm). If you wish to know more about job opportunities in the field of public history, see Beyond Academe (www.beyondacademe.com), a site designed with graduate students in history in mind, as well as the AHA's comprehensive list of employment advertisements (www.historians.org/governance/tfph/Pub licHistoryEmployment.htm).

18 Event Analysis

18.1 History in Real Time

"Those who cannot remember the past," wrote philosopher George Santayana in *The Life of Reason*—a line quoted threateningly by history teachers the world over—"are condemned to repeat it." But some might argue, a related point is also true: Those who *can* remember the past will see it repeating over and over again. The truth of this dictum is reinforced almost daily. Within hours of any important social or political event, particularly in our hand-held electronically-wired, media-saturated age, a plethora of competing historical analogies will be offered in the way of explanation by historians and journalists, amateur and professional, in newspaper editorials, across the airwaves, or on the Internet.

As an increasingly sceptical society, we have taken to calling these competing narratives "spin," and clearly political spin doctoring is often at work. The tendency toward hyperbolic historical analogizing has become a joke of sorts. Members of Internet forums and newsgroups often speak of Godwin's Law, named after Internet pioneer Mike Godwin, which states, "As an on-line discussion grows longer, the probability of a comparison involving Nazis or Hitler approaches one."[1] Donald Trump invites comparison with Hitler, not to mention P.T. Barnum or U.S. Senator Joseph McCarthy. Apoplectic analogies flourish.

Yet we should not be so quick to dismiss all attempts to analyze current events in comparison with history. Doing so serves a crucial public function, one many academic historians all too readily dismiss as a job for "popularizers." Indeed, historical event analysis is part of human nature and in some respects the very foundation of learning. Part of the way we make sense of the world around us is through historical *analogy*—by comparing present circumstances to past events in order to anticipate future outcomes. (As one popular aphorism goes, insanity is doing the same thing over and over again and expecting different results.) Few historians would argue that history is a rigidly prognostic discipline or that past events invariably yield definite, incontrovertible, and predictable results (see Chapter 7). But few historians would deny that history affords a perspective that can enlighten our understanding of present events and even guide decision makers in times of crisis.

Nevertheless, the more contentious or controversial a news event, the more likely it is to generate widely (and wildly) disparate historical analogies. Given that—despite history combining tragedy and farce, no event ever repeats itself exactly—how do we sift through and assess these competing historical claims? A recent example will make plain the difficulties inherent in evaluating historical analogies.

The Iraq War: Munich, Mukden, or Mexico?

In March 2003, after several months of diplomatic wrangling with the United Nations and European nations, the George W. Bush administration launched an invasion of Iraq, which culminated in the overthrow of Iraqi dictator Saddam Hussein and the creation of a nominally stable but prodemocratic coalition government in Baghdad. To make the case for this military conflict, the Bush administration invoked a doctrine it called "preemption," which endorsed the idea of engaging in preventive war independently for the sake of removing threats to America in advance.

The Bush administration also relied explicitly on historical analogy, most notably the example of the European acquiescence in Adolf Hitler's forced annexation of the Sudetenland (the German-speaking part of Czechoslovakia) at the 1938 Munich conference. This concession by England and France at Munich was intended to bring about "peace in our time," but ultimately forestalled war in Europe for less than a year. Since then, the Munich conference has frequently been used as an example of the danger and futility of a policy of "appeasement," and the "lesson of Munich" has been that democratic countries should not attempt to coddle tyrants.

In the months leading up to the Iraq war, several administration officials made both oblique and explicit references to the example of Hitler and Munich to make their case for pre-emptive war. In a September 2002 editorial titled "Why the West Must Strike First Against Saddam Hussein," Bush adviser Richard Perle argued that a "pre-emptive strike against Hitler at the time of Munich would have meant an immediate war, as opposed to the one that came later. Later was much worse."[2] One month earlier, Secretary of Defense Donald Rumsfeld also used the example of Munich to argue for Hussein's removal. Speaking of World War II, Rumsfeld argued, "It wasn't until each country got attacked that they stopped and said, 'Well, maybe Winston Churchill was right.' Maybe that lone voice expressing concern about what was happening was right."[3] Other administration allies were even more explicit. "When Hitler occupied the Rhineland and the Anschluss in Austria, no nation tried to stop him," declared Senator Ted Stevens of Alaska in October 2002, concluding, "I see the next Hitler in Saddam Hussein."[4]

Yet others, including many historians, believed they had found more pertinent analogies to explain the Iraq war. For example, Pulitzer Prize-winning scholar John Dower argued in the pages of *The Nation* in July 2003 that the correct analogy to explain the conflict was not the German annexation of Czechoslovakia in 1938 but the Japanese invasion of Manchuria in 1931, with the United States as Japan! The "points of resonance between the abortive Japanese empire and the burgeoning American one are striking," wrote Dower. "In each instance, we confront empire-building embedded in a larger agenda of right-wing radicalism. And in each, we find aggressive and essentially unilateral international policies wedded to a sweeping transformation of domestic priorities and practices."[5]

Similarly, esteemed historian Arthur Schlesinger Jr. saw the best explanation of the doctrine of pre-emption in remarks made 158 years earlier by a young anti-war congressman named Abraham Lincoln. Railing against American entry into the Mexican War, Lincoln had stated:

> Allow the President to invade a neighbouring nation, whenever he shall deem it necessary to repel an invasion and you allow him to do so whenever he may choose to say he deems it necessary for such purpose—and you allow him to make war at pleasure. ... If, today, he should choose to say he thinks it necessary to invade Canada to prevent the British from invading us, how could you stop him? You may say to him, "I see no probability of the British invading us"; but he will say to you, "Be silent; I see it, if you don't."[6]

Writing in April 2006, three years into the Iraq war, Schlesinger reaffirmed Lincoln's warning against pre-emption, concluding that there is "no more dangerous thing for a democracy than a foreign policy based on presidential preventive war."[7] But not all scholars concur with Schlesinger's grim indictment of pre-emption. To the contrary, diplomatic historian and Cold War expert John Lewis Gaddis argued in 2003 that:

> the doctrine of pre-emption has a long and distinguished history in the history of American foreign policy. Our doctrine throughout most of the nineteenth century—at the time that we were expanding along the frontier and confronted European colonies along the frontier, confronted Indians, confronted pirates, confronted hostile non-state actors along the frontier—was very much one of pre-emption ... So to say that pre-emption is an un-American doctrine is not right historically.[8]

The following year, Gaddis's book *Surprise, Security, and the American Experience* further defended the Bush doctrine of pre-emption as a diplomatically sound and historically rooted policy.

So, who is right? Perle or Dower? Schlesinger or Gaddis? We can examine certain claims made by each analogist—the respective military capacities of Hitler and Hussein, for example, or the actions taken by American and Japanese occupation forces in Iraq and Manchuria respectively. But since historical analogy is both a subjective art and an inexact science, our evaluation of the worth of various comparisons will depend a good deal on where we stand. We cannot expect that all members of the historical profession will agree on matters as contentious as war and diplomacy. We can only insist that historians and scholars recognize the inherent limitations within any single historical comparison and that they never falsify the past in order to win points for present policy.

Task: Choose a story from the front page of today's newspaper or the home page of a news website such as CNN.com. After reading it through, make a list of plausible historical analogies that could be used to interpret this event. In each case, compare the similarities and differences between the two events. Does one analogy fit better than another? Are these analogies mutually exclusive? In your opinion, do historical analogies illuminate or obscure current events? Can you find examples of historical analogies that informed and affected later decisions and policies?

Notes

1 Mike Godwin, "Meme, Countermeme," *Wired Magazine*, October 2, 1994 (www.wired.com/wired/archive72.10/godwin.if.html).
2 Richard Perle, "Why the West Must Strike First against Saddam Hussein," *Daily Telegraph*, September 8, 2002 (www.telegraph.co.uk/comment/personal-view/3580181).
3 David Rennie, "Remember Churchill: US Hawks Cite 'lone Stand' to Justify War on Iraq," *Daily Telegraph*, August 29, 2002 (www.telegraph.co.uk/news/world news/northamerica/usa/1405725).
4 Jim Lobe, "World War II: The Ever-Present Analogy," *Asia Times*, October 8, 2002 (www.atimes.com/atimes/Middle_East/DJ30Ak01.html).
5 John W. Dower, "The Other Japanese Occupation," *Nation*, July 7, 2003 (www.thenation.com/docprem.mhtml?i=20030707&s=dower).
6 Quoted in Arthur Schlesinger Jr., "Bush's Thousand Days," *Washington Post*, April 24, 2006 (www.washingtonpost.com/wp-dyn/content/article/2006/04/23/AR2006042301014.html).
7 Ibid.
8 "Interview with John Lewis Gaddis," *Frontline*, January 16, 2003 (www.pbsorg/wgbh/pages/frontline/shows/iraq/interviews/gaddis.html). See also Gaddis, *Surprise, Security, and the American Experience* (Cambridge, MA: Harvard University Press, 2004).

19 New Tools

GIS and CSI

19.1 Spatial History: Geographic Information Systems

History is the story of change over space as well as time. We frequently consult or create maps to show visually the terrain of history. In recent years, computers have made possible some far more imaginative and visually arresting ways to show how historical change in space occurs. More exciting is the fact that geographic information systems (GIS) can change our minds and revise the story about what happened in the past.

Historians are traditionally logocentric. They work with the printed word and normally use images only as supplements. While GIS maps are often beautifully colored and patterned eye candy, they are also powerful tools in a new science of spatial history, grounded in cartography and the *geohistoire* of the *Annales* historians (see page 35). GIS utilizes computer software to map statistical data and help us visualize history in space—neighborhood census data, "rubberizing" maps from two to three dimensions, and so on.

Mapping information is not new. John Snow mapped the cholera outbreaks of London in 1854 with striking results. But computers can integrate and apply vast databases to provide new maps of history previously impossible to imagine.

Sometimes GIS actually makes us revise our interpretation of the past. In the case of the 1692 Salem witch craze, GIS data on individual wealth, taxes, and where people lived showed that wealth was not clustered in neighbourhoods around Salem, as previously thought, but was more evenly distributed and intermixed by families. The accusers and the accused, merchants and farmers, were often neighbours. Check out the University of Virginia's Center for Digital Mapping's Salem Witch Trials Archive, available online at www.etext.virginia.edu/salem/witchcraft/home.html.

GIS maps of census data on immigrants to New York City show that the metropolitan area is now more, not less, segregated than in 1910. GIS maps of the weather, temperature, and dust storms in the Midwest of the United States show that the famous "dust bowl" of the 1930s was

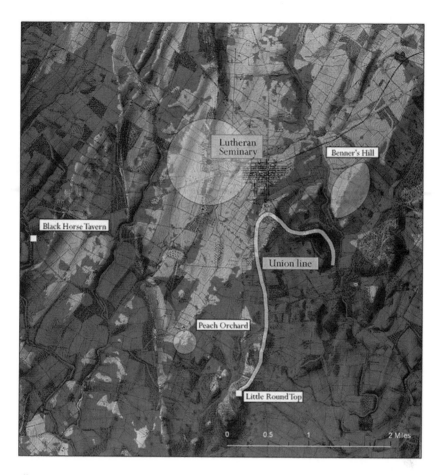

Illustration 19.1 GIS Viewshed Mapping of Gettysburg

This is what the soldiers could and could not see at Gettysburg. (*Anne K. Knowles, ed.* Placing History: How Maps, Spatial Data, and GIS are Changing Historical Scholarship [*Redlands, CA: ESRI Press, 2008*], *p. 254*)

caused not only by the great "plough up" of grassland in the 1920s, but by recurrent and normal dust storms and droughts common to the weather history of the region.

In the case of the Battle of Gettysburg, modern viewshed mapping of heights of land using five-foot contour lines helps us understand what General Robert E. Lee and his troops could, and could not, see from various points on the battlefield. In fact, Lee had a much better view of the entire terrain from the cupola of the Lutheran Seminary than contemporary accounts indicate. A similar mapping of Pickett's Charge shows that Lee had trouble seeing his advancing troops as they rose and fell along the undulating countryside and the mixed effect of his artillery barrage landing out of sight over the crest of the hill that marked the Union line (Illustration 19.1).

GIS sites are now available online. You can check out the China Historical GIS project at Harvard University at www.fas.harvard.edu/~chgis. The U.S. National Historical GIS from the University of Minnesota is available at www.nhgis.org. And the Historical GIS of Russia created by the Russian Academy of Sciences can easily be accessed at www.ihst.ru/personal/imerz/bound/bounds.htm.

Task: GIS mapping of information provides an exciting new tool allowing historians to discover and see patterns of the past they did not know existed and to re-examine received wisdom in the light of new applications of different databases. In this way they can integrate both temporal and spatial history. Pick a famous battle (Marathon, Borodino, Iwo Jima) and see if you can find a GIS mapping of the whole affair.

For Further Reading

The best introductions to GIS for historians are by Anne Kelly Knowles, ed., *Past Time, Past Place: GIS for History* (Redlands, CA: ESRI Press, 2002) and *Placing History: How Maps, Spatial Data, and GIS Are Changing Historical Scholarship* (Redlands, CA: ESRI Press, 2008).

19.2 Killer App: Crime Scene Investigation Forensics

In recent years the *CSI* series on television has brought the science of forensics into every living room and laptop as a new set of tools for investigating the past. The ubiquitous *CSI* series demonstrates the importance of human traces as historical evidence: hair, blood, bones, fingerprints, footprints, semen, and so on. Plus, DNA analysis often can prove the innocence or guilt of someone accused of committing a crime many years ago. Convicted killers have been found innocent by DNA analysis and set free after decades of imprisonment.

In the case of Napoleon I, we know that he died in May 1821 on the island of St. Helena, to which the British had exiled him. But how? Was he murdered? In the 1970s, a dentist and a toxicologist found symptoms of gradual arsenic poisoning in Napoleon's hair samples. They used neutron activation analysis, bombarding his hair samples with neutrons in a nuclear reactor. In such analysis, the hair becomes radioactive, emits gamma rays, and shows arsenic levels, in this case much higher than normal.

But so what? Arsenic was commonly used in the wallpaper of Napoleon's day and in hair conditioners. Did Napoleon simply breathe in arsenic from the wallpaper? Have a bad hair day? Or was he murdered? The case is still unresolved.

More interesting to me as a scholar of Russian history is the case of the murdered Romanov family, the last rulers of Imperial Russia. The entire family—Nicholas II, Aleksandra, and their five children, including the Tsarevich Aleksei—were machine-gunned to death in the basement of a house in Ekaterinburg in Siberia in the early morning hours of July 17, 1918. Some bones were found in a mineshaft soon afterward, but only in 1991 was a mass grave discovered, then in 2007 a second grave turned up about eighty yards away.

In 2008, the U.S. Armed Forces DNA Identification Laboratory in Rockville, Maryland, tested the remains, including a tooth of Nicholas II, the skeleton of Aleksei, and blood samples from a living descendant and distant cousin, Andrei Andreevich Romanov. The lab conducted identical tests on 4,163 other individuals for the Y-STR haplotype as a control (Illustration 19.2). Mitochondrial DNA analysis proved that the 2007 grave contained the bones of Aleksei and one of his sisters. The match of seventeen markers in the DNA of Nicholas, Aleksei, and Andrei was perfect. Consequently, all the Romanovs (and several others) had been murdered in 1918, and the stories of Aleksei and his sister Anastasia being alive and well in the United States or Europe were greatly exaggerated.

The cases of Napoleon and the Romanovs show that human remains can provide evidence to prove or disprove a case long after the event, or

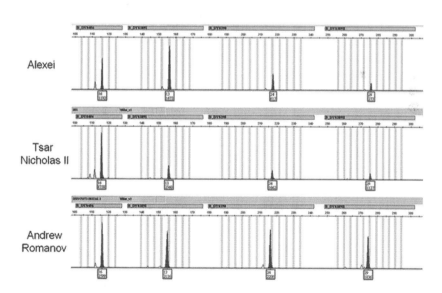

Illustration 19.2 CSI: The Remains of the Romanovs

This diagram shows the four Y-STR markers for Tsarevich Aleksei's skeleton; the tooth of his father, Tsar Nicholas II; and the blood of their distant cousin and contemporary descendant, Andrei Andreevich Romanov. (www.plosone.org)

fact, occurred. When history involves the possibility of murder, the case is rarely ever completely closed. Cold cases never die.

In 1992, Israeli, American and West German scientists analyzed the DNA samples from bones found at Embu, a village in Brazil. They concluded that the bones in fact belonged to Josef Mengele, the SS commandant and "Angel of Death" at Auschwitz responsible for the murder of hundreds of thousands of Jews. The DNA samples matched the blood samples of Mengele's widow and son in Germany. British geneticist Alec Jeffreys concluded that the family match was "beyond a reasonable doubt." Teams from around the world examined the bones, blood and teeth of a Nazi murderer and came to a final conclusion that the body unearthed in Brazil was that of Josef Mengele. Case closed.

Likewise, Jean-Jacques Cassiman, a Belgian geneticist, in 2000 examined the dessicated heart of the last king of France, Louis XVII, who allegedly died in 1795 in a Paris prison. He ground the king's heart pieces to dust, separated out the mtDNA into base-pair samples and obtained a perfect match of the DNA with the dauphin's aunt, Marie Antoinette's sister, Johanna-Gabriella. Cassiman announced that the heart mtDNA from Louis XVII and from his maternal relatives (examined by two independent laboratories) were identical. He really had died in Paris at the age of ten and the various pretenders who turned up afterwards were, in fact, pretenders. Louis' well-travelled heart in its crystal urn was returned to its crypt at the St. Denis cemetery.

Task: Find a historical event that might lend itself to forensic analysis. What kind of evidence is available? What is the controversy about? Has modern science helped to solve a riddle of history? How?

For Further Reading

If you wish to explore the Romanov murders in more detail, go online and read Michael D. Coble et al., "Mystery Solved: The Identification of the Two Missing Romanov Children Using DNA Analysis," *PloS One* 4: 3 (2009): e4838, doi:10.1371/journal.pone.0004838. See also Robert C. Williams, *The Forensic Historian: Using Science to Reexamine the Past* (Armonk, NY: M. E. Sharpe, Inc., 2013), 62–70.

20 History on the Internet

20.1 Using the Internet: Promises and Pitfalls

The Internet is one of the historian's newest tools. How can the Internet help you and other historians do your work? What are the benefits and risks of Internet research? Clearly the Internet places more information in the hands of historians than ever before. Internet sites abound for every specialized interest imaginable. You can search the bibliographies and catalogues of libraries and archives all over the world. Recent runs of journals exist online. Old documents are catalogued online and are even available to print out on your own computer. The Internet is a gold mine of both primary and secondary sources for the historian, on your desktop, laptop, or hand-held device. It is an up-to-date global encyclopedia.

Here are a few helpful sites to get you started:

- *History News Network* (www.hnn.us) offers a massive number of links to history sites sponsored by the Center for History and New Media.
- *Reviews in American History* (http://muse.jhu.edu/journals/reviews_in_ American_history) provides review articles for students of American history.
- *Library of Congress, American Memory* (http://memory.loc.gov/ ammem/mdbquery.html) gives a fantastic range of documents and images from American history and culture.
- *Institute of Historical Research, University of London, History On-Line* (http://ihr.sas.ac.uk/search/welcome.html) shows links to hundreds of sites worldwide of interest to historians.
- *National Union Catalogue of Manuscript Collections* (www.loc.gov/coll/ nucmc.html) provides links to every major manuscript collection in the United States.
- *British Library A2A Database* (www.a2a.pro.gov.uk) lists hundreds of archival sites in the United Kingdom.
- *Making of America (University of Michigan)* (http://moa.umdl?.umich.edu) indexes and often reproduces in entirety primary sources, including

journals and journal articles, focusing on nineteenth-century American social history.

- *Archiving Early America* (www.earlyamerica.com) has an enormous amount of primary source material from the eighteenth century.
- *National Archives and Records Administration Information Locator (NAIL)* (www.archives.gov) provides more than 600,000 descriptions of archival holdings.
- *Spartacus Educational* (www.spartacus.schoolnet.co.uk) is one historian's attempt to create an online textbook, with particular emphasis on recent English and American history.
- *Internet Modern History Sourcebook* (www.fordham.edu/halsall/mod/modsbook.html) includes a large collection of primary source materials for use in history classes.
- *TheAvalon Project at Yale Law School* (www.yale.edu/lawweb/avalon/avalon.htm) offers a comprehensive archive of legal, historical, and diplomatic primary resources.
- *Jensen's Web Guides* (http://tigger.uic.edu/~rjensen/0.htm) are lists of links assembled by University of Illinois historian emeritus Richard Jensen, particularly useful for finding American history resources.
- *JSTOR: The Scholarly Journal Archive* (www.jstor.org) allows historians to peruse and search the full text of hundreds of scholarly journals in their field.

Internet sites are often criticized for being uncritical, self-published, and not peer reviewed. Surely Internet users must be careful (as with published material). But the historical material available today on the Internet is simply unprecedented in its scope and value. The Internet is a major tool of any working historian and history student. Most historians use the Internet as a starting point for research and bibliographical aids, since, in the end, there is no substitute for the library and the archive.

An excellent guide to the Internet for historians is Dennis A. Trinkle and Scott A. Merriman, eds., *The History Highway*, 4th ed. (Armonk, NY: M.E. Sharpe, 2006), which runs 696 pages and provides descriptions of thousands of websites. An accompanying CD-ROM includes live links to every site.

Task: Log on to an Internet site devoted to some aspect, event, or personality of history. Who created the site? Was the site peer reviewed? By whom? How does the site relate to books and articles found in a library? Does the site tell you any more than printed sources? What other sites does it suggest?

20.2 Wikipedia and "Wikiality"

One of the most intriguing and controversial attempts to make the Internet useful for historians and laypeople alike is the Wikipedia phenomenon. Initially created in 1995, Wiki is software uploaded to a website's server that allows any visitor to add to or edit the material presented there and that tracks the changes that these visitors make to the site. In 2001, in an attempt to use Wiki to create an "open source, collaborative encyclopedia, open to contribution by ordinary people," a team of Internet entrepreneurs led by Jimmy Wales and Larry Sanger started Wikipedia (www.wikipedia.org). In the past five years, this online encyclopedia has become one of the most wide-ranging and comprehensive resources on the Internet. The English version now includes over one million visitor-penned articles, and it has spawned several foreign-language sister sites.[1]

The idea of an infinitely expandable open-source encyclopedia, available for free to anyone with a computer and Internet access, has captured the imaginations of many historians. Indeed, in lieu of short papers or reading responses, some professors now assign their students to create Wikipedia entries on a historical person or event, so the world can share in the knowledge the students obtained from the class. But obviously, an encyclopedia that anyone can change at will, virtually anonymously, harbours not only immense promise but also the potential for vast abuse. So do Facebook and Twitter.

In November 2005, John Seigenthaler, a retired journalist, Vanderbilt University professor, and former assistant to Robert Kennedy, wrote an editorial for *USA Today* that illustrated both the dangers of using Wikipedia for historical research and the harm the site can cause to individuals who find themselves written about. Seigenthaler described his dismay when he visited his own entry at Wikipedia and discovered the following patently and egregiously false statement about him therein: "For a brief time, he was thought to have been directly involved in the Kennedy assassinations of both John, and his brother, Bobby. Nothing was ever proven." Shocked by this "Internet character assassination" and the lack of accountability it suggested, Seigenthaler angrily decried Wikipedia as a site too often "populated by volunteer vandals with poison-pen intellects," and he argued that it was more useful as a tool for slander than for historical research. (Ironically, Seigenthaler's editorial resulted in doubling traffic to Wikipedia.) Although the author of the false remark—a 38 year-old operations manager in Nashville who mistook Wikipedia for a gag website—came forward and apologized to Seigenthaler a month later, the incident nevertheless underscored how the malleability of information posted at Wikipedia can lead to highly dubious assertions, and even outright lies, being taken as historical fact.[2]

As Wikipedia has continued to grow and expand despite the Seigenthaler incident, several comedians have poked fun at this crucial weakness of the website. The humorous online newspaper *The Onion* published a July 2006 cover story declaring that "Wikipedia Celebrates 750 Years of American Independence," while television personality Stephen Colbert caused a furor in August 2006 when, while explaining the concept of "Wikiality," he altered several Wikipedia entries in the middle of his show, including the entry for George Washington. "If I want to say

George Washington didn't have slaves, that's my right. And now, thanks to Wikipedia, it's also a fact," commented Colbert while changing the entry, which subsequently read: "In conclusion, George Washington did not own slaves."[3]

Colbert's meddling was quickly fixed by other Wikipedia users. Most researchers are apt to spot such large mistakes as these. Nevertheless, given the significant possibilities for errors in Wikipedia entries, the jury remains out on the usefulness of the website for historical research, and almost all historians would agree that, at least for now, Wikipedia is rarely if ever acceptable for use as a citation resource.

Wikipedia remains a worldwide collaborative filter that tries to assemble the true facts and delete the false ones, a giant conspiracy to have its articles agree with reality. Historians need to make good use of it, even if they do not cite it as a source.

Task: Go to www.wikipedia.org and read over a few entries on historical subjects of your choosing, for example, the entries under "history." Does the information therein seem correct? Is it comprehensive? Is it biased? Who wrote it? Who altered it? How does it compare to what you might find in a published history textbook or encyclopedia? How, in your opinion, should historians approach Wikipedia or other open-source Internet resources when conducting research?

20.3 Blogging the Past (and Present)

Another potential tool for history on the Internet is the blog. A blog (short for "Web log") is a frequently updated website in which one or multiple authors post links and commentary on a given subject, usually more informally than in writing published "offline." Since their advent in the late 1990s, blogs have mushroomed exponentially across the Web and now number in the millions. There are now blogs written on almost every conceivable subject, from politics to painting to podiatry, including, of course, history. While their research use is limited, blogs allow historians a forum to comment on and discuss issues of historical or contemporary importance without the need of a publisher and to interact with both their colleagues and the public across large distances. Blogs provide a global example of history as an argument without end, to use Peter Geyl's phrase (see page xiv). Only now the argument can be instantaneous, anonymous, and interactive.

If you are interested in reading blogs maintained by historians, the History News Network (HNN) has created a comprehensive and user-friendly history "blogroll" at http://hnn.us/blogs/entries/9665.html. HNN also hosts a number of its own historical blogs, most notably the collective group effort at Cliopatria (http://hnn.us/blogs/2.html). The blogger Ralph Luker surveyed the origins and uses of blogs for historians in his May 2005 article, "Were There Blog Enough and Time" (www.historians?.org/Perspectives/Issues/2005/0505/0505tec1.cfm).

Task: Visit a few of the blogs listed on HNN's blogroll above. How do the authors' approaches to their subjects differ from what you might find in a published textbook or monograph? Do you find blogs useful or informative as tools for understanding history? What are the similarities and differences between conventional publication and publication on the Internet?

Notes

1 "Wiki.Org: What Is Wiki" (http://wiki.org/wiki.cgi7WhatIsWiki); "Wikipedia: History of Wikipedia" (http://en.wikipedia.org/wiki/History_of_Wikipedia). In a telling comment on the dangers of using Wikipedia for historical research, at the time of this writing (August 2006) Wikipedia's About and History pages have been protected from alteration by new or anonymous users.

2 John Seigenthaler, "A False Wikipedia 'Biography,'" *USA Today*, November 29, 2005 (www.usatoday.com/news/opinion/editorials/2005–11–29-wiki-pedia-edit_x.htm); "Wikipedia: History of Wikipedia"; Katharine Q. Seelye, "Wikipedia Prankster Confesses," *Seattle Times*, December 15, 2005 (http://seattletimes. nwsource.com/html/nationworld/2002677060_wiki11.html). Some advocates of Wikipedia have attempted to counter Seigenthaler's criticism by arguing that he did not use Wikipedia's open-source ability to change his own entry. They also point to a December 2005 study by *Nature Magazine* that found that the number of errors at Wikipedia and in the *Encyclopedia Britannica* were roughly comparable. Jim Giles, "Internet Encyclopaedias Go Head to Head," *Nature Magazine*, December 15, 2005 (www.nature.com/nature/journal/v438/n7070/full/438900a.html).

3 "Wikipedia Celebrates 750 Years of American Independence," *The Onion*, July 26, 2006 (www.theonion.com/content/node/50902); Frank Ahrens, "It's on Wikipedia, So It Must Be True," *Washington Post*, August 6, 2006 (www.washingtonpost. com/wp-dyn/content/article/2006/08/05/AR2006080500114.html); James Montgomery, "Can Wikipedia Handle Stephen Colbert's Truthiness?" *MTV News*, August 3, 2006 (www.mtv.com/news/articles/1537865/20060803/index.jhtml).

21 TMI: Too Much Information

We often complain that the Internet and online sources have produced a flood of information so enormous that it threatens to drown the historian. Critics write about information overload, glut, fatigue, and anxiety in a universe of what author David Foster Wallace called "total noise." But the new universe also produces meaningful signals that the historian can search for, and interpret, to the benefit of the craft of history. Falsehoods abound on the Internet. But so does the peer review process that can refute them. The very idea that history is information can stimulate historians to rethink the past. And the information age itself is already becoming the object of historical study and research.

21.1 History as Information

History appears in print as a series of books, paragraphs, words, and letters, along with supplemental images. But since World War II, the rise of information theory and computer science has made us realize that history consists of even more basic bits, or bytes, of information that can be combined into letters and words, numbers, narrative, and argument. Information pervades everything, from genetics and neuroscience to logic and cybernetics. In a way, the universe is information—10^{90} bits of information, by one estimate, and counting, an infosphere.

Think about it. If history is information, then the historian is recovering messages (evidence) from the past to be transmitted to readers by other messages (history) in the present. These messages contain both signals (meaningful evidence to support an argument) and noise (the colorful and brutal random details of life and death). The historian composes messages (statements of fact or interpretation, argument, or narrative) and transmits them by book, article, or online blog post to the recipient or reader. Networks of readers await publication. Networks of reviewers sharpen their critical knives for the journals, providing feedback to the historian. Networks of other historians plug along on their own projects.

Illustration 21.1 Selecting Signals and Filtering Out Noise
The historian now has endless information and must select and filter the signals from the noise. (http://commons.wikimedia.org)

Misinformation can instantly "go viral" on the Internet and create fake history worldwide. So can the corrections to that fake history. Historical information is highly selective. The historian sifts through mountains of evidence to find significant information and signals worthy of incorporation in the narrative argument. With computers, those mountains of evidence become ever higher, and we can see farther than ever before through the fog of the past. We use powerful search engines to do our research online. We "Google" for specific information about the past and any search engine may produce hundreds of entries that could be of interest. With computers, the historian can do history faster and farther than ever before, but not necessarily better.

The ordinary language of the historian disguises the fact that the historian transmits messages in code and symbols, following the conventions of the craft. History builds upon prior messages and histories to give more meaning, or provide new evidence, in a new version of the old past. The alert reader gets more out of history from a prior knowledge of historiography around the topic. Read in context, messages carry more meaning. Thanks to computers, historians have an accessible and searchable network of evidence about the past at their fingertips.

Then why cannot we reduce history to text messaging? Imagine Paul Revere's coded message: "1 f by lnd, 2 f by c." This message is meaningful, but hardly readable. We need noise as well as signal to make history come alive. If that makes the narrative longer, so be it. Brevity is for logicians. Historians cannot and should not reduce history to a combination of zeroes and ones, or the 140 characters of Twitter, even though they may be the atoms and bits of the information, evidence, and meaning we seek. Tweets are for those who cannot read or write well and at length. But historians should filter the meaningful signals from the random noise. Who else can do it better?

Task: Find a sentence or two from any good history book on your shelf. Try to convert the language to information, as in a text message. What is lost? What is gained? Will you write history any differently if you think of it as a form of text messaging?

For Further Reading

James Gleick, *The Information: A History, A Theory, A Flood* (New York: Pantheon Books, 2011).

21.2 Hacking History: The Deluge of WikiLeaks

What are historians to make of the massive data dump of previously secret military and diplomatic documents through the WikiLeaks website? Is WikiLeaks a new tool for historians?

WikiLeaks is largely the product of a small group of computer hackers and journalists led by Julian Assange, an Australian-born shape-shifter, global nomad, and anarchist claiming to bring transparency and openness to governments around the world. For years, he enjoyed asylum at the Ecuadorian embassy in London. Despite his rhetoric about accurate history being the only way to truth, Assange is a paranoid dictator of a secretive online organization whose brand is transparency, but which constructs its own version of the truth by selecting and constructing facts that suit its political purpose. Since 2006, WikiLeaks, aided and abetted by a young U.S. soldier in Iraq named Bradley (now Chelsea) Manning, currently an ex-convict in the United States, and many other anonymous sources, have put on the Internet hundreds of thousands of classified documents focusing on the wars in Iraq and Afghanistan, including 251,282 U.S. diplomatic cables and 391,832 Iraq war logs.

The WikiLeaks motto is "Help us create a just and corruption-free world," and the company accepts donations. WikiLeaks is a business and has an agenda. It provides an Internet platform that guarantees whistle-blower anonymity, but not historical accuracy.

The massive selective dump—beginning on November 28, 2010—is both a dream and a nightmare for historians. Never before (or at least not since the Pentagon Papers appeared in 1975) has such a treasure-trove of evidence been made public for historians to research. But never before has the research been so daunting, requiring historians to explore a wilderness of search engines, passwords, and encryption to distinguish the significant from the insignificant. Historians may feel as if they are locked in a room with the entire contents of the National Archives coming at them through a fire hose.

Moreover, the documents are not as transparent and revealing as they might appear to be. Most are bureaucratic and military memoranda written in the jargon of the day that present a version of the truth (body counts, the killing of civilians, friendly fire incidents, portraits of key world leaders) that protects the author from possible criticism or retaliation. The authors have their own agendas. The documents are carefully selected by the leakers (mainly to expose government wrongdoings) and then carefully edited by journalists (mainly to protect confidential sources). WikiLeaks documents are not simply raw data.

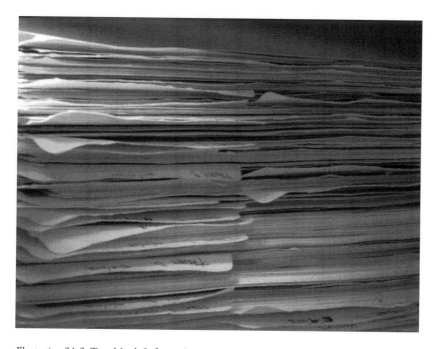

Illustration 21.2 Too Much Information

The traditional historian faced a data dump in paper. Now the dump is worldwide online 24/7. (http://commons.wikimedia.org)

Here is a selection from a WikiLeaks document:

Friday, February 12, 2010, 15:39
SECRET SECTION 01 OF 03 MOSCOW 000317
SIPDIS
EO 12958 DECL: 02/11/2020
TAGS PGOV, PREL, PHUM, PINR, ECON, KDEM, KCOR,RS"> 8
SUBJECT: THE LUZHKOV DILEMMA
Classified by: Ambassador John R. Beyrle, Reason 1.4 (b), (d).

10. (8) According to XXXXXXXXXXX, Luzhkov [Mayor of Moscow] is following orders from the Kremlin to not go after Moscow's criminal groups. For example, XXXXXXXXXXXX argued that it was only a public relations stunt from Putin to close gambling. XXXXXXXXXXX said he did not see the sense in suitcases of money going into the Kremlin since it would be easier to open a secret account in Cyprus. He speculated that the Moscow police heads have a secret war chest of money. XXXXXXXXX said that this money is likely used to solve problems that the Kremlin decides, such as rigging elections. It can be accessed as a resource for when orders come from above, for example, for bribes or to pay off people when necessary. XXXXXXXXXX postulated that the Kremlin might say to a governor that he can rule a certain territory but in exchange he must do what the Kremlin says.

The document is problematic. On the surface, we have a report from the American embassy in Moscow, classified by the ambassador, which passes along gossip from anonymous sources. To the historian, it is not news that crime and corruption persist in post-Soviet Russia. The allegation about a secret war chest of Moscow police is unsubstantiated. Governors having to obey Kremlin orders are hardly news either. What is most revealing is how American diplomats collect and report alleged information about Putin's Russia. And we do, after all, have a secret document from U.S. diplomatic traffic previously unavailable. But should historians use stolen documents posted online by anti-authority hackers?

Russian trolls have been meddling in foreign elections for years, notably in the 2016 U.S election. They have hacked into European elections for a decade or more. These hackers are often funded by the Russian government and make sustained efforts to produce disinformation, fake news, malignant web sites and other mischief. Unlike WikiLeaks, Russian trolls create their own world of fake history and lies, rather than simply release documents they steal on the Internet. They operate in the best tradition of the Soviet KGB and GRU intelligence agencies.

The WikiLeakers (and now OpenLeakers) are generally young computer hackers with a deep distrust of government authority. They may have produced a database of hundreds of millions of words, but they too have an agenda. The anonymous submission of leaked and stolen documents to a website is not exactly a firm foundation for historical research. But there is some gold in the hills if you know how to pan for it.

Task: Find a Wikileaks document at cablegate.wikileaks.org for your research. Is it authentic? Can you use it? Should you use it? Who is the author? Where is the original document? How has it been edited during the release and publication process? How do you know? Why do you think WikiLeaks selected it for release?

For Further Reading

David Leigh and Luke Harding, *WikiLeaks: Inside Julian Assange's War on Secrecy* (New York: Guardian, 2011); Micah Sifry, *WikiLeaks and the Age of Transparency* (Berkeley, CA: Counterpoint, 2011). A good insider account is Daniel Domscheit-Berg, *Inside WikiLeaks* (New York: Crown, 2011).

Illustration 21.3 Margaret Hubbard Chadwell, the author's maternal grandmother, in her wedding dress in 1904.

21.3 Private Parts: The Intrusion of History

Historians have long been familiar with stories about Cleopatra's nose, Catherine the Great's horse, or Adolf Hitler's missing testicle. But how significant are the private parts of history in matters of decision-making or agency? Do we really need to know *everything* about individuals in the past?

Historical agents who make things happen are human beings, just like the rest of us. They have their private lives, idiosyncrasies, sex life, and fantasies. Until fairly recently, we did not pay much attention to the titillating details of history, and we especially gave a pass to living U.S. presidents. No one discussed in print the facts of Franklin Roosevelt's polio or John Kennedy's Addison's disease, let alone their active extramarital sex lives. Then came Senator Gary Hart's *Monkey Business* and President Bill Clinton's dalliance with a White House intern to entice a curious and willing public. Now psychohistorians and *paparazzi* have made every sordid detail of private life fair game to feed an insatiable media frenzy. Donald J. Trump, a narcissistic hedonist and womanizer, makes previous U.S. presidents look like monks.

Computers continue to shrink our privacy. Facebook, YouTube, Skype, and Twitter broadcast as much of our own—and public figures'—private lives as anyone could want. Companies of data miners dig through online files and mailing lists seeking gold, or people's identities and Social Security numbers, whatever they can find. The sheer volume of pornography and sexting on line makes almost everything private public. Trolls in chat rooms post inflammatory off-topic messages. High school students are bullied and ridiculed with personal insults, photographs, and videos worldwide in nanoseconds. In August 2010, Facebook Places was widely attacked for revealing where users or their "friends" were located at any time, convenient information for stalkers or criminals.

The threat to privacy from the Internet has become so intrusive that a number of new search engines are marketed to erase our history:

- Internet History Eraser 8.0: "a privacy tool to protect you."
- Evidence Blaster: "erase your Internet history, for good."
- CyberScrub: "erase online Internet web history."
- CCCleaner: "maintain your privacy by cleaning your entire Internet history."
- HistorySweep: "how to clean history now."

In the past, we might try to have an errant publication recalled or shredded. Now we have an Orwellian world of cyberspace where our history never happened, should we wish to erase, blast, or clean it up.

Until now, we have generally associated history with our memory of the past. Now with a keystroke we can forget it ever happened, at least for ourselves.

Revelations about the private lives of dead individuals can be merely titillating or newly significant. Peculiar habits and features may help explain how individuals acted as historical agents, or not. We have traditionally had gossip columns and the rumour mill to pass around the private secrets of the community. Now we have the Internet, a constant deluge of self-advertisement, pornography, sexting, gossip, bullying, and lies. None of this noise is of particular interest to the historian except as a dump of data to be mined, sifted, or ignored.

Privacy information is overrated. Does it matter to historians that Abraham Lincoln may or may not have had some homosexual proclivities? For years historians have noted that he had an unpleasant marriage and slept in the same bed with male friends, notably Joshua Speed, a young lawyer in Illinois. "I slept with Speed," he openly admitted. At age twenty, as a joke, he wrote an eight-line poem about two men who get married. And his relations with the various women in his life were often difficult.

But there is not enough evidence to sustain the argument of C.A. Tripp in *The Intimate World of Abraham Lincoln* (2005) that Lincoln was "predominantly homosexual." The word *homosexual* did not exist in Lincoln's day. Men slept with each other often on the frontier, where beds were difficult to come by. Tripp was not a historian but a sexologist colleague of Alfred Kinsey, who studied the sexual activities of Americans in great detail, voyeurism cloaked in science. Tripp, an advocate of gay liberation, twists and ignores the facts to suit his political agenda.

The historian can safely ignore Lincoln's sexual preferences in favour of the public life of America's greatest president, saviour of the Union, liberator of the slaves, and author of the Gettysburg Address. Until new evidence proves otherwise, the Lincoln we know will prevail.

The Internet provides us with too much information about private lives, the endless exhibition of our common humanity and inhumanity online. On rare occasions something might turn up that is significant to the historian. But more likely Internet gossip simply whets our appetite, stimulates our prurient curiosity, and shows that our age and the Internet have virtually eliminated privacy. And that is historically significant.

Task: Choose a famous historical figure from the past. How much information can you find on line about the person's private life? Is that information historically significant or merely intriguing? If it seems significant to you, how?

For Further Reading

"Privacy Is History—Get Over It," *Wired* 4: 2 (February 1996). Also, Victor Mayer-Schonberger, *Delete: The Virtue of Forgetting in the Digital Age* (Princeton: Princeton University Press, 2009).

21.4 Twitter

Twitter is a growing source of information overload since its founding in 2006 as an American on-line news and social networking service on which users post and interact with their "followers" using brief messages called "tweets." Headquartered in San Francisco, Twitter by 2012 had a hundred million users posting 340 million tweets daily. Tweets were instant, frequent, and short, limited to 140 characters until November 7, 2017 (the 100th anniversary of the Bolshevik Revolution in Russia) when the limit was doubled to 280 characters. A year later, on November 7, 2013, Twitter began trading stock as a company on the New York Stock Exchange.

Starting in 2012, Twitter partnered with Yandex, the leading Russian computer platform for advertisements, founded in 1997 with its data-base operations housed in Finland. Twitter users acquired a #hashtag and a @username to contribute their tweets to "trending topics." By 2017, Twitter had a global base of 328 million users. The Kremlin-backed oligarch Yury Milner invested millions in both Facebook and Twitter, which one observer compared with the old CB (Citizens Band) radio system. The Russians were able to meddle successfully in the 2016 U.S. Presidential Election by spreading disinformation and fake news in cyberspace. Among Russian-developed Twitter addicts was Donald J. Trump.

While blurting out millions of tweet-storms worldwide, Twitter also generated a huge database that historians could use. Many were searchable and could be downloaded for future use, a massive archive of daily opinion that could be checked and compared with the more standard primary sources on line or in print. Tweets are now legally admissible in court and increasingly used by historians. They represent too much information only if and when historians are unable to discover valuable statements of fact within the data bases they can now search. Twitter generates both noise and signals. And any Trump tweet-storm can reach an audience of millions worldwide in nanoseconds without going through the usual media channels.

Disinformation is also rampant on the Internet. Russian trolls disseminate made-up stories about non-existent events from computers in St. Petersburg. U.S. political parties create totally fake web sites allegedly supporting their opponents. Artificial Intelligence (AI) makes possible novel forms of deception: computer-generated speech (MelNet), neural fake news, face-swaps and lip-synch fakery. Anything can be photoshopped. Political handlers can make rival politicians appear drunk and disorderly. Crowd size can be as large or small as you wish. Truth and falsity are often indistinguishable. Hackers and fraudsters greatly outnumber those attempting to combat virtual frauds online that can go viral around the globe in seconds. There is no money in detecting fraud, but much in fakery. The historian working on the Internet is increasingly susceptible to deception and misinformation. She can no longer assume the truth of an image or the reliability of a piece of evidence. In the postmodern era, disinformation is a weapon of mass deception. Historians beware!

22 Epilogue
The End of History?

History remains the study of continuity and change over time in the past. Often the pace of change (e.g., computers, the Internet, and the "too much information" challenge) seems radical, novel, and overwhelming. But the continuities of the historians' craft persist, and we need to remember them, especially in the age of the "sixth extinction" that may well mark the end of history and the effects of human technology on our planet, known as the Anthropocene (Illustration 22.1).

Technology is double-edged. Computers provide historians with virtually endless amounts of information that they cannot control, but also with apps and search engines that enable them to access and research precisely what they want. Chat rooms and blogs enable them to communicate with each other. Historians using science can take a new look at old crimes and re-examine the evidence. Technology pits the national security of states against the transparency of hacking and cryptocurrency. It erodes privacy and uncovers evidence that may or may not be significant for understanding the actions of historical agents and actors.

We have moved from secrecy to transparency, always the friend of the historian. Governments continue to lie, but a computer-savvy global public exposes the lies instantly on the Internet and establishes its own websites to compete. Even with too much information, history still provides an essential set of tools for understanding the past and arguing about that understanding.

We also see historians collaborating on projects more than in the past. Given the vast amounts of information available and the new tools, historians may well be encouraged to work together in teams, rather than in isolation in their cubicles or at their desks.

The fact that history is sometimes computable information does not mean we can reduce it to text messaging. History remains linear prose, not retrievable bytes, an art as well as a science. Without the historian filtering the signals from the noise of the past, who will distinguish the two? We continue to make the music of history, composing history between the sounds of silence and the total noise of information cacophony.

Illustration 22.1 Climate Angels at an Extinction Rebellion, Australia, March 22, 2019

The history of planet earth goes back more than four billion years. There were no humans until less than half a million years ago. Virtually all the species on earth by then no longer existed. Today species vanish at an accelerating rate largely due to human activity. Mass extinction of species is part of history. Our own species, *Homo sapiens*, is the all-time ecological serial killer and super-predator on earth. Fossil fuels and their carbon emissions are already producing global warming and climate change that is accelerating.

History is a modern activity conducted by a tiny group (historians) to study the modern period of planet earth when human beings appeared (around 350,000 years ago). The historical past of earth may be traced back four billion years, but history itself emerged as a discipline only in the last few millennia as a conscious activity of some *Homo sapiens* fascinated by documentary evidence, archives, and libraries. History began with the cognitive revolution of 70,000 years ago and continued through the scientific revolution after 1500 and the industrial revolution after 1800. Historians try to explain how or why humans organized themselves into mass-cooperation networks with a common language and alphabet. Our historian's toolbox is very modern indeed. It applies to a tiny part of our planet during a tiny time period.

Moreover, history deals with a chaotic past that we explain with the "hindsight fallacy." We know the outcome. We can usually explain *how* an event happened by reconstructing a series of events that preceded that event. But finding the causes that explain *why* an event happened is more difficult. We must demonstrate that the event in question was caused to the exclusion of all other possible outcomes. There may be one or more possible causes lurking in the midst of chaos. Which causes really mattered? Were they recognized at the time?

In the end, the chaos of history is quite unpredictable. We can discover and speculate about many alternative outcomes that simply fail to materialize at all. History *is what it is*, to use the current cliché.

Speaking of the end, the craft of history often involves speculating about a future end-time ahead of us. Perhaps most famous speculation is the portrait of the Biblical Apocalypse in the *Revelation of St. John*, but there are many more end-time chronicles as well. They predict a story of flood, famine, nuclear war, pestilence, starvation, temperature rise and fall, and environmental degradation. Nuclear weapons and climate change make such an end-time a real possibility. Is history coming to an end? Will historians become participant-observers who chronicle that end from the evidence of fragments found? Or simply more fragments?

Robert Nathan presents such an end-time fantasy in his lively story *The Weens* (1960). With his tongue firmly in cheek, the American novelist writes of a vanished western civilization of five thousand years ago. The Weens lived in the We, or U.S. Nathan allegedly joins archaeological expeditions that produce diggings of lost cities at Yok, Bostin and Oleens. The expeditions were funded by the Konegi Foundation. The surviving Weens live in a reconstructed civilization that lacks any music.

Less amusing is Nevil Shute's terrifying *On the Beach* (1957), a novel that portrays a post-nuclear war landscape of modern Apocalypse. Set in Australia at the end of World War III (1963), the novel features survivors traveling in submarines, suicide pills, and a world dying slowly of radiation poisoning. The subject of nuclear fiction has become the object of study by literary critics and historians.

****

Historical end-time achieves perspective if we look back a few million years or so to an evolving world of mass extinctions of diverse species of organic life. In 2010, scientists discovered a finger bone fragment in the Denisova Cave in the Altai Mountains of Siberia. Analysis of bone mtDNA showed a being of a species distinct from both Neanderthal Man (400–40,000 years ago) and modern humans (*Homo Sapiens*), but genetically related to both. The Denisova Cave was named for a hermit named Denis who lived in the cave in the eighteenth century. Soon more bones, teeth and fossils turned up in a great arc stretching from Spain through Siberia and Tibet to Java and Australia. The technology of modern history had unearthed an entirely unknown species, *Homo Denisova*, akin to both Neanderthals and modern humans by virtue of descent from a common ancestor that lived about a million years ago.

In 2019, another research group in China used protein analysis and discovered collagen fingerprints linked to Denisovan Man. Uranium decay-dating estimated the age of the collagen to be 160,000 years. Genomic sequencing suggested the Denisovan Man was genetically linked to Neanderthals and modern humans. Modern scientific study thus has discovered an entirely novel species that lived worldwide and is kin to humans. Genetics concludes that our historical past is far more ancient and widespread than we knew. *Homo Sapiens* have been around for some 350,000 years but have only been recording and writing history for the past few millennia.

Humans are super-predators who have destroyed much of their environment by hunting, fishing, deforestation, pollution, and warfare. They wiped out their predecessors, including Neanderthal and Denisovan men. Some believe that with the industrial revolution we have entered the *Sixth Extinction*, a Holocene Age or Anthropocene Age in which we humans are systematically destroying life on earth through over-population, over-consumption, hunting animals, burning fossil fuels, and raising the land, sea, and air temperatures as well as carbon emissions. Plate tectonic shifts, the decline in biodiversity through species extinction, greenhouse-gas emissions, deforestation, rising temperatures from an expanding sun, and antibiotic-resistant diseases all play a role. But the driver of the Sixth Extinction is humankind.[1]

Extinctions are not novel. There have probably been five to twenty mass extinctions in the past 540 million years. The fossil record provides evidence of the Ordovician-Silurian extinction (450 mya, or million years ago); the Late Devonian extinction (375–60 mya); the Permian-Triassic extinction of 252 mya that killed off 90 percent of all species on planet earth; the Triassic-Jurassic extinction of 201 mya; the Cretaceous-Paleogene extinction of 66 mya that destroyed the dinosaurs and may have been caused by an asteroid striking the earth from space; and the Holocene (or sixth) extinction in which we now live and which is largely cause by human activity.

Humans have also been the perpetrators of earlier extinctions, but the major explanations or causes of extinctions have been non-human: flood-basalt events that include volcanic eruptions; rising and falling sea levels; melting glaciers; and asteroids. We call our present phase of extinction "Anthropocene" because human activity plays such a major role in the ongoing destruction of our planet. Whatever the causes, well over 95 percent of all species that once lived on earth are now extinct because of natural or human shocks to the biosphere that reduce biodiversity. Only one Sumatran rhino remains in a zoo to contemplate its extinction, if it can. The little brown bat was once ubiquitous in northern New England and is now nearly extinct. And humans continue to be both the agents and the victims of their own extinction. We are an invasive species that writes history.

Yet the Endangered Species Act (1974) and other human activity have hopefully deferred the extinction of species. There are more California condors flying today than a few decades ago. Wild turkeys and fishers have recovered their populations in New England. The Pangea Project suggests that global warming and ocean acidification could provide reverse engineering that links the disappearance of islands and coastlines with tectonic plate shifts that return us to one huge continental land mass. Some think we can resurrect Neanderthal Man by using their DNA. Future historians may write about the non-extinction of endangered species, as well as their extinction. But they will still be doing history using the tools in their toolbox.

Task: Find out what you can about a past mass extinction and write a very brief history of that event and its causes? Do the same for an endangered species that was saved temporarily by human action. What role do historians play in chronicling mass extinctions or endangered species? What evidence do they use? Are we really living in end time? If so, what's a historian to do?

Notes

1 Elizabeth Kolbert, *The Sixth Extinction: An Unnatural History* (New York: Henry Holt, 2014).

Glossary

alternate facts   Facts chosen to support assumptions, conspiracies or ideologies that completely contradict historical facts and evidence to the contrary

anthropology   The study of humankind; a discipline related to history that utilizes linguistic, material, and mythological evidence to study human origins

archaeology   The recovery of material evidence for human life and culture

archive   A repository for historical documents, artifacts, or images

argument   Persuasive logic that is based on premises, supported by evidence, and leads to a conclusion

artifact   An object made by humans that is of historical or archaeological interest

bias   An opinion that hinders judgment and is not based on argument or evidence; prejudice

bibliography   A list of books, articles, and unpublished manuscript and archival sources normally placed at the back of a historical monograph

biography   The life history of one particular individual, including an account of the individual's time and place

book review   A published critique of the work of one historian, normally by another historian

cartography   The study of maps

cause   Something that produces, or leads to, an event, idea, or action

chromosome   A linear strand of DNA that carries and transmits genetic information

chronicle   A narrative listing of historical events in chronological order, normally by date

chronology   A listing of dates and events in the order they occurred

citation   A reference to a particular source or work

cliometrics   The quantitative study of history emphasizing numbers and mathematics

conspiracy theory   An explanation of past events that assumes a plan or plot, with or without appropriate evidence

conventional wisdom   Historical knowledge that is commonly accepted until revised by historians subsequently

crime scene investigation (CSI) The major application of science and forensics to the historical investigation of crimes, often years after they were committed

culture The art, religion, literature, music, and other creations and beliefs of a society

database Electronic collection of historical sources, images, sounds, records, bibliographies, or other historical data

deep fakes False and misleading Internet information or images manipulated by computer technologies to introduce disorder and chaos into cyberspace

dissertation A major original work of historical research and writing required for the doctor of philosophy (PhD) degree in history

DNA Deoxyribonucleic acid, which contains genetic information in a cell, replicates itself, and determines hereditary characteristics; can establish identities and relationships among individuals, living or dead

document A written source (letter, memorandum, book, article, grocery list, etc.)

draft An unrevised piece of writing, subject to future revision until a final draft is complete

edit To make stylistic and substantive suggestions or corrections to a manuscript or paper; to help revise

empathy Understanding another person in another time and place

evidence Material that supports an argument, normally drawn from primary sources

evolution Gradual change and progression over time

explanation A demonstration or argument showing how or why an event occurred

facsimile A copy of an original

fact An established and verifiable piece of information about the past

fair use Reproduction of a copyrighted work for educational or research purposes

fake news A derogatory term used to disparage news or history when the facts are critical of, or do not support, an argument, individual or ideology

fiction An imagined or invented story

file An ordered collection of documents in an archive

footnote An acknowledgment in the text of a source where information or interpretation was found

forensics The use of science to confirm or refute evidence of past events, commonly used in criminal investigations

forgery An invented document that falsely claims to be something it is not

fossil record The history of life on earth using as evidence the remains, traces, or imprints of organisms preserved in sedimentary rock over the past four billion years

genealogy A historical record of the descent of a family or individual from ancestors; lineage or pedigree

genome A complete set of chromosomes

geographic information systems (GIS)   The computer science of mapping statistical data sets in visual form, useful in spatial history and seeing change over time in space

global history   See world history

hagiography   Study and writing of the lives of saints; a biography that idealizes its subject

historian   One who researches evidence and tries to understand the past, often constructing a narrative, argument, or analysis of past events, ideas, or people

historical event   An occurrence in the past, selected and made significant by the historian

historicism   The belief that the meaning of history is internal, not external, to history

historiography   The study of the history of historical writings

history   The study of the past; a nonfictional account of the past

idealism   The belief that history is primarily what human beings thought or intended

index   A list of entries at the back of a book indicating on what pages something related to each entry may be found

interlibrary loan   A book, article, or manuscript copy obtained from one library for use in another library, often by photocopy, microfilm, or microfiche

Internet   The global network of information accessed by computers.

interpretation   A conclusion based on evidence that gives meaning; historians may have different interpretations of the same evidence

journal   A scholarly periodical that publishes current research

law   A rule that determines, explains, or predicts a recurrent course of history

manuscript   A handwritten text; an author's printed text prior to publication

master narrative   The dominant and accepted story of past events

meme   An idea, ideology, value, or fashion that may or may not endure over time

memoir   An autobiography; an account of one's own life

memory   The recollection of the past

metahistory   An explanation of all history in terms of one factor (economics, class, civilizations, progress, freedom, great women, etc.)

microhistory   The history of a single event or community in great detail

monocausal   Having one cause

monograph   A single volume or book investigating a fairly specialized historical topic

multicausal   Having many causes

narrative   A modern literary-critical term for story, relating a sequence of events

note   A summary, quotation, citation, or comment written down as a record of a text, image, or sound being considered

note taking   A process whereby the historian selects from sources, and writes down, what is to be remembered and possibly used in a subsequent history

objectivity Judgment based on evidence without personal bias

online catalogue An indexed guide to or listing of historical sources and writing, often linked to other catalogs or websites

oral history History based on oral interviews of surviving witnesses or participants

ordinary language Language in common or everyday use by most people

outline A skeletal framework for a paper, article, book, or argument

paleontology The study of fossils, bones, shells, exoskeletons, stone imprints and DNA as evidence regarding the ancient history of planet earth

paradigm An accepted set of questions framed by a community of inquiry

paraphrase To say the same thing in different words

past What has happened until the present, not necessarily observed or recorded

peer review The critical feedback provided by other scholars in one's field regarding one's own work; published book reviews in scholarly journals are a normal part of peer review

periodical Journal appearing at regular intervals

permissions Rights to reproduce or republish words or images owned or copyrighted by another publisher or author

philosophy of history An analysis of the ways in which historians make assumptions, use language, frame questions, or otherwise employ theories to help explain the past

plagiarism Presenting the words or thoughts of another as if they were one's own without proper acknowledgment; a form of lying, cheating, and stealing

positivism The nineteenth-century belief that history is a science, can test laws of human behaviour, and can establish the truth about the past

postmodernism A recent attitude toward modernity and history that minimizes or denies the external existence of truth, past, and fact except through present narrative and text

prediction A statement of what will happen in the future

proofread To examine a text to correct mistakes in spelling, grammar, or content; to read prior to publication or submission in order to improve

public domain Accessible to all; not protected by copyright

question A query asked by the historian of the sources

quotation The words of another author or person indicated in the text by quotation marks at the beginning and end of those words

quotation marks The symbols (" ") used to signify that the words are those of another author

record A trace of the past, normally written at the time for posterity

relativism The belief that there is no absolute truth, only relatively true statements believed by those who make them

research paper A limited exploration of a particular topic whose findings are based on original research in primary and secondary sources

revise To improve by changing (1) the style and content of a piece of writing, or (2) the accepted interpretation (conventional wisdom) of a particular historical topic

revisionism   Historical research and writing that contradict the conventional wisdom about a historical topic

revolution   A sudden, dramatic, and often violent change in the order of things

rough draft   A first attempt at writing, subject to future revision until a final version is completed

selectivity   Choosing from among many sources of information or ideas the few that appear to be significant in some predetermined way

Sixth Extinction   The current and final mass extinction of species on earth, involving the destruction of the planet and its inhabitants. Also known as the Holocene or Anthropocene.

scepticism   Being unwilling to accept anything on faith; doubt

source—primary: a document, image, or artifact that provides evidence about the past provided at the time; and **secondary**: a book, article, film, or museum that displays primary sources selectively in order to interpret the past. Many sources may be both primary and secondary with respect to different entities

speculation   Drawing a conclusion without the benefit of evidence or facts; imagination

summary   A short version of a text, argument, or document that conveys ideas and information in brief

table   A graphic way of showing trends, quantitative results, or other data

text   Written or printed words; the body of a work distinct from preface, footnotes, appendix, or index; a textbook

textbook   A book that presents a large amount of material about a subject based upon the research and writing of many people

thesis   An argument; also, shorthand for a dissertation

topic   An area or field of historical inquiry and research. A topic is not a question. Historians ask, and try to answer, different questions in order to understand a topic

Twitter   A computer platform and company that limits itself to very short, frequent and instant bursts of individual "tweets" of opinion in cyberspace and on the Internet

WikiLeaks   Website platform generated by Julian Assange and other computer hackers to bring transparency to classified documents worldwide; journalistic exposés useful to historians in some cases

Wikipedia   Online open-source encyclopedia that may be continuously revised and updated by anyone

world history   History that extends beyond the boundaries of Europe and the U.S. and focuses less on nation states than on trans-national patterns of trade, disease, slavery, migration, diasporas, agriculture, and industrialization.

World Wide Web   A global electronic information network accessible by computer and linking the user to databases of interest

zero-sum   In game theory, the idea that one player's gain is another player's equal loss

Bibliography

Appleby, Joyce, Lynn Hunt, and Margaret Jacob. *Telling the Truth about History*. New York: W.W. Norton, 1994.

Archiving Early America. www.earlyamerica.com.

Arnold, John H. *History: A Very Short Introduction*. Oxford: Oxford University Press, 2000.

Aveni, Anthony. *Empires of Time: Calendars, Clocks, and Cultures*. New York: Basic Books, 1989.

Bancroft, George. *History of the United States from the Discovery of the American Continent*. Vol. 9. Boston: Little, Brown, 1857–1866.

Bates College website on plagiarism. www.bates.edu/pubs/plagiarism.

Bede, Venerable. *Ecclesiastical History of the English People*. London: Penguin Books, 1990.

Bellesiles, Michael A. *Arming America: The Origins of a National Gun Culture*. New York: Alfred A. Knopf, 2000.

Benjamin, Jules R. *A Student's Guide to History* (11th ed.). Boston: Bedford Books, 2010.

Berdyaev, Nikolai. *The Meaning of History*. Translated from the Russian by George Reavey. Cleveland: Meridian, [1936] 1962.

Berlin, Isaiah. *The Hedgehog and the Fox: An Essay on Tolstoy's View of History*. New York: Mentor, 1957.

Blackmore, Susan. *The Meme Machine*. New York: Oxford University Press, 1999.

Bloch, Marc. *The Historian's Craft*. New York: Alfred A. Knopf, 1953.

Bonnell, Victoria E. *Roots of Rebellion: Workers' Politics and Organizations in St. Petersburg and Moscow, 1900–1914*. Berkeley: University of California Press, 1983.

Braudel, Fernand. *On History*. Chicago: University of Chicago Press, 1980.

British Library A2A Database. www.a2a.pro.gov.uk.

Brodie, Richard. *The Virus of the Mind: The New Science of the Meme*. Seattle: Integral Press, 2001.

Brown, Norman O. *Life against Death*. Middletown, CT: Wesleyan University Press, 1957.

Burke, Kenneth. *The Philosophy of Literary Form* (2nd ed.). Baton Rouge: Louisiana State University Press, 1967.

Butterfield, Herbert. *The Whig Interpretation of History*. London: Penguin Books, 1931.

Carr, E.H. *What Is History?* New York: Alfred A. Knopf, 1961.

Clark, Elizabeth. *History, Theory, Text: Historians and the Linguistic Turn*. Cambridge, MA: Harvard University Press, 2004.

Clark, Jonathan. *Our Shadowed Present: Modernism, Postmodernism, and History*. Stanford, CA: Stanford University Press, 2003.

Cohn, Dorrit. "Fictional versus Historical Lives: Borderlines and Borderline Cases." *Journal of Narrative Technique 19*: 1 (Winter 1989): 3–24.

Collingwood, Robin G. *The Idea of History*. New York: Oxford University Press, 1943.

Costello, Paul. *World Historians and Their Goals: Twentieth-Century Answers to Modernism*. Dekalb: Northern Illinois University Press, 1993.

Cowley, Robert, ed. *What If? The World's Foremost Military Historians Imagine What Might Have Been*. New York: Putnam, 1999.

Davis, Natalie Zemon. *The Return of Martin Guerre*. Cambridge, MA: Harvard University Press, 1983.

Davis, Natalie Zemon. "On the Lame." *American Historical Review 93* (June 1988): 572–603.

Domscheit-Berg, Daniel. *Inside WikiLeaks*. New York: Crown, 2011.

Dray, William H. *Philosophy of History* (2nd ed.). Englewood Cliffs, NJ: Prentice Hall, 1993.

Edelman, Gary E., and Smith, Timothy H., eds. "The Lore of the Sharpshooter." In *Devil's Den: A History and a Guide*. Gettysburg, PA: Thomas Publications, 1997.

Eley, Geoff. *The "Goldhagen Effect": History, Memory, Nazism—Facing the German Past*. Ann Arbor: University of Michigan Press, 2001.

Eliade, Mircea. *Cosmos and History: The Myth of the Eternal Return*. New York: Harper and Row, 1959.

Evans, Richard. *In Defense of History*. New York: W.W. Norton, 1999.

Finlay, Robert. "The Refashioning of Martin Guerre." *American Historical Review 93* (June 1988): 552–571.

Fischer, David Hackett. *Historians' Fallacies: Toward a Logic of Historical Thought*. New York: Harper and Row, 1970.

Fischer, David Hackett. *Paul Revere's Ride*. New York: Oxford University Press, 1994.

Gardiner, Patrick. *Theories of History*. New York: Free Press, 1959.

Geyl, Peter. *Debates with Historians*. New York: Meridian, 1958.

Gilderhus, Mark T. *History and Historians: A Historiographical Introduction* (7th ed.). Upper Saddle River, NJ: Prentice Hall, 2010.

Gleick, James. *The Information: A History, A Theory, A Flood*. New York: Pantheon Books, 2011.

Gordon-Reed, Anne. *Thomas Jefferson and Sally Hemings: An American Controversy*. Charlottesville: University of Virginia Press, 1997.

Gray, Paul. "Other People's Words." *Smithsonian 32*: 12 (March 2002): 102–103.

Hacker, Diana, ed. "Managing Information; Avoiding Plagiarism." In *The Bedford Handbook* (5th ed., pp. 554–562). Boston: Bedford Books, 1998.

Harari, Yuval Noah. *Sapiens. A Brief History of Humankind*. New York: Random-House, 2014.

Hexter, J. H. *The History Primer*. New York: Basic Books, 1971.

Hexter, J. H. *On Historians*. Cambridge, MA: Harvard University Press, 1979.

History News Network. http://chnm.gmu.edu/hun.

Hunt, Lynn. "French History in the Last Twenty Years: The Rise and Fall of the Annales Paradigm." *Journal of Contemporary History 21* (1986): 209–224.

Hutton, Patrick H. *History and the Art of Memory*. Hanover, NH: University Press of New England, 1993.

Iggers, George. *Historiography in the Twentieth Century: From Scientific Objectivity to the Postmodern Challenge*. Middletown, CT: Wesleyan University Press, 1997.

Institute of Historical Research, University of London. History On-Line. http://ihr?.sas. ac.uk/search/welcome.html.

Jenkins, Keith. *The Postmodern History Reader*. London: Routledge, 1997.

Jenkins, Keith. *Refiguring History: New Thoughts on an Old Discipline*. London: Routledge, 2003.

Keegan, John. *The Battle for History: Re-fighting World War II*. New York: Vintage Books, 1995.

Knowles, Anne Kelly, ed. *Past Time, past Place: GIS for History*. Redlands, CA: ESRI Press, 2002.

Knowles, Anne Kelly. *Placing History: How Maps, Spatial Data, and GIS are Changing Historical Scholarship*. Redlands, CA: ESRI Press, 2008.

Kolbert, Elizabeth. *The Sixth Extinction. An Unnatural History*. New York: Henry Holt, 2014.

Kracauer, Siegfried. *History: The Last Things before the Last*. New York: Oxford University Press, 1969.

Kubler, George. *The Shape of Time*. New Haven: Yale University Press, 1962.

Leigh, David, and Luke Harding. *WikiLeaks: Inside Julian Assange's War on Secrecy*. New York: Guardian, 2011.

Library of Congress. American Memory. http://memory.loc.gov/ammem/mdbquery?. html.

Linenthal, Edward T., and Tom Engelhardt, eds. *History Wars: The Enola Gay and Other Battles for the American Past*. New York: Henry Holt, 1996.

Lipstadt, Deborah. *Denying the Holocaust: The Growing Assault on Truth and Memory*. New York: Free Press, 1993.

Lunsford, Andrea, and Robert Connors, eds. "Recognizing Plagiarism and Acknowledging Sources." In *The New St. Martin's Handbook* (pp. 494–497). Boston: Bedford/ St. Martin's Press, 1999.

MacLean, Nancy. "The Leo Frank Case Reconsidered: Gender and Sexual Politics in the Making of Reactionary Populism." *Journal of American History* 78: 3 (December 1991): 917–948.

Maclean, Norman. *Young Men and Fire*. Chicago: University of Chicago Press, 1992.

Mayer-Schonberger, Victor. *Delete: The Virtue of Forgetting in the Digital Age*. Princeton: Princeton University Press, 2009.

Middleton, Arthur Pierce, and Douglass Adair. "The Mystery of the Horn Papers." *William and Mary Quarterly*, 3rd ser., 4 (October, 1947): 409–443.

Monmonier, Mark. *Mapping It Out: Expository Cartography for the Humanities and Social Sciences*. Chicago: University of Chicago Press, 1993.

National Archives and Records Administration Information Locator (NAIL). www.nara. gov/nara/nailhi.html.

National Union Catalogue of Manuscript Collections. http://lcweb.loc.gov/coll/ nucmc.html.

Neustadt, Richard E., and Ernest R. May. *Thinking in Time: The Uses of History for Decision-Makers*. New York: Free Press, 1985.

Nitpickers. www.nitpickers.com/movies/nitpicks.

Novick, Peter. *That Noble Dream: The "Objectivity Question" and the American Historical Profession*. New York: Cambridge University Press, 1988.

O'Brien, Tim. *The Things They Carried: A Work of Fiction*. New York: Penguin, 1990.

Onuf, Peter S., and Jan E. Lewis, eds. *Sally Hemings and Thomas Jefferson: History, Memory, and Civic Culture*. Charlottesville: University of Virginia Press, 1999.

Plumb, J. H. *The Death of the Past*. Boston: Houghton Mifflin, 1970.

Poster, Mark. *Cultural History and Postmodernity: Disciplinary Readings and Challenges*. New York: Columbia University Press, 1997.

Reardon, Carol. *Pickett's Charge in History and Memory*. Chapel Hill: University of North Carolina Press, 1997.

Rendell, Kenneth W. *Forging History: The Detection of Fake Letters and Documents*. Norman: University of Oklahoma Press, 1994.

Reviews in American History. http://muse.jhu.edu/journals/reviews_in_american_history.

Rollins, Peter C. *Hollywood as Historian* (2nd ed.). Lexington: University Press of Kentucky, 1998.

Roth, Randolph. "Guns, Gun Culture, and Homicide: The Relationship between Firearms, the Uses of Firearms, and Interpersonal Violence." *William and Mary Quarterly*, 3d ser., *59*: 1 (January, 2002): 223–240.

Schama, Simon. *Dead Certainties (Unwarranted Speculations)*. New York: Vintage, 1992.

Schlereth, Thomas. *Material Culture Studies in America*. Walnut Creek, CA: Alta Mira, 1995.

Schlereth, Thomas, ed. *Material Culture: A Research Guide*. Lawrence: University Press of Kansas, 1999.

Scott, Joan. *Gender and the Politics of History*. New York: Columbia University Press, 1989.

Seaver, Kirsten A. *Maps, Myths and Men: The Story of the Vinland Map*. Stanford, CA: Stanford University Press, 2004.

Shermer, Michael, and Alex Grobman. *Denying History: Who Says the Holocaust Never Happened and Why Do They Say It?* Berkeley: University of California Press, 2000.

Smith, Bonnie G. *The Gender of History: Men, Women, and the Practice of History*. Cambridge, MA: Harvard University Press, 1998.

Stern, Fritz J. *The Varieties of History: From Voltaire to the Present*. New York: Meridian, 1956.

Stoianovich, Traian. *French Historical Method: The Annales Paradigm*. Ithaca, NY: Cornell University Press, 1976.

Storey, William K. *Writing History: A Guide for Students* (2nd ed.). Cambridge, MA: Harvard University Press, 2003.

Tosh, John. *The Pursuit of History: Aims, Methods, and New Directions in the Study of Modern History* (5th ed.). London: Longman, 2010.

Toynbee, Arnold. *A Study of History*. New York: Oxford University Press, 1957.

Trinkle, Dennis A., and Scott A. Merriman, eds. *The History Highway* (4th ed.). Armonk, NY: M.E. Sharpe, 2006.

Ulrich Thatcher, Laurel. *The Age of Homespun: Objects and Stories in the Creation of an American Myth*. New York: Alfred A. Knopf, 2001.

University of Michigan. Making of America. http://moa.umdl.umich.edu.

Van Hillier, E. "Acknowledging Sources and Avoiding Plagiarism." http://uwp.duke.edu/sources.html.

Weston, Anthony. *A Rulebook for Arguments* (2nd ed.). Indianapolis: Hackett, 1992.

White, Hayden. *Metahistory: The Historical Imagination in Nineteenth-Century Europe*. Baltimore: Johns Hopkins University Press, 1973.

White, Hayden. *The Content of the Form: Narrative Discourse and Historical Representation*. Baltimore: Johns Hopkins University Press, 1987.

Whitrow, G.J. *Time in History*. Oxford: Oxford University Press, 1988.

Williams, Robert C. *Lovewell's Town. From Howling Wilderness to Vacationland in Trust.* Topsham: Just Write Books, 2007.

Williams, Robert C. *The Historian's Toolbox. A Student's Guide to the Theory and Craft of History* (3rd ed.). Armonk, NY: M.E. Sharpe, Inc., 2012.

Williams, Robert C. *The Forensic Historian. Using Science to Reexamine the Past.* Armonk, NY: M.E. Sharpe, Inc, 2013.

Williams, Robert C. *Stealing Van Gogh: The Russian Collection, Soviet Confiscation, and American Reception of Night Café.* Overland Park and Kansas: The Heritage Consulting Group, 2015.

Williams, Robert C. *Topsham, Maine: From the River to the Highlands.* Topsham: Just Write Books, 2015.

Williams, Robert C. *From Away: The Maine Origins of a Russian Historian.* Topsham, Maine: Just Write Books, 2019.

Williams, Robert C. *Useful Assets. The Trump Family, the Russians and Eurasian Organized Crime.* Topsham, Maine: Just Write Books, 2019.

Wilson, Norman J. *History in Crisis? Recent Directions in Historiography.* Upper Saddle River, NJ: Prentice Hall, 1999.

Windschuttle, Keith. *The Killing of History: How a Discipline Is Being Murdered by Literary Critics and Social Criticism.* Paddington and Australia: Macleay, 1996.

Winks, Robin W., ed. *The Historian as Detective.* New York: Harper and Row, 1968.

Wright, Robert. *Nonzero: The Logic of Human Destiny.* New York: Vintage, 2000.

Zenzen, Joan. *Battling for Manassas: The Fifty-Year Preservation Struggle at Manassas Battlefield Park.* State College: Pennsylvania State University Press, 1998.

Index

Note: Page locators in *italic* refer to figures and in **bold** refer to tables.